the secret life of

# FREDDIE MILLS

**Michael Litchfield** is the author of several true-crime and current-affairs books. His background is rooted in investigative journalism. He worked as a crime correspondent for several national newspapers and was contracted to *Time/ Life* magazine to investigate the Mafia's infiltration of the Bahamas government. At one stage, a contract was taken out on his life and he was smuggled out of Nassau on a cruise ship to the US, where he was kept for a time in a safe house before being repatriated. Back in the UK, his books on the bombing of Pan Am Flight 103 over Lockerbie and the biography of the controversial Chief Constable of Greater Manchester, Sir James Anderton, coupled with the Northern Ireland terrorist issue, were highly acclaimed, staying for several weeks in the top ten non-fiction bestsellers' lists. His last staff newspaper appointment was as political editor in London with Northcliffe Newspapers. His most recent book for John Blake Publishing is *The Murder of Lord Shaftesbury* (2016), the extraordinary, if unedifying, true story of the passionate love affair that ended in high society's most shocking murder.

# the secret life of
# FREDDIE MILLS

**NATIONAL HERO.
BOXING CHAMPION.
SERIAL KILLER.**

## MICHAEL LITCHFIELD
**AUTHOR OF *THE MURDER OF*
*LORD SHAFTESBURY***

JOHN BLAKE

Published by John Blake Publishing,
3 Bramber Court, 2 Bramber Road,
London W14 9PB, England

www.johnblakebooks.com

www.facebook.com/johnblakebooks 🅕
twitter.com/jblakebooks 🅴

First published in paperback in 2017

ISBN: 978-1-78606-445-5

British Library Cataloguing-in-Publication Data:

A catalogue record for this book is available from the British Library.

Design by www.envydesign.co.uk

Printed in Great Britain by CPI Group (UK) Ltd

3 5 7 9 10 8 6 4 2

Papers used by John Blake Publishing are natural, recyclable products
made from wood grown in sustainable forests. The manufacturing processes
conform to the environmental regulations of the country of origin.

Every attempt has been made to contact the relevant copyright-holders,
but some were unobtainable. We would be grateful if the appropriate
people could contact us.

John Blake Publishing is an imprint of Bonnier Publishing
www.bonnierpublishing.com

# CONTENTS

# ACKNOWLEDGEMENTS

First and foremost I must thank Bob Berry, who was a detective sergeant with Scotland Yard's Murder Squad during the 1960s, for his friendship and invaluable assistance. Without his input and guidance during those heady, crazy days of the Swinging Sixties, this book would have been impossible.

More recently, I was given immense help by staff of the British Museum in London. Their kindness, diligence and willingness to help at all times with good humour were much appreciated.

Finally, but of course not least, I owe a debt of great gratitude to my editor at John Blake Publishing, the incomparable Toby Buchan. His patience, understanding and calming influence, as always, have made it a joy to write for him.

# AN EXPLANATION

Readers might reasonably ask how I can remember conversations of so long ago that weren't recorded electronically or with contemporaneous notes. The answer to that is with the reverse question: How could I possibly forget? With a subject of this enormity, a rollercoaster saga of such staggering magnitude inexorably building to a climax that defies the laws of imagination and plausibility, it is inevitable that the zeitgeist of those times have crystallised in my memory, rather than dimming and withering. Of course I have been helped by police records and media microfilm, but the most illuminating elements of this narrative come from my own personal involvement and the dialogue in which I was a participant. Of course, some words and phrases will be inaccurately juxtaposed, but to paraphrase would squander the quality of characterisation; speech, for example, the argot of gangland London was very personified.

One mystery that remains is what happened to the tape-recording of a confession to John du Rose (shortly before he became Deputy Assistant Commissioner at Scotland Yard) by the serial killer, who was never charged, for reasons that will become clear. The reflex is to find his cover-up implausible. Surely the natural reaction would be for him to have revealed his historic coup in his autobiography and bathe in the kudos? Not so. The problem for devious du Rose was that the tape was a double-edged sword. He had a confession and had the man cornered – literally, in a Masonic bar, but instead of arresting him there and then, he struck a deal, with a special, trusting handshake. To have exposed the existence of that tape and to admit that he had allowed the serial killer to walk away, would have damned du Rose for ever, making him 'The Idiot of the Yard', rather than bathing him in glory. And he knew it, more than anybody. So I guess the recording was destroyed. In his favour, he would have been acutely aware, from an earlier disaster, that a confession on its own would not have been enough.

Nevertheless, instead of the real plural killer being named, blamed and shamed, du Rose fingered an innocent. A 'disposable' man, someone unable to fight back because carbon monoxide fumes from his car in a locked garage had silenced him, to du Rose's cynical and sickening advantage.

MICHAEL LITCHFIELD

# PROLOGUE

For more than half a century, since his mysterious death, the memory of Freddie Mills has been preserved and polished like a national treasure.

Freddie was a winner. A national hero. A world champion. He fought his way to the top from humble beginnings. He was proud of his heritage. He was proud of his family. He was proud that he conquered the world in the name of his country. And his country was proud of him.

In life, his image of a lovable rogue was carefully crafted. His tousled black hair, craggy features and cheeky grin endeared him to millions, even those with no interest in pugilism, or who even hated it for its raw violence. He transcended all class and cultural frontiers. Lion-hearted to the last, the epitome of true grit... or so it seemed. So goes the legend, unfortunately a mirage, a myth of gigantic proportions.

Since the twilight days of his sporting career, he was dogged by dark rumours which followed him like a menacing stalker. Some worse than others, one of them unspeakable, though never established publicly. Until now.

Time is not always a healer. Even after so long, skeletons in cupboards can start to rattle, refusing to lie down and finding new life. And so it is the case with Mills.

Although to the unsuspecting reader it may seem that Mills does not appear on stage in this saga until relatively late, let me assure you that his footprint is on every page, so too his darkling shadow.

From the beginning to the end, this is the narrative of a Freddie Mills that a cabal of influential people tried to keep secret; sadly, a shamed hero.

Hence the title of this book, *The Secret Life of Freddie Mills*.

Tragically, in many respects, no longer a secret.

# CHAPTER 1

# A SUSPECT

The two detectives were waiting for me in the living room of my home in Kempston, a first-time-buyers' suburb of Bedford. My first impression was that the strangers were a pair of cold-call salesmen, probably flogging life insurance or double-glazing. They were too smart to be Jehovah's Witnesses. Not smart enough to be clean-cut Mormon cheerleaders.

I was annoyed that my wife, Pearl, had allowed them over the threshold. When hustlers came calling, she was normally quick at hoisting the drawbridge: 'Not today, thank you; I'm afraid one of my husband's hungry pet pythons has just got loose.'

Pearl was in the room, head lowered disconsolately, standing uncomfortably in front of an armchair by the fireplace, her back to the small fence-enclosed garden, where our toddler daughter, Joanne, was playing on her tricycle. Pearl seemed to be deliberately eschewing eye contact with me, which signalled a faint alarm.

The men had stood up in unison from the settee as I entered

the room. It was just after lunchtime on a Saturday and I'd been into town to place a wager on a horse, having had a strong tip from racehorse trainer John Bartholomew, who was based in Kent. We'd become close friends since I'd started an investigation on his behalf to establish that a charlatan solicitor had defrauded him of a sizeable inheritance from his late father's estate. Bartholomew Snr had been the mentor of Fred Winter, who rode – and later trained – horses for the Queen Mother, with several Grand National winners to his name.

'We're detectives from Bedford police station, but we're acting on behalf of Scotland Yard, on a very serious matter,' said the obvious senior of the two men. 'You are Mr Michael Litchfield?'

If Scotland Yard hadn't been mentioned, I might have replied facetiously, 'Well, I'm not the milkman. He only calls after I've gone to work.' Instead, I just said, 'Yes', simultaneously throwing my wife daggers that pleaded, *What the hell's going on here?* But still she had her eyes focused on her slippers.

'And you do live at this address?'

Again a flippant reply was invited, *No, I'm just the burglar,* but wisely I refrained. I was picking up bad vibes. Two detectives in my house on a mission for Scotland Yard; this was no trivial matter like a motoring offence or an unpaid parking fine. This had to be heavy-duty stuff, something endorsed by Pearl's edginess.

'I do,' I said simply, answering the second question, as if repeating my wedding vows.

'I'm afraid it's necessary for you to come with us to the police station in order to clarify the situation,' said the spokesman, stiffly. What *situation*? No subject had been mentioned. 'What's this all about?' I asked. Did my wife know? If she did, she wasn't saying. All telepathic communications between us had been broken. I don't know if it's possible to feel oneself going pale, but if it is that's exactly how I felt. Bloodless.

# A SUSPECT

'I think the subject is one you'd rather not have aired in front of your wife, sir. It's essential you come with us to the police station in order to clarify things.' The transparent code within this mischievously *considerate* comment would have been deciphered in an instant by an adolescent: sexual misbehaviour, at the least. Such a statement, although devoid of facts and substance, was so loaded that it came across as a damning indictment. The web of mystery being woven was far worse than an out-in-the-open clarification or accusation.

Pearl blanched.

At this point I suggested driving myself to the police station and rendezvousing with them there, hoping for a private catch-up moment with Pearl before I set off. This proposition was met by a united shake of heads and at least one smirk, which translated to, *What do you take us for, provincial prats?*

'That isn't the way we do things in serious cases of this nature,' I was told.

Again the reference to *serious*! My brain was turning into a runaway train. I was losing control of all the competing and racing machinations, with no way of applying the brake. The freedom of making choices had already been taken from me. Already I was a prisoner, but within invisible walls, trapped in a scenario I didn't understand and that was beyond my comprehension. For as long as I can remember I've suffered from claustrophobia, and this situation was rapidly becoming claustrophobic for me, although I wasn't entombed – not yet.

Whatever this was all about, it had to be a mistake, I kept reasoning to myself. Maybe a simple matter of mistaken identity. The harder I concentrated on the permutations, the less sense it made and was far from being a salve. Whatever the *offence,* clearly it had been committed in London, where I worked.

'I think we'd better go, sir.' No more wriggle-room remained.

I cannot remember if they introduced themselves by name or showed me ID, though I'm sure they must have, probably early on. One thing was certain: although the word *arrest* hadn't been used, that's exactly what was happening. I went either voluntarily or in handcuffs. These cops were not for turning or deterring.

Just as we were about to leave, there was an hysterical, clichéd caricature movie moment. Pearl crossed the room purposefully, gripped my hand and, blushing, said, 'Whatever you've done, I'll stand by you.' Briefly the tension snapped because, for me, that moment was so comical that I couldn't prevent myself from laughing.

'Darling, I don't know what you're imagining, but I'm no murderer or rapist,' I said, trying to lighten my load as well as hers.

Instantly, I spotted the exchange of telepathic messages passing between the two towering police officers.

'Of course you're not,' Pearl said, rather light on conviction, I thought, as she returned my hand.

'I'll sort it,' I promised. 'See you soon.'

I could have sworn that Pearl flicked away a tear.

We left the house rather resembling a hanging party, one detective leading the way and the other behind me: a sandwich formation, with me as the filling, the tasty bit. (The death penalty had not yet been abolished, something I was to reflect upon very shortly.)

Not a word was spoken during the fifteen-minute drive until we were manoeuvring into a reserved slot in the central police station's parking zone. All the way my blitzed brain had been a hive of frenzied activity. I'd come to the conclusion that whatever the crime – or suspected offence – my purported involvement had to be an administrative error. Or maybe they had reason to believe that I'd witnessed something, inconsequential to me but of relevance to Scotland Yard's investigators. Reasonable assumption, surely? *Yes, that's most likely the answer,* I assuaged myself, though I must confess that my thoughts were in disarray, like garments in a tumble dryer, going round and round, tossed one way, then another.

'You ought to know that we've had a look at your vehicle in your garage,' said the senior detective, who was sitting beside me in the rear of the unmarked car.

At the time I owned a grey-blue minivan, not because I needed it for my job but because it had been cheap to buy second-hand and economic to run. The significance of the van and its colour would only become apparent weeks later.

'Forensics may have to tow it up to London for fingerprints and fibres to be lifted, also any stains will need testing. That's just one of the reasons why we didn't want you driving it and touching it any more. It might even have to be dismantled.'

The scenario was darkening by the minute. 'What for?' I queried, in relation to the possible need for my vehicle to be impounded. The answer was evasive. Some banter followed. Not idle banter from them, though; they were sharply focused. I remember being bemused by a question about painting; did I do much.

'I'm no artist,' I said naively, which was a hoot to them.

They were talking about painting and decorating, one of them said. Although I managed a self-deprecating chuckle, I wasn't the least amused or comforted, just more confused.

At the police station, I was escorted upstairs to the office of a detective inspector, a middle-aged man, with the easy-going, dangerously disarming doctor's bedside manner. He was at his desk, busying himself with folders and documents, behaving as if I was invisible and he hadn't noticed my occupation of a chair directly opposite him. The other detectives stood like sentinels inside the door, as if to prevent a rash attempt at escape.

Finally, he looked up. 'Ah, Mr Litchfield, thank you for dropping in!'

'*Dropping in,* isn't how I'd explain my presence here,' I said, to which he smiled, recognising the game that was being played, all on his terms. We shook hands. No one could possibly have been more affable. *Don't drop your guard,* I lectured myself. *This is Danger Man, the intelligent one, the brains of this place.* I started thinking of him as a snake and I had to be as smart and quick as a mongoose.

Right from the start he had the appearance and mannerisms of a methodical civil servant and I was there just to help fill in some forms, as if applying for a passport or something trivial like that. He repeated the routine of checking my full name and address, date of birth and marital status, then enquired what I did for a living.

This was the defining moment when the mood and tempo in that office changed palpably, like a fever suddenly subsiding and the mercury dropping like a stone. I explained that I was a crime correspondent for a national newspaper (*The Sun,* then a serious broadsheet that had morphed from the *Daily Herald,* a crusader for the Labour Party and the trades union movement, and now embraced within the *Daily Mirror* empire, divorced from its old owners, Odhams. This high-quality *Sun* was soon to be bought by the Australian press mogul Rupert Murdoch and reborn as a raunchy tabloid, with a different semi-naked Page Three Girl each day as its insignia.)

'Any crime case in particular you're currently covering on a regular basis?' the inspector asked, as if making polite small talk, simultaneously offering me a cigarette, which I eagerly accepted. I was one of those chain-smoking obsessives who felt naked without a coffin nail between my lips or fingers. The inspector had no doubt that I would pluck a cigarette from the packet, like a mouse being lured into a spring-trap. This was an old police trick of which I was unfamiliar, highlighting my callowness. His confidence was based on the culture of the age: tobacco seemed more essential to Western survival than oxygen. Pubs were smog zones because of the cigarette smoke. So, too, were restaurants, where diners would smoke between courses, finally lighting cigars when coffee and port were served. The movies made smoking *cool*, something the smart-set did on dates, just before and immediately after having sex, in the office, on trains, buses, liners, aeroplanes and even on the beach. Huge advertisements on London buses and hoardings, displayed prominently in towns, urged the nation to light up and inhale the fumes of the good life. So the inspector was on to a safe bet that I would bite the bait.

'Yes, the London "Nudes Murders",' I said, making use of the flame of a flick-lighter that was proffered by one of the sentinels, yet another little test, which I was to learn I'd failed. This whole experience was a learning curve about the nuances of police interrogation techniques. At the time, though, the last thing on my mind was the value of the free education that few other writers would receive in these potentially dire circumstances. The relevance of the death sentence not yet abolished was later to chill me to the core when I pondered upon the possible consequences. I was first assigned to the 'Nudes' investigation a year before, immediately following the first freakish crime.

The body of Gwynneth Rees had been discovered naked on 8 November 1963. In each successive case, there was a yawning gap between the date of the murder and the appearance of the corpse, an important feature of the serial killer's modus operandi that will be elaborated as the narrative unfolds. I shall continue to use the term 'serial killer' although the label wasn't coined until the mid-1970s by FBI agent Robert Ressler. Mythology has it that Ressler came up with the tag while listening to a lecture at

Bramshill, the British Police Academy. The lecturer was focusing on different categories of crimes occurring with distinctive patterns. This coincided with a realisation by the FBI in the USA that a pandemic was evolving and a new killing culture spreading: perpetrators not murdering for traditional motives, such as jealousy, greed, hatred or revenge, but for pleasure, even as a hobby, though mainly with strong sexual stimulation. In view of Jack the Ripper and others, serial killing wasn't a new phenomenon; it was more a revival.

Ever since the slaying of Rees there has been conflict among criminologists and police historians as to whether this was indeed the first or second killing in the series. There are those who believe that number one was Elizabeth Figg in 1959. I am in the opposite camp, but more on that later. Back to Bedford police station…

Suddenly, like a conjuror pulling a white rabbit from a hat, the inspector produced a plastic, transparent evidence bag and slid it across the desk to me, saying deadpan, 'Have you ever seen this before?'

Seasoned detectives rarely ask a question without already being in possession of the truthful answer.

I know it's a cliché, but I really could not believe my eyes. If ever *gobsmacked* was a justifiable description of a reaction, this was the occasion. In the bag was a white envelope which I had ripped into tiny pieces and stuffed into an ashtray on a late-night train from London St Pancras to Bedford, a distance of fifty miles north, a few days earlier. Unknown to me, another passenger in that open-plan carriage had scooped up all those pieces from the ashtray after I'd alighted, taken them home and pieced them together, like a completed jigsaw puzzle, and then Sellotaped everything in place. After reading what was written on the back of the envelope, he or she had gone hotfoot with it to Scotland Yard, no doubt hoping that there might be a reward and glowing publicity in the pipeline: *Sherlock Holmes Train Passenger Solves 'Nudes Murders' Mystery!*

I was so astonished that it took me some time to compute the scenario and compose myself.

'You're unsettled,' observed the inspector.

'You bet!' I replied, my voice quaking.

'I also noticed when you took the cigarette I offered you that your hand was shaking nervously.'

Ah! The trick.

'Also when one of my colleagues here lit the cigarette for you.'

Trick number two! Corroborating the result of trick number one.

'If there's something you want to get off your chest, now's the time to do it,' he said paternally. 'The longer you leave it, the harder it will become to open up about it.' His voice and manner were soothing; he had style and certainly knew how to entice one into the confessional. He was reclining, fingers interlaced, talking to me just like a solicitous father or a priest delivering a soothing homily. *Trust me. I'm your friend. I want to help.*

Here I was being encouraged to confess to being a serial killer, the monster the media – me included – had dubbed 'Jack the Stripper', as evil as Jack the Ripper and just as hard to catch. In view of the spine-chilling spectre of the judicial rope and noose, mocking these detectives would not have been a smart course of action. Here I should explain the significance of the pieced-together envelope. On the front was my name and address, typed, and on the reverse side I had listed the names of all the victims, *so far,* in chronological order and the dates on which the women disappeared and the corpses were later discovered: Gwynneth Rees (alias Tina Smart), 8 November 1963; Hannah Tailford (alias Terry Lynch), 2 February 1964; Irene Lockwood (alias Sandra Russell), 8 April 1964; Helene Barthelemy (alias Helen

Paul and Teddy), 24 April 1964; and Mary Fleming, 14 July 1964; all prostitutes with police files.

However, there was much more incriminating 'evidence' against me on that rescued envelope. I had scribbled certain sensitive details relating to the killer's specific MO that were not yet in the public domain, deliberately held back by the police. These juicy delicacies were known only to detectives at the top of the food chain, amounting to no more than a dozen senior officers, including forensic specialists and a Home Office pathologist.

In homicide investigations, it was common practice the world over for the police to withhold from the press, and therefore the public, certain key elements of which only the perpetrator could be aware, apart from the few top guns running the investigation operation.

Doubtlessly detectives at Scotland Yard were hoping that the envelope that had been passed to the Bedford police would prove to be my death certificate: a unique form of smoking gun.

As I sat staring at that envelope, chilling images scrolled through my head like a speeded-up documentary movie: a court chaplain placing on the head of a judge a black cap, made of silk and measuring nine inches square, which was always worn by the judge when passing the death sentence. Always there would be a melancholy, cathedral silence, broken only by the stony-faced judge reciting the 'gallows litany' that was as precise as a piece of Masonic ritual: '...There is only one sentence which the law permits me to pronounce and that is that you be taken from this place to a lawful prison, and thence to a place of execution, and that you be there hanged by the neck until you are dead. And may the Lord have mercy on your soul.' Bang on cue the chaplain, head bowed, would round-off the grim ritual with a solemn, 'Amen.'

Still fresh in my mind was the trial and execution in Bedford of

# A SUSPECT

James Hanratty, known as the A6 or Deadman's Hill murderer. He shot dead a married scientist and seriously wounded his young mistress, who was left paralysed for life, in a lay-by. After the hanging in Bedford prison on 4 April 1962, I interviewed the prison chaplain, 'Ref' Bearman – he was known more as 'Ref' than Rev. because he was an official football referee, in addition to his teaching duties at a local public school and gaol pastoral care work.

There was something inhumanly ghoulish about those procedural rites, so meticulously and cold-bloodedly structured by the state, for the final hours before the hangman pulled the lever to open the trapdoor to oblivion. Flashbacks of that conversation with Bearman seemed so germane as I sat in the office with those detectives, maybe in the same seat Hanratty had occupied before being charged.

About two days before a hanging a messenger would leave the Home Office in Whitehall on a motorbike bound for the prison where the execution was to take place. In his possession would be a box that he had to guard with his life, the contents so morbid to those in the *know,* yet meaningless to most of the population. Two reels of rope, the product of John Edgington and Sons of the Old Kent Road, London. Ropes for the very special purpose of hanging people. One of the ropes would be new. The other would have already been used, whether or not around someone's neck, I am unsure. The point of the choice for the hangman was that some executioners, proficient in this ancient black art, preferred rope that had been tried and tested, mainly because it had no stretch remaining, thus ensuring a clean break of the neck.

Upon the ceremonious arrival of the messenger at the gaol, the governor would take charge of the box and lock it in his office safe. At four p.m. precisely, on the day before the rope would snap a human neck, breaking the vertebrae, the box of grisly tricks would be removed from the safe, coinciding with the arrival of the hangman and his mate. They would examine the ropes and read the physical statistics of the condemned prisoner, which would have been meticulously prepared by the medical officer. Despite being in possession of these details, the hangman always wanted to peer for a few minutes into the cell through what was known as the 'Judas Hole'. Veteran executioner Albert Pierrepoint said that in those few minutes, he got a 'feel' for the person he was going to kill and could accurately assess how he would react during the seven paces to the rope and when the noose was slipped over his hooded head.

The execution chamber was always next door to the cell where the condemned prisoner spent his last few weeks, watched over by two warders day and night. A door connected the two rooms, but was traditionally hidden by a wardrobe. During the final evening, after one of the ropes had been selected, the drop would be tested, with sandbags deputising for the 'dead man talking' in the next cell. The bags would be filled with the exact amount of sand to equal the weight of the victim, and the length of the rope adjusted accordingly. The sandbags would be left hanging overnight in order to stretch the rope, removing any stretch, so the sudden jerk would be instantly lethal – if all went to plan. Then to dinner and a few beers for the state's professional killers, during which warders would be regaled with bleak 'jokes' about how previous prisoners had 'messed themselves' even before they encountered their brutal fate.

The hanging team always slept in the prison, usually with the two warders who would take over the 'last watch'. Reveille was six-thirty. The first task was to untie the sandbags and place them in a corner, near to a stretcher; this was in the 'drop zone'. Then it was up the steps to the trapdoor, on which chalk marks were made where the prisoner's feet should be positioned. After that was accomplished satisfactorily, it was breakfast-time, nearly always eggs and bacon. As Pierrepoint once told an interviewer, 'You can't do this job on an empty stomach.'

About ten minutes before the 'drop', the hangman and his assistant, the governor, two prison officers, the chaplain and maybe the county sheriff or his/her deputy, would assemble quietly in the hanging chamber. Any conversation was conducted in whispers.

As soon as the governor gave the thumbs-up sign after checking his watch, the hangman would strut briskly and purposefully into the condemned prisoner's cell through the main door, binding his hands behind his back. Simultaneously, one of the 'death watch' warders would push the wardrobe to one side, while the other opened the secret door to the prisoner's nemesis. In full, stark view would be the hanging rope. From that moment everything would happen fast. Seven measured paces to the trapdoor. Legs strapped at the ankles. A close-up encounter between hangman and his victim, eye-to-eye, smelling each other's breath, and for one the smell of fear. Like a conjuror producing a white rabbit from a hat, the hangman would pull a hood from his pocket to blind his helpless victim. The noose would be slipped over the hood, knotted, and the rope run through a metal eye and tightened. A rubber washer would be manoeuvred along the rope to hold the noose in place. A nod from the governor and the hangman would pull the lever, causing a distinctive clatter as the 'trap' opened beneath the tethered and blindfolded prisoner. The body would plunge from view, leaving the sad little group mesmerised by a gently swaying rope, resembling a pendulum.

There was still more work for the hangman. He was responsible for releasing and stripping the body for an inquest the same morning, a mere formality, with the medical officer confirming that death was the result of 'judicial hanging'. The body would be buried within the grounds of the prison.

Legend has it that just before Neville Heath was hanged in Pentonville prison, north London, in 1946, he asked for a whisky when the governor enquired if he had one last wish before dying. Just before the governor left the cell to fetch the drink, Heath is said to have added cheekily, 'While you're at it, you might as well make it a double, old chap.' I'm sure I would have asked for the whole bottle.

All this knowledge on such a gruesome subject was counter-productive for me that afternoon in Bedford police station. Ignorance may not have been bliss, but it would have been preferable.

Nonchalantly, in fact almost apologetically, the inspector asked for an explanation about my jottings on the back of the envelope.

Without histrionics, I explained that I'd been to the daily press conference, held early every evening, Monday to Friday, at Shepherd's Bush police station, the operational headquarters in west London of the long-running investigation. Politicians and the public were braying for a result, especially the female nightwalkers in the red-light territory where this serial killer stalked. The conference on the evening in question was led by Detective Superintendent Bill Marchant. There had been an almost tangible edginess among the top brass because there was an intuition flowing through the team that another corpse was overdue.

The killer had settled into a rhythm, roughly a three-monthly killing cycle. Forensic psychologists had expounded on the theory that the killer would emotionally 'feed off' each crime and would remain satiated for several weeks, comparable to an animal squirrelling away sustenance for a given period. Gradually, however, his hunger would return until he was consumed by a lust to strike again, thriving on the publicity, being an anonymous star; quite possibly someone who was a nonentity in his work and a failure as a husband and father. The urge and tension would mount until he could no longer be contained and he would be out of control, hunting on the streets again virtually robotically.

Helene Barthelemy's body had appeared in April. We were now into November. The clock was ticking. Marchant and his team feared that they were probably into the final countdown to number six. In fact, the killing could quite easily have already occurred and the wait now was for the killer to release the body from his lair and dump it, almost certainly within view of the River Thames. The fact that no prostitute had been reported missing was of little significance. Most of them were rootless. Their lifestyle tended to be nomadic. Usually they were little more than marionettes, dancing to the tune of their ponce. And ponces weren't known for their pastoral philosophy. Cops and police stations were anathema to them. Therefore, if one girl of a stable did a runner or just disappeared, it was unlikely for her 'master' to contact the police and fill out an official missing person's report.

Marchant made the usual noises. 'We are closing in. Never before has there been so much coordination between so many police divisions and nationwide cooperation.' Very Churchillian. 'The trail hasn't gone cold. It would be wrong to give the public that impression. We're confident we're on the right track.'

'What *track* is that?' I'd asked.

'Sorry, but that has to remain confidential at this stage. We don't want to alert *our man* that we have him in our sights; well, almost. You boys will be the first to know, I promise, when we've banged-up *our man*.'

There were no *girls* among us, so Marchant wasn't guilty of being sexist, although being macho was his nature. The nature of them all.

'So you think you know the identity of the killer?' I'd pressed, already being a pain.

'I wouldn't go that far,' he'd said cagily. 'But we're building a shortlist.'

That *was* news.

A *Daily Express* reporter beat me to the obvious follow-up question: How many names were there on the shortlist?

'Can't tell you,' was the anticipated, pithy reply. He meant *won't* rather than *can't*.

Someone else asked for a 'steer' – four, six, eight, ten, twelve, a thousand?

'We hope to be trimming it substantially within the next few days when all alibis have been bottomed-out,' Marchant had blagged.

'From what number?' I'd tried again.

'No more than a dozen.'

Well, that was something; a ballpark figure, at least.

Each answer had spawned more questions. I was eager to learn how the shortlisted men had become suspects. Had they police records for sex crimes, for example. Marchant had already 'let slip' too much, he confided artificially, as if we'd milked him further than he'd intended to allow, which was nonsense, of course. Officers of Marchant's rank and experience were shrewd and manipulative when it came to handling the media. He knew exactly how to play the press, to make reporters believe they had squeezed more out of him than he realised. Both sides wanted something; a bargain if possible. Everything came at a price, though. Marchant gave what he had to *sell* – nothing more at any price – and we paid by giving him the particular publicity he was angling for. I had many more questions, but not for him; they were stored up for a rendezvous later that evening with my special contact – or mole –who was deep within the elite murder squad.

# A SUSPECT

We met in a pub less than a quarter of a mile from Shepherd's Bush police station. He was a detective sergeant. Having police officers on a newspaper's payroll was an integral part of press and police culture of the times. Payments to my mole went openly on my expenses' account and would have been seen and accepted by the Inland Revenue. Senior officers were content to accept a bottle of whisky and a brace of pheasants at Christmas. No harm done. No investigation compromised. No lies told, except in ruses to snare villains. These gifts, not bribes, were seen as just another means of oiling the wheels of the working world. More importantly, it paradoxically gave the public a better deal in terms of transparency than in today's sterile and over-sanitised and zealous restrictive practices. Gone are the days when detectives had special relationships with crime correspondents, with two-way trust assiduously cultivated and nursed solicitously. Now the press have to rely on evasive statements from press bureaus, which merely encourages journalists to speculate and, in doing so, may easily compromise a delicate, softly-softly police operation.

During my covert meeting with the detective sergeant following Marchant's press conference, we consumed quite a few beers. That was the evening he tipped me off about the 'Deep Throat' modus operandi, which had never been hinted at before, not even during the inquests, when the pathologist who performed the post-mortem examination was legally required to give precise details at the public hearing of the cause of death.

In each case, the coroner had simply recorded death due to asphyxiation. In retrospect, it is astonishing that the media, including myself, hadn't led a chorus for greater amplification and clarification. After all, *asphyxiation* is so generic. I think we had all gone along like lemmings with the assumption that the hapless prostitutes had been strangled or suffocated with a pillow.

None of the relatives of the deceased hired a solicitor to cross-examine the pathologist at the inquests. Most likely this was due to lack of funds and not a callous act of disinterest.

As my insider informed me, the conspiracy of silence – or economy of detail – had been orchestrated with military thoroughness. Of course it couldn't have been achieved without the cooperation of pathologist and coroner. In fact, the full facts, the entire story, were contained within a tightly knit inner circle, a cop cabal of top brass, coincidentally nearly all Freemasons, plus a couple of detective sergeants who were also 'on the square'. Scotland Yard even had its own Freemasons' Lodge, meeting once a month on Friday afternoons, autumn until spring. After the ceremony in the 'temple', members would dine (known as the festive board) in one of their favourite restaurants, where they were treated to a concessionary rate, and the imbibing would continue unabated into the wee hours of Saturday. The cop Masons were humorously known within the Met as the 'Untouchables'.

There is no suggestion here that Freemasonry among the murder squad elite bred corruption or in ay way detracted from their investigations. However, it did bind together the 'brethren' into a club in which total loyalty to one another was expected, in accordance with the oath they had taken at their initiation, as long as their undertakings were lawful. However, human nature being what it is, jealousy was generated among those officers who weren't in the brotherhood, particularly those who had applied to join but had been blackballed, resulting in defamatory rumours doing the rounds, even in Parliament and among the press gang.

Inevitably, one theory was that the killer was a Freemason cop who was being shielded by his fellow 'brethren' in the murder squad. On a similar theme, there was a fable that the serial killer was a prominent businessman who was known to senior Met cops through Freemasonry and, once again, was being protected out of misguided loyalty to the secret society that boasted royalty among its ranks. (Since then, Freemasonry has become much more open and rather than being a secret society it is promoted as a society with secrets.) There was never anything to give credence to these malicious stories. There was nothing unusual about them, however; they were typical of those doing the rounds during Jack the Ripper's rampage.

At first I could not believe what I was hearing from my always reliable source – that the murder weapon was the perpetrator's penis. This was just too far-fetched. Certainly it wasn't something that I could contemplate putting in copy to my news editor, Ken James, a Welshman with a shock of pure white hair who was, at thirty-five, the youngest on national newspapers at that time to hold his pivotal position. The news editor was the beating heart of the news-gathering process of every newspaper. His ability determined the strength of the product. My view, as perhaps a rather reckless 'publish and be damned' Young Turk, was that James was feckless, a man who did his best to duck 'what if we've got it all wrong' nightmares. A very different animal from fellow Welshman Hugh Cudlipp, who edited the tabloid *Daily Mirror*, famous for its Andy Capp caricatures and the venomous snake-bite 'Cassandra' column.

I really thought that my mole was winding me up, that the beer had set fire to his lurid imagination, with the inevitable flames of fantasy. These murders preceded Linda Lovelace and the classic porno movie *Deep Throat*, later to become the sobriquet for the mole within the White House who was keeping the *Washington Post* apprised of all the black arts relating to President Richard Nixon's presidency and the scandalous Watergate cover-up. So it was understandable for me to think that my informant was joking, in bad taste, admittedly, but drink worked wonders on inhibitions and shibboleths. Seeing my reaction, he managed one of those instant sobering-up feats and eyeballed me with penetrating sincerity, making it clear that he wasn't jesting.

Of course I asked the obvious question: why hadn't the killer been castrated, surely the instinctive, self-defensive response by any woman having her windpipe blocked in such grotesque fashion? The answer was that in each case an instrument had been deployed to restrain the women from being able to bite and was the reason why a number of the victims had front teeth missing.

'How much of this could I publish?' I asked, really testing the veracity of what I'd been told because I knew it would never get into print in my family newspaper, unless it was released in the form of an official statement, such as from Scotland Yard or a coroner at one of the inquests.

'None of it,' he replied definitively. 'Not yet. Not until I give you the thumbs up. It's something you have in the bag, so you can work out why certain things are happening.' He knew it was safe to confide in me because if I reneged on the code of trust I'd never get anything else from him or anyone else in the murder squad. My name would be circulated and I'd be on the outside, a pariah for ever.

Something more plausible and usable at that stage was the news that similar paint marks had been found on a number of the bodies, indicating that they had been stored in the same place, possibly a garage or workshop. 'You mean I can write that?' I said.

'It could be helpful, but don't attribute the info to me; it might make the warped bastard overreact and do something stupid in panic. You never know. Optimism is a healthy drug.'

On the envelope, in addition to the victims' names and a few personal particulars, I had scribbled *penis weapon* and *body paint marks*, neither of which meant anything to the Bedford officers, but had most certainly resonated with Scotland Yard's A team.

The Bedford bunch were merely emissaries of the Yard. Their task was to pull me in, put me through the tumble dryer, and make a judgment. Did my story stack up or was it threadbare?

No provincial police force cares to make a fool of itself by having a serial killer in its grasp and casually letting him go, something that occurred years later several times with the West Yorkshire Police. The inspector quizzing me was only too aware that if he released me and later it transpired that I was the perpetrator, who was being hunted nationwide, his career would end on a bonfire of profanities. Someone at the Yard, not Marchant or one of the lead detectives, had instructed the Bedford police to hang on to me if in any doubt. This communique from the Yard had come from a deskbound middle-ranking officer to whom my name and address meant nothing. Why should it? Even if the envelope had been seen by my Yard insider, there would have been no reason to immediately make the connection; he had no idea that I lived outside London.

The Bedford inspector asked for the name of the Met officer I'd gone to a pub with, 'just to verify your story'. *Bollocks!* I thought. I replied affably, 'You don't really expect me to divulge *that* source, do you? If I did, I'd be out of a job.'

He smiled whimsically, 'Well, I had to try,' adding, 'So what made you dispose of the envelope if it had valuable references for you?'

I went through the sequence of events methodically and chronologically. I left the pub between nine and nine-thirty, took a cab to St Pancras railway station, where I caught a slow, suburban, stopping train to Bedford, using my season ticket, which I produced for the police inspector's benefit. I'd been dozing fitfully for about half an hour when the train reached Luton and the noise of slamming doors woke me. Making use of the time, I copied the notes on the envelope into my notebook.

Somewhere after Luton, I decided there was no point retaining the envelope and 'you know the rest,' I said.

'The person who took the envelope to the police has alleged in a statement that you were behaving suspiciously,' he remarked, eyeballing me, the way you see it done on TV, watching for a nervous tic or tell-tale evasiveness.

'I wasn't behaving *suspiciously*, I was pissed,' I countered testily. I was content to be self-deprecating when it was to my advantage.

By now we were playing the game of who blinks first. I was gambling that he wouldn't wish to make an ass of himself. He could have locked me up, 'pending further inquiries', but my newspaper would have had a lawyer down to Bedford within an hour and the situation would have snowballed. I knew from personal experience that the murder squad then was a gigantic, leaking battleship. All crime correspondents on national newspapers had their own moles, at various levels of seniority in the Met. The hottest leaks came from middle-rank informers, especially those who felt they were undervalued and underpaid.

Although the inducements were small beer, it was nonetheless a cottage industry and for that to have been made public would have sunk many a ship. So I knew I had leverage, an insurance policy that afforded me comprehensive cover.

Decision-time had arrived for the inspector. He seemed to toss a coin in his head and it came down on the side of common sense.

'Let's go to the canteen for a cup of tea,' he suggested, his demeanour now chummy.

At one point in the conversation in the canteen – just the two of us – he prodded the evidence bag containing the envelope and speculated, 'Something as crazy as this affair is how the maniac will probably eventually be caught.'

He was wrong, of course.

## CHAPTER 2

# SHADOW BOXING
# WITH 'NIPPER'

As we finished our cups of tea, I said to the Bedford inspector, 'So what happens now?'

'I'll have someone drive you home.'

*So I'm off the hook.*

'What about the envelope?' I asked.

'Goes back to the Yard.'

'And how long will they keep it?'

'Probably until someone's nicked and convicted. No use to you now, is it?' The question was rhetorical. 'Eventually it'll be destroyed with tons of other rubbish.'

We returned to his office for him to make arrangements for a driver to ferry me home. 'Wait there a minute,' he said, as if an afterthought had suddenly occurred to him mid-stride. 'I'm just going to make a private call. Won't be a minute.' Obviously it concerned something he was anxious for me not to hear.

'I've just spoken with the Yard,' he said, on his return. 'They still want to speak with you direct. Not urgently. Nothing to worry about.

*Oh, yeah!*

'If they were still taking this seriously, they'd have sent a posse down right away to collect you,' he continued convivially, seeing my frown. 'I've outlined the situation to them. They saw the funny side of it.'

*But I hadn't!*

'Then why do they still want to question me?' I queried.

'Just to officially sign it off, so to speak. To see that you really *are* the Michael Litchfield they know about. You know what they're like up there; reckon we provincials are cowboys, with straw sticking from our ears.'

'So why have they left it to you to interview me in the first place?' I said logically, so I thought.

'Because this is our turf,' he replied protectively, as if talking about his garden or vegetable allotment.

I had already shown the inspector my Scotland Yard press card, but I could see that there was no future in further protests.

'So what's the arrangement?' I wondered aloud.

'You're to report to Chelsea police station, at eleven on Monday morning.'

'Chelsea police station?' I double-checked, because this seemed strange. If not the Yard, I could fully understand Shepherd's Bush, but Chelsea... Who was there who could possibly have a finger on the pulse of the 'London Nudes' investigation? I was soon to find out.

'You should ask for Detective Superintendent Leonard Read. He'll be expecting you.'

'Nipper' Read, the legend! He was one of the shrewdest detectives in the history of British policing, a real-life Sherlock Holmes, a cerebral cop who was making his name as a gangland-buster. He didn't waste his time on the small-time racketeers. He went for the jugular of London's most toxic and cut-throat criminals, in particular the infamous Kray brothers, who through bribery and every interpretation of corruption, including torture, had evaded justice for years. 'Nipper' was to prove their nemesis. However, unlike many Met detectives of that vibrant, heady period, he did it the honourable way; no planted evidence, no witnesses induced to perjure themselves and no 'verballing'.

Interviews weren't recorded electronically for some time to come and many defendants were said by the police to have confessed to a crime when that was a lie, hence the cry, 'I've been verballed.' Even Jimmy Evans, who was a career criminal, a specialist in safe-blowing, who also castrated the gangster George Foreman with a shotgun as revenge for bedding his wife, testified in his autobiography to 'Nipper's' honesty. 'A straight cop', which was a very special commendation from a villain who wrote that he 'hated every copper' and as a breed they were 'scum'.

My wife (we divorced several years later) was peeping around the net curtains in our living room when I scrambled as fast as possible out of the unmarked police car on my return from Bedford police station.

Before I was even halfway up the path to our house, she'd opened the front door and was hovering on the threshold to greet me with an outpouring of relief.

'Thank God you're back!' she cooed. 'You were gone so long, I was having kittens. I was getting frantic. I couldn't call a solicitor because none of them are open on Saturdays. Any other day, including a Sunday, I could have phoned your office for help,' she added.

I was pleased that she hadn't been able to do either. Calling out a solicitor would have started to make the whole thing official and all informality would have been zapped. As for my news editor, Ken James, I wasn't sure that I wanted him to know. It could have proved embarrassing for me, having disposed of the leaked, sensitive information in the careless way that I had. Better to allow it to run its course and see where it went. I'd lost all track of time and had no idea that I'd been *entertained* by the Bedford police for almost four hours. As hosts, they couldn't be faulted.

Naturally Pearl was gagging to be regaled with the uncensored version of events. What was it all about? Was it a case of mistaken identity? Was I worried? Had I been treated fairly? Was it all sorted?

After I'd finished my account, which had been punctuated with a peppering of interruptions, she gasped in an uncontrived astonished tone, 'They didn't *really* believe you were *that* monster, surely?'

'They feed on hope,' I said,' I said, trying to be blasé. 'Sometimes that's all they have for sustenance.'

Of course when I slipped in the little matter of having to see 'Nipper' Read in London on the Monday, she was horrified. 'So you're still a suspect? You're *not* off the hook. You're scaring me.'

'It's just protocol,' I said breezily, endeavouring to keep any self-doubt camouflaged.

Pearl stood with her back to the gas fire, our wedding photograph on the simple mantelpiece, a shaky hand to her chin and our daughter nestling into her side, pestering to be cuddled. In reverie, she said absently, 'I can't get this out of my head: a wife somewhere might be standing just like I am, with her husband, perhaps chatting about what they can do for a bit of Saturday-night fun, and all he's interested in is who he can next kill, when and where. Scary, isn't it?'

What could I say? Nothing seemed appropriate, until she pondered aloud, 'Do you think *he's* married?'

I refrained from saying, 'Just like *me*, you mean?' Instead,

I told her that Marchant had been counselling every species of shrink. 'They all have their pet theories and you pays your money and takes your choice.' There were those who believed that London's new Jack was a prosaic husband and father, probably holding down a normal, regular job, though most likely a mundane one, but was a sexual deviant unfulfilled by sex with his wife. So he began frequenting brothels, where the prostitutes were prepared to indulge his outré taste and then one day he was infected with VD. Perhaps he passed it on to his wife, she accused him of whoring, banned him from her bed and the marriage disintegrated, for which he blamed not himself but the hookers, leading to a vendetta. That was a popular scenario trotted out over and over, just as much by pub-shrinks as qualified ones.

'Reasonable,' Pearl commented. 'I don't mean it's reasonable what he's doing, but the theory seems plausible.'

All the theories were plausible, but they wouldn't help the police one jot until they had *him* in their headlights.

After more windmills of the mind and now cuddling Joanne, she asked, 'And what are other shrinks saying?'

One popular storyline was that he was a loner, single, never been married, rejected by women, clumsy with his attempts at relationships, mocked in the workplace and couldn't keep a decent job, of low intelligence but canny and vulpine, perhaps kicked about as a kid.

'And suddenly he sees himself as all-powerful,' she cottoned on.

The backers of this trend of thought argued that for the first time in his life he was the dominant one, seeing himself as the alpha of all alphas. He was in control. He gave the orders and dished out the punishment. He stalked the streets at night and alone decided who lived and who died. Such power was not only intoxicating but also orgasmic. The point stressed by these theorists was that this was more sexually gratifying for him than the climax, the killing, which was quite possibly a let-down, frustrating bathos. In this sense, he wasn't a sex maniac. Sex wasn't the driver. Any sexual satisfaction was a bi-product.

By the end of that eventful Saturday, I'd completely forgotten about the horse I'd backed. In fact, I never did learn about its fate. But I did remember its name: *Surprise Packet.*

* * *

'Nipper' Read greeted me as if we were inveterate drinking pals. Beaming from behind his desk, he said, as he shook hands with the vigour of a cocktail-barman at work with his shaker, 'Good of you to drop by.' Same patter as at Bedford; perhaps it's in the training manual. Just as if I'd turned up to a charity coffee morning. 'I hope I'm not keeping you from anything important,' he continued apologetically. 'I can't imagine we'll be long. Just a formality. Red tape. One of the admin nightmares of climbing the ladder. Oh, well...'

My instinctive reflex to *it's just a formality* was to reinforce my guard and shore up my alertness. I had learned very quickly that nothing was ever *a mere formality* for the police during a multiple-murder inquiry. If it had indeed been a trivial matter, I wouldn't have been sitting opposite 'Nipper', who was already a Scotland Yard grandee and the only detective in London to chill the hot blood of the murderous Kray brothers.

Despite his disarming chumminess, we'd never met before. Indeed, we were also destined never to cross paths again. The first impression he made on me, apart from his cheerfulness, came from his stature. For some inexplicable reason, I was expecting to be confronted by an intimidating colossus, armed at least with a thumbscrew. Of course, his nickname should have been clue enough. He appeared so strikingly diminutive, though that may have been exaggerated because he was slumped in his leather-padded chair, jacket slung over the back, and the sleeves of his spotlessly clean and starched white shirt rolled up. Nipper was also very dapper.

And there on his desk, taking centre stage, taunting me, was *that* ubiquitous evidence-bag containing the wretched envelope, the little demon that was haunting me like a fiendish leprechaun.

Nipper began by prodding the plastic bag and saying something to the effect that, 'I bet you'll never throw away another envelope on public transport.' He was still all smiles and bonhomie. Not once was this unlaboured cordiality to diminish. 'If you wrote about this, no one would believe you.'

'Certainly it wouldn't work in fiction,' I said. 'Not a chance of suspending disbelief.'

After some thought, he said, bonding seamlessly, a master craftsman, something I had to admire, 'Funny old phrase that. 'Why can't they just say *unbelievable*?' The question was rhetorical and directed more at himself than me. 'I guess *unbelievable* wouldn't be sufficiently bookish.'

Finally, he returned to the relevant tramlines: 'You're obviously aware we've had a comprehensive report from our colleagues in Bedford. I hope they didn't spoil your weekend.'

We were still circling one another metaphorically like animals sniffing for a sign of weakness, one cunningly predatory and the other hedgehog-defensive.

'No, no,' I said. 'They were most hospitable. The tea was even drinkable.'

Suddenly he was effusive with an apology. 'Good heavens, I haven't offered you a coffee. You must think me rude. Can I get you one?'

I thanked him and we went through the customary social ritual of whether I preferred it black or white, sugar or no sugar, and if yes to sugar, then how much. This was truly surreal. If his ploy was to bamboozle me, then he was conclusively successful. It was all so polite and civilised that, instead of my being mellowed, I was anxiously expecting a trapdoor to snap open beneath my chair at any moment.

He was articulate and urbane, nothing remotely resembling the movie image of top gangbusters. I was soon to discover that many of the lodestars of the Yard confounded public perception. Flying Squad supremo Tommy Butler, for example, was another small man, though very different in character from Nipper. Despite his exalted public persona and the rollercoaster saga of his abortive attempts to extradite Great Train Robber and prison escapee Ronnie Biggs from Brazil, Butler had a reputation among London's underworld for being a bigger villain than the civilian criminals. In Soho, it was common knowledge that Butler, known none too affectionately as the 'Grey Fox', regularly pocketed bribes from hitman Freddie Foreman, and £30,000-plus of the stash recovered from the Great Train Robbery was locked in his personal safe at the Yard and not added to the rest of the hot loot harvested from raids by honest officers. The money recouped was only ever a fraction of the original stolen two and a half million pounds at a time when a new house in the Home Counties could be bought for three grand.

Read and Butler will feature prominently throughout this narrative, so it is worth pausing at this point to grasp their significance and counterpoint personas.

After his retirement, Nipper Read wrote an autobiography, in which he was scathing of the 'Grey Fox', writing that 'in one way' Butler was 'the worst detective I've ever come across.' How about that for an uppercut to an ego? Read elaborated,

'He was so secretive.' Diluting the poison, but only marginally and momentarily, Nipper conceded that Butler was a 'great investigator', only to return to the arsenic with a withering assault on Tommy's inability to inspire a rapport with his grafting worker-bees and that he was a hopeless team player:

'Really opening up and having a conference, saying, "Listen, chaps, this is what it's all about" would have been as alien as cutting his own throat. He was obsessed by security. He would never tell his men what was happening where or when.

'Occasionally he would join his team for a drink, but it was only occasionally. He was a very private man and no one was ever really close to him. Unmarried, he lived with his mother, but home was really the CID office.'

These negative features of Butler were soon to luridly fire certain people's susceptible and vindictive imaginations.

Read complained that Butler shut himself in his office upstairs in Paddington Green police station in the evenings and officers downstairs would hear him thumping his typewriter for hours, as if involved in a two-fingered punch-up. 'Downstairs we could hear the tapping of the machine,' Read recounted reproachfully. 'No one knew what he was doing.' The vision penned by Read was of an anti-social, obsessive maverick, devoid of any gregarious instinct or skills of social interaction.

Perhaps Butler was something of an elusive enigma, because Read softened his tone at one point, stressing the 'enormous affection' people had for Tommy 'because on the face of it, he was such a lovely man.' *On the face of it* was the prelude to more venom. He was really suggesting that Butler wasn't all that he seemed; that he was a sham or, at best, a chameleon. 'He had a good sense of humour and a nice attitude. The police and detection were his only obsessions.'

There are, of course, some inconsistencies in Read's assessment of Butler, but clearly these two contemporary giants of the Yard were not of the same breed.

Some readers might be confused when I refer to officers like Nipper Read and Tommy Butler as Scotland Yard icons and then describe them working from a *foreign* police station, such as Paddington Green or Chelsea. In those swashbuckling, *romantic* days, the top guns were nomadic. They would 'set up shop' in any Met police station that was conveniently located for the investigation they were heading and they would handpick a team, possibly drawn from several divisions within the metropolis.

Likewise, the murder squad comprised detective super-intendents and detective inspectors who were stationed throughout London. They would be assigned to homicides almost on a rota basis or where they happened to be camped at the time of a crime. There were no regional crime squads, so investigations into provincial murders would be sub- contracted to Scotland Yard and delegated to one of the murder squad doyens to take charge. Murder squad was an umbrella title for a whole circus of specialists, operating from many locations, who would come together when called upon. The lead detective, always deferred to as the Guv'nor, would cherry-pick his team from a vast pool of talent. Each lead detective would have his favourites for major roles; a parallel were the casting directors of Hollywood blockbusters, who would tend to favour professionals he/she had worked with successfully before and trusted implicitly.

Jack Slipper, another fabled Yard cop who dovetailed effectively with Butler in the worldwide dragnet for the Great Train Robbers, also had some harsh words in his blunt memoirs, *Slipper of the Yard*, for the 'Grey Fox'. Like 'Nipper', he best remembered Butler as a secretive night owl who worked late hours and insisted on being left alone. 'Night was his best time,' he recalled. 'He never came in early in the morning, but if he did it was best to keep out of his way. Often, if you passed him in the morning, he'd walk right by you, or he might just growl. He had quite a few odd habits, but one in particular was the way he used to go home at night. Late in the evening, he'd sometimes go down to the Red Lion, a pub just near the Yard, for a drink before going home. He wasn't much of a drinker and, by Squad standards, you'd say he didn't really drink at all! He didn't smoke either [though he died from lung cancer, aged only fifty-seven] but he'd drop into the pub occasionally to be sociable. Then, if he'd sent his driver off earlier, he'd take a lift with whoever was last on duty. He was a single man and he lived with his mother in a little house in Washington Road, Barnes, near Hammersmith Bridge.'

Apparently, Butler would never allow the driver to drop him off outside his mother's house. Neither would he ever invite another cop into his home, even if they had known one another for years and had worked countless investigations together. In fact, he went to extreme lengths to ensure that he was never seen in a police car near his neighbourhood. Whatever the weather – rain, hail, snow, ice or fog – he would order his late-night chauffeur to stop the car at least half a mile from where he lived. 'Just here will do nicely,' he'd say, said one retired detective sergeant. 'We might even be a mile from his terraced place. I don't reckon it was a case of his being ashamed of being a copper; quite the reverse, he was chuffed by his status in society and his achievements. It's my opinion, and lots of people speculated over the years about his weird habits, that he was protecting his old mum.

'I think he feared that if locals got to know who he was and how he earned his crust, his mum could become a target; even be kidnapped and held hostage as a bargaining tool, especially when he was rounding up those cowboys [the Great Train Robbers]. I mean, if any friend or relative of the gang got hold of the old girl and stashed her in a coal-cellar, say, somewhere in the East End, just imagine the leverage they'd reckon they had over Tommy. They would think they'd struck gold, an insurance policy that guaranteed their freedom. But it wouldn't have been, you know. He'd have allowed the bastards to slit his old mum's throat rather than let a villain get the better of him. I believe he feared his own response to anyone making off with his old ma, so he went to extremes to keep the risks to a minimum. No villain would ever be allowed to manipulate him, however high the stakes for potential personal loss.' On that score, it appeared that this ex-cop's loyalty and reverence to the 'Grey Fox' was misplaced.

The evidence is strong that Butler was milking money seized from the Great Train Robbers as and when they were captured to cushion and sweeten his retirement.

Shortly before his retirement, Butler was arrested in Juan-les-Pins, a swanky jet-set resort next to Antibes and between Nice and Cannes on the French Riviera. A female sunbather reported him to the police for ogling the hundreds of bikini-clad women – most of them socialites – through high-powered, military-issue binoculars and also taking reels of photographs. In other words, he was suspected of being a creepy Peeping Tom and a possible stalker threat to women. He had caught the attention of many people because he was 'at it' for four hours continuously, not even a break for a drink or a snack.

Of course he protested vociferously when two officers frogmarched him to their wagon and pitched him headfirst through the rear doors, landing at the feet of two snarling Alsatians, much to the appreciation and amusement of the aggrieved beach-beauties. Butler's knowledge of the French language was limited to *oui* and *s'il vous plaît*, neither of which was appropriate, so the gendarmes hadn't a clue what he was ranting about.

When he was asked by the chief of the local gendarmerie to explain his behaviour, Butler confidently produced his Scotland

Yard warrant card and claimed to be on the trail of Bruce Reynolds, the mastermind of the Great Train Robbers, who was on the run. Butler had good reason to believe that Reynolds was high-rolling on the Riviera, funding his casino-gambling, champagne-guzzling and high-class whoring with his lion's share of the stolen loot, equivalent to £45 million in 2016.

Although Juan-les-Pins was only a modestly sized resort, with a summer population of around seventy-five thousand, swollen by opulent tourists, the police chief was no simpleton and neither was he impressed, much to Butler's chagrin, by the reputation of Scotland Yard; in fact, if anything, it was a red flag to a bull. The chief was particularly rattled by Butler's insinuation that the two buffoons who had arrested him had probably allowed one of the world's most 'Wanted' men to slip through the net yet again. Yet another blow to the *etente cordiale*!

For a start, the chief, whose English was adequate, was sniffy about the warrant-card, suggesting, quite legitimately, that it could easily be a forgery. He actually told Butler that he was a 'funny-looking policeman,' asking sardonically if his grey, rapidly receding hair was a disguise for undercover work.

Despite Nipper Read writing that Butler had a 'good sense of humour', on this occasion he wasn't the least amused.

'If you don't believe who I am, call Scotland Yard,' Butler said trenchantly.

The reply was a steady, 'I intend to.' Followed by, 'And while I do, you can wait in one of the cells.'

Butler was incandescent. The great 'Grey Fox' locked in a grotty, foreign dungeon-style cell, suspected of being a beachcombing pervert! The UK was not yet in the Common Market, the precursor to the EC.

Butler's version was that he was quickly put through on the phone to one of the commanders at the Yard and, after genial handshakes, a grovelling apology and salutations, he was shown the door, into the street, binoculars and camera returned. Only later did he discover that the film had been removed from the camera.

The cynics at the Yard weren't conned by Butler's story. First, he was on holiday. Before leaving, he hadn't advised anyone of his plans and itinerary. True, whenever on leave in the UK, he was as restless as a flea without flesh on which to picnic. Work was Butler's vocation and vacation. The Yard's senior bureaucrats weren't the least surprised to learn that Butler had used his leave to go robber-stalking on the Continent, leaving his mum to fend for herself...

There had been a plethora of anonymous reports that Reynolds had been spotted on the Riviera, a blonde in tow, which figured. Of course the Côte d'Azur covers a wide area; to say, 'I saw Brucie boy living it up on the flippin' Riviera' was vastly different from alleging that he'd just been spotted in Soho. Because of Butler's cagey modus operandi, only he knew the hotspots of the Reynolds supposed sightings. Saint Tropez, Antibes and Cannes would have been the obvious ones, so it could be logically assumed that Butler had been scouting in the most likely area, if indeed Reynolds was one of the big spenders among the new-moneyed playboys and girls in the ritzy South of France, once the preserve of international aristocrats.

The promenade in Juan-les-Pins was very similar to the one in Nice, and British in ambience. Once a fishing village, the resort had morphed dramatically into a pleasure playground for the idle, nouveau riche, vacationing Hollywood actors and starlets, voluptuous hookers, big-hitter thieves and more than a fair share of parvenus. Locals would picnic in the shade of the forest of pines, leaving the tourists to fry on the silky sand and the decks of garish yachts.

Butler was a pro-active predator. If there were no promising leads, he would follow his nose; writers would call it acting on a hunch, an impulse, which, make no mistake, had served him well in the past. Despite the vague and variable reports that placed Reynolds on the Riviera, it was Butler's hooked nose that navigated him there.

To Butler, the Riviera was Bruce's type of scene; it *smelled* right: glorious beaches, a night-life of sumptuous clubs and classy casinos, the mesmerising rattle of roulette wheels under glittering chandeliers, and underdressed women: a colony of shapely, bronzed bodies. Everyone there for enjoyment, exactly what the robbery was designed to finance.

Then there was the celebrated Hotel Le Provençal, of which Charlie Chaplin had been a patron. Yet more than all this, it was something else that Butler fancied would have been the irresistible magnet for Reynolds. The Grey Fox knew that Reynolds's sobriquet in the London netherworld was 'Napoleon'. Not too many professional British villains would have known that Napoleon Bonaparte had once resided on the coast between Antibes and Juan-les-Pins. Reynolds was by far the most intelligent of the Great Train Robbers and Butler doubtlessly surmised that the Napoleon of London's gangland would be unable to resist the lure of following in the footsteps of his illustrious progenitor. Butler probably reasoned that Reynolds would be unable to resist the concept of returning as 'Napoleon' to Antibes, following in the Emperor's footsteps; so delusional. Perhaps even a personal challenge to Butler to see if he could decode Reynolds's movements and motives.

And Butler was right. Reynolds *was* there. On the beaches. Sauntering along the promenade with an arm embracing the bare flesh of a suntanned female. Impressing his escort with reckless wagers in the casinos. Sipping vintage champagne where once Charlie Chaplin had drunk. But here is the oddity: the chief of police in Juan-les-Pins had the films developed that had been confiscated from Butler and his long-lens camera and every shot was of a sunbathing female, many of them topless; there was not a single frame of a man.

The rolls of film were mailed to the Met Commissioner at Scotland Yard, while copies were retained. What was said in the missive to the Commissioner is not known to me, but probably the negatives were handed to Butler and that was the end of the matter. Naturally, there was much mirth among the senior ranks who were *in the know*. 'Dirty old Peeping Tommy' was the jibe by those mandarins at the Yard who disapproved of Butler's methods. 'A typical, hypocritical voyeur' voiced one commander. 'Tommy up to his old tricks!' was the kinder locker-room expression of the few who hero-worshipped him. As for Butler, it was a storm in an empty teacup. Such was his standing, he could walk on water and not get his feet wet.

Just for the record, Reynolds had assumed the name of Keith Miller, living first in Mexico and Canada, before heading for the French Riviera, which was much too close for comfort. When Butler finally caught up with him, it was in respectable Torquay, known as the *English Riviera,* where Reynolds was the quiet and neighbourly Mr Keith Hiller. 'Hello, Bruce, it's been a long time [five years, to be exact],' said the Grey Fox triumphantly. With a resigned shrug, Reynolds answered, *'C'est la vie.'* Butler's stunt on the real Riviera was history. Results were the only measure of a man – and increasingly women – in police forces. Reynolds had evaded detection overseas for so long, but like so many ex-pat criminals, especially cockneys for some reason, he was drawn to the womb of his homeland – and downfall.

Police protocol dictated that if investigators wanted to encroach on another force's turf to follow leads, then there should be collaboration. It was simply a matter of common courtesy; you didn't go plunging into someone else's backyard to collect your ball without consulting the householder; the police principle was based on that basic premise. The French police, through Interpol, were well aware of the long-running hunt for Reynolds, yet Butler hadn't informed any of the French law-enforcement agencies that he would be snooping around their south coast, which, if he had, would have spared him the embarrassment that occurred. Butler probably considered himself on a busman's holiday and therefore etiquette didn't apply. If he never told his own team what he was up to, why should anyone be surprised that he didn't confide in the French?

When Butler retired, much of the media related the story of his pursuing Reynolds on the Continent while on holiday as an example of his dedication to duty; a copper to the core. Of course, they weren't privy to the full story.

I have dwelt on Butler's foibles because of their burgeoning relevance to the Nudes Murders as the considerable and bizarre twists and turns unfold.

\* \* \*

During my encounter with Nipper Read at Chelsea police station, it was soon apparent that one of the reasons for having me there was to provide him with a natural opportunity to launch a fishing expedition to try to establish the identity of my mole. I cannot imagine that he ever really expected me to betray my source, but he was far more persistent and persuasive than the Bedford detective inspector. 'It'll just be between the two of us,' he said, almost with hand-on-heart sincerity, the way a TV chat show presenter would jokingly say the phrase to a celebrity guest, with chuckles from the audience. 'It won't go any further than this room,' he added, with the technique of a very smooth salesman. 'I'm just intrigued.'

For all I knew, and indeed cared, he could have meant what

he was saying; just cajoling something out of me to be stored in his own, private memory-file. Butler wasn't the only Yard detective to squirrel away little secret nuggets about colleagues, information that could be traded for a future favour. My mole might have been useful to someone like Nipper in a different way, deploying him as a conduit for something he wanted making public, while at the same time distancing himself from the leak. If that was indeed why Nipper wanted me to finger my inside source, it would have worked to my advantage to have cooperated, but I couldn't take the chance. Playing poker with Nipper wasn't to be recommended.

Read's attempt at camaraderie continued unabated until he finally ran out of steam, time and coffee. 'Maybe we can do business together in the not too distant future,' he said, with a sort of last throw of the dice. 'I can understand why you're so trusted by *what's his name*?' We both broke into laughter at his own *Carry on Cops* clumsy effort to con the name from me.

We parted cordially with a warm handshake and a matey slap on the back for me.

I was almost out of the door of his office when there was a comic Lieutenant *Columbo,* of TV fame, replicated sketch, but in reverse: 'One last thing...'

I hovered on the threshold, door ajar.

'I needed to see your face for myself; that was very necessary. This wasn't a waste of time for me; I'm sorry, though, if it has been for you.'

He was already scribbling notes in a buff folder, head down, enigmatic as ever.

As I stepped into the murky street, my head was buzzing with the tantalising words, *I needed to see your face for myself...* what could he have meant? Was it some kind of warning? Or threat? Or could it have been a coded message?

I did not have long to wait for the answer.

## CHAPTER 3

# THE 'SOLICITOR'

Two days later, on the Wednesday, I returned from a long, liquid lunch to my newspaper office in Endell Street, off Long Acre in Covent Garden, to be told by a female journalist that a friend of mine had called and left a message, saying he hoped to see me in the Jack of Clubs at around eleven that evening.

'All he'd say was to tell you it was Jack calling,' said my colleague, Liz Prosser, a Birmingham-bred general news reporter, and a very capable one, too. Women reporters on the original *Sun* newspaper weren't allowed to be on duty after nine p.m. and were certainly not considered fit for the crime beat, very much a male preserve. Emulating the police forces of that otherwise social-revolutionary era, Fleet Street was a very macho jungle with an extremely low glass ceiling. Instead of doing night shifts, female journalists would nip across Endell Street to the Cross Keys pub for gin and tonics. The landlady, Annie Hulbert, was known with enormous affection as 'The Banker' because she

43

would bankroll any impecunious *Sun* journalist. The cardinal sin, however, was to spend any of her loaned money in another Covent Garden pub, the penalty for which was permanent expulsion.

'Jack' was the alias for my Yard informant, real name Bob Berry, a murder squad detective sergeant, well-built with a military bearing and moustache; not someone to tangle with physically. The media had dubbed the serial killer 'Jack the Stripper', a none-too-subtle play on Jack the Ripper. So 'Jack' had seemed the natural pseudonym for my mole to adopt when making contact and simultaneously disguising his identity.

The Jack of Clubs, in Brewer Street, Soho, was a regular meeting place for us when the rendezvous had to be in the evening. The club, a basement establishment, was next to Isow's restaurant and the club's name perpetuated the 'Jack' theme in the relationship with my Yard insider, which somehow added to the frisson.

Jack Isow, a Polish Jew, whose name at birth was Joseph Isowitski, owned both the restaurant and the nightclub, which was the responsibility of his affable son, Norman. Both premises created a reputable oasis in the middle of a desert of decadence. The restaurant, which was frequented by celebrities, including Adam Faith, Tom Jones, Frank Sinatra, Liberace, Marilyn Monroe, George Raft and Diana Dors, was on the corner of dank and dingy Walkers Court, home to the Raymond Revuebar, a grubby porn shop and a wallet-emptying clip joint.

Jack Isow had made his money as a major player in the black market during and immediately after the Second World War. Having made his pile dubiously, he could afford to don the demeanour of respectability. He had bought property shrewdly in Soho at knockdown prices, including what had once been the Doric Ballroom in Walkers Court, at this time a no-go alley for decent folk. The one-time Doric Ballroom had deteriorated into a crumbling shell of a building and Isow, chubby, balding and avuncular, couldn't believe his luck when Paul Raymond, itching to rent it for the launch of his planned striptease and burlesque shows, cheerfully tied himself to a twenty-one-year lease.

The doorman at the Jack of Clubs always unnerved me. He was ex-heavyweight boxer George 'Nosher' Powell and he was built like a Centurion tank. Despite my being something of a habitué there, I don't believe I was ever treated to a smile from him. He trebled-up as doorman, cloakroom attendant and bouncer. If, when trying to be sociable, I asked if it was busy downstairs, the most I'd get from him was, 'So-so'. More often, though, it was a dismissive grunt.

Downstairs, I was greeted by the manager/head waiter, Mr Pino, an absolute charmer, always immaculately dressed in a dinner suit and black bow tie. We shook hands, exchanged pleasantries, before he said, 'Your friend is already here. He's at your usual table.' He knew there was no need to escort me. This club was not anything resembling a basement dive. True, there were 'hostesses' – about six of them – but they weren't hustlers; such predatory behaviour would never have been tolerated by the courtly Mr Pino. Closed long ago, I'd venture that this nightclub, its girls and clientele, were the most decorous in the whole of Soho. There was never any hard sell. If a 'hostess' was invited to join a customer at his table, she would be expected to ask for champagne, preferably a magnum, but if the punter preferred a less expensive wine or even a beer, then that was his prerogative and there would be no hassle. The hostess would charge a 'companionship fee', but that was between her and the client, and none of it went to the club. In most other London nightclubs, the head waiter would expect a backhander from every hostess who was booked out. Another rule at the Jack of Clubs was that no hostess was permitted to leave the establishment until after the second cabaret performance. If she then chose to go elsewhere with a customer, then that was her affair. The hostesses were regarded as freelance traders and this protected the club management from any accusation of living off immoral earnings.

By *usual table*, Mr Pino meant one of those nearest to the foot of the L-shaped stairs and just inside the club proper. The room was oblong in shape, with candlelit tables around three sides. At the far end, centre, was a dais to support a small band – pianist, drummer, saxophonist and the leader. The resident singer was Jo Marney, whose recordings were often played on the radio. She had dark hair, sultry features and a perfectly pitched, powerful voice. At the start of the evening, between ten and eleven, the hostesses always sat together gossiping at a table near the band and just in front of one of the two swing-door entrances to the kitchen and fire escape. In a Soho nightclub, *fire escape* was a euphemism for a route to flee should the premises be targeted by gangland mobsters, which did occur there on one occasion.

'Jack' was nursing a pint of bitter. Another full pint glass was on the table to his right, where I'd be sitting next to him on the upholstered, bench-seat. 'I got you one in,' he said, matter-of-fact.

Before making inroads into my drink, although thirsty, I produced a packet of cigarettes, which was the customary way to begin any kind of social rendezvous, with man or woman. It was more than convention, rather a rite, an integral part of Western culture and anyone who didn't smoke was considered anti-social or trapped in a time warp of adolescence.

'See who's in, over there,' he said, nodding towards the far end of the smoky room and to our right of the band, which was just assembling.

The only light came from the table candles and my eyes hadn't yet adjusted to the darkness.

'Tell me,' I said. 'I can't see a thing yet.'

'It's that nutter Frankie Fraser, with one of the house-tarts. Splashed out on a magnum of bubbly, too. Must have just slashed someone somewhere or chopped off a head with an axe and is celebrating.' All said deadpan.

'A bit early for him to be in,' I commented.

'Nothing or nowhere is ever too early for that nuthead bastard.'

Eleven o'clock was early for nightclubs. Generally, they didn't come alive until around midnight, after the pubs had closed and theatregoers had been to a restaurant for supper and were rounding-off their evening clubbing.

At the Jack of Clubs there were two cabaret spots each night, Monday through Saturday – at midnight and two a.m. That night it was the Irish comedian Dave Allen, who had his own TV show. The following week it was to be the Australian singing star Frank Ifield, followed by the pop pianist Russ Conway.

'Could be trouble tonight if Fraser gets pissed and aggressive,' I speculated, prophetically.

Jack laughed mirthlessly. 'He'll have been pissed before breakfast.' Then a change of tempo and focus. 'How did you get here?'

Puzzled, I replied, 'Cab.'

'From the office?'

'Sort of. Is there a problem?'

'Could be,' he said gravely. 'Depends. Could you have been followed?'

'It's always a possibility, but I doubt it,' I answered after a little thought, trying to compute and untangle this strange line of questioning. 'I didn't leave the office by the main entrance. I went through our library and down the rear staircase, out into Drury Lane. Lots of the reporters use that in the daytime when they want to sneak out unnoticed for a sly drink in Milo's'.

Milo's was a basement drinking club beneath a small, shabby restaurant that sold very basic Maltese dishes. Milo, the proprietor, who hailed from Malta, was short, silver-haired, and softly spoken, a married, family man who, to my knowledge, wasn't involved in any of the rackets for which the Maltese had become infamous in Soho. His wife ran the restaurant while he served behind the bar downstairs, which was one of the favoured watering holes for detectives from nearby Bow Street police station.

'Jack' relaxed. 'Good boy,' he said, not the least patronisingly.

I started to relate to him the saga of the envelope and the encounter at Chelsea police station with Nipper, but long before I'd finished he held up a hand, like a traffic-cop, saying, 'I know all about that sparring. That's why we need to talk.'

'Surely it's all over, done and dusted?' I assumed.

'That's what you're *supposed* to believe. Don't be a wanker.'

Now I drank quickly. I needed alcohol on the brain.

He reminded me of a story that had appeared in the national press in April that year about the murder squad being keen to trace and question a punter of prostitutes, known to the street-walkers in the Shepherd's Bush/Notting Hill area as 'The Solicitor'. On a sheet of blue paper he listed his sexual requirements, with his payment proposition of £40. The sheet of writing paper would be handed to the whores he approached or those who accosted him. One of them had handed this 'evidence' to officers investigating the 'Nudes Murders'.

'Basically, this freak wanted to stick *it* in the tarts' mouths,'

'Jack' said bluntly. 'As you know from me, oral sex has become pivotal to this case, right?'

'Right,' I agreed, 'but how does this solicitor concern me?' I queried, simultaneously catching a waiter's attention and ordering two more beers.

'We don't think he is a solicitor, though he could be. Although the tarts where the killer kerb-crawls are desperate for business, most of them won't do mouth jobs. I don't blame them. How do they know where *it's* been? We have a decent description of the fella from at least four of the girls: small and balding, aged forty to fifty. Speaks well. Dresses OK; smart enough to pass as a lawyer. The point is, Nipper wanted to see you close up.'

And it dawned on me: because of the envelope pantomime, Nipper Read needed to eliminate me from the possibility of being 'The Solicitor'. What a hoot! It didn't make a scrap of sense, I was twenty-five with a head of brown hair and the Yard was looking for a grey, balding middle-aged man, forty at the youngest. What was I missing? Nothing, in fact, bar the Yard's pedantry.

'I know exactly what you're thinking, but the Yard doesn't trust any force outside the Smoke. Also, Nipper wasn't the one originally liaising with Bedford. I've no idea whether your age was asked for. Communication isn't one of our strengths.' He went on to tell me that my notes on the envelope had been compared to the 'Solicitor's' handwriting.

'And?' I said, confident of the response.

'There were many more differences than similarities. Definitely not a match; nothing like. Neither do your fingerprints compare with any on the blue paper.'

Fingerprints! My fingerprints!! This generated more thinking time for me, before I observed, 'There must be loads of fingerprints on that stuck-together retrieved envelope of mine. How do they know which are my prints? I've never had my fingerprints taken.' I was bemused.

'Perhaps not formally,' 'Jack' said, grinning and smacking his lips. 'But they're on file now, bank on it.' He was playing me like a fish on the end of his line, taking his time reeling me in. I really couldn't figure it, so finally he helped me out.

'Monday morning, Chelsea police station, in Nipper's office, drinking coffee from a fine china cup, right?'

A switch was flicked in my head and on came the light; I saw it all. 'Jack' needn't have continued with his explanation, though he did, sort of bragging on behalf of the Met. The cup had been cleaned of all fingerprints before it was handed to me by a sweet-smiling woman PC. Afterwards, it was handled only by officers wearing gloves. A science detective in the forensics lab lifted just two sets of prints from the cup, mine and those of the female PC. The final simple task was to compare my fingerprints with all those on the 'Solicitor's' blue paper. Just the way it's done in a Miss Marple TV series. In police-speak, Nipper had been informed that I was a non-runner.

'The last of all the checks on you related to your vehicle,' 'Jack' said,' returning to the stilted language of cops' evidence from the witness box. The registration number had been put into the system at the Shepherd's Bush incident room. All numbers of kerb-crawlers during the past six months had been logged. The registration number of my vehicle did not feature among them.

'You're clean,' he announced jovially.

I wouldn't have gone that far, but this was no occasion to argue against that testimony. 'God!' I exclaimed. 'They've really done a comprehensive job on me in a very short time.'

'Had to be done,' he said, solemnly now. 'You know why, as well as I do.'

The clock was ticking. All the dead ends were leading to

another death. Another body was due any day, if they were right about the calendar cycle, the build-up of pressure in the serial killer's abnormal and perverted libido. The murders were becoming as regular as a menstrual cycle, as if the killer was ruled as much by his chemistry as the derangement of his brain.

'Jack' confirmed that still no girl had been reported missing from the streets, but that was meaningless and gave no comfort. The comings and goings of street whores was a deciduous process, comparable to crop rotation. But if there ever was a harvest, it was never reaped by the girls, only their handlers.

We then came to the main agenda for our meeting. 'Paranoia had set in. The hierarchy were 'tearing out their hair' trying to pinpoint the leaks in the Squad.

'Are you worried?' I wondered aloud, but quietly, though there was zero chance of our conversation carrying.

The band was playing, Jo Marney was belting out a hit song of the period, sashaying to the rhythm, the room was filling, all the hostesses had been hired, the waiters – mostly Italians – were in and out of the kitchen, as if trapped in a revolving door, and Frankie Fraser was loud-mouthing.

'What do you think?' said 'Jack', wrapping his answer in a rhetorical question.

'Are you saying you want out, to come off the payroll?' I asked him, taking the initiative.

'That's not what I'm saying,' he was eager to clarify. 'It's just that we have to be much more circumspect from now on.'

He was drinking faster than me and was ready for another refill, which I organised, leaving myself out of this round, needing a clear head. As a means of exonerating himself and exorcising any guilt complex, he chatted about the history of 'pipelines to the press' from the Yard through 'informal, private arrangements', sanctioned conduits, clearly to sanitise his role and to appease his conscience. 'Jack' thought we should have a moratorium until 'things cool down'. He was also in favour of our 'mixing up' our meeting venues, which was fine by me. I had the distinct impression that he was not overwhelmingly confident of my ability to detect someone who had been professionally trained in the nifty and indeed shifty art of shadowing people.

Apparently, the chiefs weren't opposed to leaks to the press per se, but they had to be authorised, sometimes comprising deliberate misinformation in the hope of fooling the killer and luring him into making a fatal mistake; all very Machiavellian and melodramatic. 'Jack' also fancied that there was an element of jealousy, that some of the senior ranks were miffed by the perks that were seeping into the pockets of their juniors. So we agreed that I should wait to hear from him and not try to make contact for the next few weeks. After his third pint, he left. Naturally, the tab was mine, which would be reimbursed by my newspaper through the normal channels: my expenses account.

I decided to stay to see Dave Allen's cabaret performance. He straddled a stool to tell his jokes, exactly as he did on TV. We knew one another from Singapore, where he'd been on tour and I was stationed there with the RAOC (Royal Army Ordnance Corps), doing National Service. We'd met most evenings for drinks at the Orchard Hotel, where the entertainers were staying. In addition to being in the British Army, I was moonlighting on the *Straits Times*, Singapore's national morning newspaper that did its utmost to mirror the UK's broadsheet *Daily Express* as it was during Beaverbrook's ground-breaking reign, and I'd given a plug to Allen and the others in the troupe. Here, in the Jack of Clubs that evening, I sent a note to him in his dressing room, inviting him to join me at my table for a reunion after his midnight spot.

Moments later, there was a commotion upstairs: shouts,

threats, swearing and what sounded like a scuffle. Mr Norman – that's how Norman Isow was referred to deferentially by the staff – came hurtling down the stairs two at a time. He took Mr Pino to one side for a breathless briefing. At one point, I heard Norman say, 'For God's sake, don't let Frankie upstairs, whatever you do. Whatever it takes, keep him occupied down here. As many drinks on the house as he wants.'

Nodding continuously, Mr Pino wore the pinched face of a very frightened man, though he kept his sangfroid throughout this crisis. Norman, still in panic mode, bounded upstairs, where the ruckus appeared to have subsided. Suddenly, it was all quiet on the Brewer Street front, except for the band, Jo Marney's caressing tones, and Frankie Fraser lording louder than ever.

Later that night, after my reunion with Allen, I learned that murder and possibly all kinds of other mayhem had been averted by 'Nosher' Powell, who had put his own life on the line by denying entrance to the club to Ronnie and Reggie Kray, something never heard of in Soho and considered tantamount to suicide by those in – and on the fringe – of the West End underworld. No man in his right mind who cared for his own life ever denied entrance to the swaggering, swashbuckling, gun-toting Krays. It was simply beyond even fantasy, yet it had just happened. A crossroad had been reached in the quicksand power-struggle of Soho. What next?

I was reliably informed that the stand-off went something like this:

Ronnie: 'Is that mad bastard Frankie in tonight?'

Nosher: 'Frankie who?'

Ronnie: 'Don't fuck with us, Nosher. How many Mad Frankie's do you know?'

Reggie: 'We know Fraser's in, down in the pit.'

Nosher: 'You're wrong. He's a no-show tonight, so far.'

Ronnie: 'And you're a fucking liar. We'll go take a look for ourselves.'

Nosher: 'No you won't.'

Ronnie: 'And who's going to fucking stop us?'

Nosher: 'Me. For one thing, you're not wearing ties.'

Reggie: 'You what?'

Nosher: 'You're not properly dressed.'

Ronnie: 'Why you fucking arsehole. Carry on like this and you'll get what we've come to give Frankie – a fucking bullet in the head; not his brain 'cause he don't have one. Even if we was just in our bleeding underpants nobody would dare stop us coming in.'

Nosher: 'I'm sorry, boys, but I'm going to have to ask you to leave now.'

Ronnie: 'Arsehole! We'll be back.'

Reggie: 'Yeah, wearing Old Etonian ties.'

Ronnie: 'Is Frankie wearing a tie?'

Nosher (not falling for that insulting trick): 'I told you, he's not in.'

Ronnie: 'Oh, yeah, so you did. We'll be seeing you, Nosher. Can't promise *you'll* be wearing a tie, though, by the time we part company.'

Reggie spat on the floor just before they kicked open the glass doors at the club's entrance.

The cloakroom assistant that night had the memory for dialogue of a *Mastermind* contestant. 'Please don't let on where you got this info from,' she said. I never have.

Nosher was about the only person in the world who could have survived such a vitriolic confrontation with the murderous Krays in a test of mental strength. But Nosher had been born without the human and animal instinct of fear. His daytime job for years was as a daredevil movie stuntman. He sparred with world heavyweight boxing champions Muhammad Ali and Joe Louis, and appeared in the film *Emergency Call*, in which he fought Britain's light-heavyweight champion Freddie Mills, who is to have a special place in this book, as do the Krays. At various times Nosher was personal bodyguard to movie goddesses Ava Gardner and Sophia Loren, then billionaire philanthropist Paul Getty. Nosher wrote a truly colourful memoir in 1999, which was published by Blake. He died in 2013, aged eighty-four, having outlived and outsmarted the Krays.

The Krays were renowned for never backing down on a threat. If they warned, 'We'll be back', you could count on it. This, however, was a rare occasion when their menacing word was *not* their bond. Maybe that was due to the fact that they had genuine respect for anyone who had been a part of the boxing fraternity. Nevertheless, although the Krays didn't return to the Jack of Clubs, their troops did. Unknown to Nosher, they arrived mob-handed, posing as out-of-town businessmen determined to make the most of a night away from their wives. There were eight of them, occupying two tables. The cabaret had just begun when they contrived a dispute and 'staged' a fight, upturning tables, smashing glasses, terrorising the clientele and sending the cabaret act, band and waiters scuttling for cover in the kitchen. Odds of eight to one weren't manageable even for a Goliath like Nosher. The club had to be closed for the rest of the night and the message was clear: the Krays had left their calling card and indelible handiwork. The Krays, the kings of the West End's underbelly, were preparing to demand a cut in the weekly takings of the Isow operation.

Jack Isow was an old hand and Soho survivor. He was familiar with the protection racketeers and their age-old MO, and was too stubborn at his age to genuflect to the gangster parasites who sucked the blood from those who had used their own initiative to build successful businesses. Against that, a wise old owl like Isow knew only too well that to put up two fingers to the Krays was to commit commercial suicide. When there were brawls in nightclubs, the word soon spread and business dried up. This was probably the crossroad at which the Isows decided to turn away from Soho.

People today may fail to understand why the police weren't called on the night that the Krays turned up at the Jack of Clubs intent on shooting Frankie Fraser, but this is to be unfamiliar with the 1960s London clubland culture. The Krays would have denied the stand-off with Nosher, they would have laughed at the accusation that they were gunning, literally, for Fraser and, finally, many of the police, especially those working out of West End Central, were on the Krays' payroll and as crooked as an Alpine hairpin bend.

The gangs, such as the Krays and Richardsons, did their own policing. Frankie Fraser, who was only five feet, four inches tall, was shot, as promised by the Krays. The bullet tore Fraser's mouth apart. His life was saved by Marilyn Wisbey, daughter of the Great Train Robber Tom Wisbey, who was with him at the time. Risking her own life, she rugby-tackled Fraser to topple him and the second shot whistled over both their heads. Fraser survived to die of natural causes, aged ninety. One of the most violent and sadistic of all London villains, he'd been certified insane on three separate occasions and had served more than forty years in prison. Certainly he'd murdered at the behest of the Richardson Syndicate, for which he was a fixer, and one reason why the Krays went to the Jack of Clubs to shoot him. When once charged with murder, he escaped the hangman because key prosecution witnesses were frightened into refusing to testify against him in court. The professional hitman who did accept the contract to shoot Fraser was undoubtedly Jimmy Moody, yet another protagonist in the 'Nudes' murder mystery.

Meanwhile, the tension in the murder squad was well founded. The serial killer *had* already struck again. The body came to light on 26 November 1964. My 'Jack' was lying low, doing his job and allowing his bosses to do all the talking to the press. They had plenty to say, but it was mostly all bluff and fluff. Yes, they had another nude body. Yes, they had the same old, repetitive clues. No, they didn't have anyone in custody in connection with these crimes. Several suspects, but none of them more likely than the man tearing up an envelope on a late-night train...

## CHAPTER 4

# AND THEN THERE
# WERE SIX

D ennis Sutton was looking for something that was missing,
but he found much more than he'd set out to find, much
to his horror.

The time was one-thirty p.m. on Wednesday, 25 November. A
miserable, murky day in central London that was soon to become
considerably bleaker for the edgy murder squad.

Mr Sutton was employed as Assisted Civil Defence Officer at the
Civil Defence Corps headquarters in the basement of Kensington
Central Library in Phillimore Walk, just off the fashionable High
Street. He was shivering in a public car park at the rear of the
library. Hands in pockets, cussing about the cold and a dustbin lid
that had gone 'walkabout', he headed disgruntledly for the concrete
building which served as the Civil Defence's control centre.

'Gotcha!' he exclaimed aloud to himself as he spied the out-
of-place dustbin lid behind the concrete building, among various
debris and illegally dumped rubbish, including used condoms
and soiled nappies.

Shaking his head in disgust, he picked up the dustbin-lid – and froze. Unbeknown to him, he had just stumbled across victim number six in the 'Nudes' series, Frances Brown, whose undernourished body was already severely decomposed. Maggots had infested most of her flesh, including her head. Naturally, she was naked, which, after all, was the killer's signature; his voice and announcement to the world, *Yes, it's me again. Take notice. Just as you were beginning to think it was safe to go out after dark once more... The police, those plodding flatfoots, are no nearer to catching me than on day one. Aren't I clever? More sleepless nights for the Yard dickheads. And more bodies to come, too!* Below her torso, she had been crudely concealed by chunks of concrete, broken pieces of wooden furniture, twigs and leaves.

Mr Sutton dropped the dustbin lid and ran.

The police swooped on the scene like moths drawn to a campfire. The speed of events from thereon was as swift as a relay race, with the baton (in this case, the body) passed with smooth changeovers along the chain of command so that by five o'clock that same Wednesday the post-mortem examination had already begun in the Hammersmith mortuary, led by Home Office pathologist Professor Donald Teare, one of the 'Three Cadaver Cavaliers', the nickname among the morgue humourists for the venerable pathology professors Keith Simpson, Francis Camps and, of course, Teare.

Just like all the previous victims, she was small, a mere inch over five feet tall and weighing a maximum of seven stone, although this had to be an estimate in view of the defiled condition of the body. Old scars on the right lung indicated to Teare that she had once suffered from tuberculosis. Brown's viscera provided an explicit insight into her unhealthy lifestyle. Teare speculated that a recent kidney infection, pyelonephritis, could have been caused by a dose of VD.

Gallbladder stones were common in middle-aged women, especially those with a liking for fatty food and prone to a daily tipple, but rare for a twenty-two-year-old. The single stone plucked from Brown's thick-walled gallbladder was blamed by the pathologist on a poor diet and persistent dehydration, almost certainly the result of excessive alcohol consumption. A very pertinent fact for the detectives was that she was missing three lower front teeth and there was no indication how – or indeed when – they were extracted. Exterior injuries were minimal, consistent with the previous five killings in the series. Crucial to Marchant and his team was cause of death: would this also be compatible with the others? Marchant hoped so or it would introduce confusing anomalies into the methodology. A change of signature – or indeed a completely new one – would not be welcomed; in fact, it would be a nightmare. A nightmare heaped upon an already existing nightmare. The police have historically had a penchant for consistency and regularity.

Gone were her nose, eyes and much of her face, probably due to scavengers such as rats and urban foxes, plus the maggots, of course. Nailing the cause of death, beyond all doubt, was proving elusive: no blow to the head, no gunshot or knife wounds, no evidence of manual strangulation, such as contusions made by thumb-pressure, no reason to suspect poisoning, although that could be confirmed only by toxicology tests which would take days. Then Teare spotted the spread of pink pigmentation below Brown's chin and signs of minor haemorrhages in the larynx, but no fractures. He now had the crucial answer to the number-one question: she had died from asphyxiation. Just like the others.

Not of too much interest to Teare, but very much so to Marchant, was the roll of paper that had been thrust into the dead woman's vagina. Was there some kind of message in that gross act of defilement? Certainly not a written one because the paper was plain white, without a mark, not even a semen stain. If only it had been blue and matched the texture of the 'Solicitor's' notepaper, Marchant lamented.

Brown was identified by her fingerprints, which should have been a routine task, considering her bulky file of convictions for soliciting. No novice, this one. An old hand at a mere twenty-two. That was the Swinging Sixties for you, everything embroidered to an evocative patchwork of apocalyptic milestones that symbolised the zeitgeist of the times: the assassination of President Kennedy, the Great Train Robbery, the Profumo/Keeler political sex scandal, the Zodiac killer in the USA, the Beatles phenomenon, the drug-popping revolution, the birth of Flower Power (Make Love Not War) and the sensational revelations of orgies with peers of the realm cavorting with call girls. Also spurring the pulse of the British public were the first James Bond film and the Hitchcock thriller *Psycho*.

Very little was routine or as it seemed in the chaotic London netherworld. The police were quick – possibly too quick – to identify victim number six as Margaret McGowan. The truth is that she had worked the streets under a range of aliases: Frances Quinn, Nuala Rowlands, Donna Sutherland, Anne Sutherland, Susan Edwards and Frances Brown. With the media snapping at the heels of the police for personal details of the latest victim, Scotland Yard ran with the name that had appeared most recently on her list, like movie credits, of convictions. Even the *Police Gazette,* the coppers' own bible, seemed confused about Frances Brown's true identity, naming her as Margaret McGowan, which was just one of her aliases.

To be fair, even the prostitutes soon lost track of who they really were. In fact, they ceased to have an identity; they were strapped to a treadmill and once on, there was no way off: well, not entirely true, six of them had been removed within a few months, but not of their own volition. For those left, the daily grind ground them down inexorably: little sleep, rubbish food, whisky, purple hearts (the speed drug of choice in that bewitching era), more whisky, grubby, soul-blitzing business, front seat of cars, back seat of cars, up against a wall in an unlit alley, in a park, on the banks of the Thames, under a tree, more street-trawling, tired feet, aching heart, finally home to a slapping from the ponce for not having earned enough, for being a 'lazy cow', for wasting 'dosh' on drugs and booze. Every day, in their dreams, they vowed to stop the world and jump off, finding a life where venereal disease and daily degradation were not the ensign of their trade, the badge of dishonour. But few ever did get off because it *was* just a dream. For most, the treadmill was a relentless downhill slope towards some form of unspeakable oblivion.

Jack the Ripper, east London, 1880s; Jack the Stripper, west London, 1960s; eighty years and about eight miles apart, but very little change in lifestyle and prospects among the sediment of the capital's society.

As for the mistaken identity, there was no excuse for Deputy Assistant Commissioner John 'Four-Day Johnny' du Rose of Scotland Yard sloppily perpetuating the name error in his autobiography, *Murder was my Business*, which was published in 1973, a full eight years after the reign of terror in cosmopolitan west London came to an abrupt and untidy end. One can only assume that the book was ghost-written and the great man was too busy or idle to checks the proofs. It seems that he was as cavalier in his writing as in his previous day job at the Yard.

Du Rose was soon to take over from Marchant as the General, appointed as the swashbuckling overall leader to bring about the equivalent of an 'Operation Overlord' D-Day invasion that would bring this war on London's west front to a swift conclusion. This was how his appointment was sold to the public and politicians, who jointly were becoming restless and beginning to wonder if the legendary Scotland Yard was still up to the job. The Yard had always been seen as the trailblazer for police forces around the world, but now that image was becoming tarnished, mocked even. Jack the Ripper had outsmarted the Yard, along with all criminologists, and now Jack the Stripper was making a mockery of the allegedly greatest police force worldwide.

The initial task facing the investigators after the murder of Frances Brown was formidable: three unknown quantities, of equal value, had to be resolved as quickly as possible: when had she last been seen alive, by whom, and how long had she remained undiscovered in the public car park? Marchant was also keen to learn as much as possible about her background, though this was unlikely to have any bearing on her death, an assumption that was to be dramatically challenged within a few hours, especially as the autopsy had shown that she had most certainly not been raped just prior to death, nor had she even indulged in sexual intercourse, strange indeed when that was apparently her calling and only reason for patrolling the streets at night.

Soon it became apparent to detectives that Brown must have disappeared on Friday, 23 October. They discovered that she had been drinking whiskies most of the evening in the Warwick Castle pub around Shepherd's Bush with a kindred spirit, blonde Beryl Mahood. They had tottered out together into the fresh evening air at around eleven p.m., when it was time to clock-on for the night whoring shift. It is understandable that they needed to be drunk in order to provide some of the depraved services that their forthcoming clients would be seeking.

Brown was Scottish-born, Mahood an exile from Liverpool. Huddled together, they headed towards the junction of Westbourne Park Road and Portobello Road. Two men in separate cars were slyly kerb-crawling, perhaps not obvious to the untrained eye but clear as a pawnbroker's sign to those two women. One of the men emerged from his car and gestured for the women to follow them into Portobello Road. Although driving separate vehicles, it was readily apparent that the men were together. When Brown and her companion caught up with the potential punters, they were parked in Hayden's Place, a dim mews.

Brown suggested that she and Mahood should travel in one car, while the second punter followed. The destination would be Chiswick Green. However, the men disagreed and as money was king they got their way. According to Mahood, Brown climbed into a Ford Zephyr or Zodiac 'or something similar, anyhow', while the second car was light grey in colour, but she had no idea about the make or model, except it had a gear lever on the steering column and a 'convenient' bench-seat in the front.

The Zephyr or Zodiac or whatever led the way. Traffic was heavy with the usual end-of-the-working-week revellers. Headlights dazzled. Friday-night fever was kicking in. And for two young 'working-girls', fuelled by whisky, there was no fear. Fool's Paradise never ceased sucking in the guileless.

Just east of Shepherd's Bush Green, the first car, with Frances Brown aboard, disappeared from view, lost in the traffic congestion. It didn't matter. Nothing had been proposed about a foursome. This was private enterprise; all is fair in love and whore.

Frances Brown, out of sight, already almost out of mind, had gone, not to be seen again until Dennis Sutton went looking for the lost dustbin lid.

Mahood told detectives days later, 'When we lost Frances and her bloke, the man I was with said something like, "It doesn't matter. He knows where to find me at the flat."'

What did it matter that they were separated? They were big girls now. This was their territory. They could take care of themselves. The punters were the mugs. Fortunately for me, neither Nipper Read nor John du Rose knew that my first home when I married in the early 1960s was a flat in Palace Gardens Terrace, which joined Church Street in Kensington, just around the corner from the car park where Brown's body had been hidden. Now that would have been a coincidence too far for Nipper and 'Big John' to have swallowed easily, which demonstrates just why circumstantial evidence, without any other backup, should be treated cautiously.

# CHAPTER 5

# DID ANYONE CARE?

Although Frances Brown had been removed from the streets of west London on Friday, 23 October and never returned to them, it was another eight days before her disappearance was made known to the police and even then she wasn't reported as a missing person; more that she was a ruddy nuisance, a pain in the butt.

Her whereabouts seemed to be of complete indifference and insignificance to the man she'd been sharing her grotty life with, on and off (more off than on), Dublin-born Paul Quinn, a scaffolder by trade and layabout by nature, at 16a Southerton Road, Hammersmith. He was aggrieved at being left holding the baby – quite literally.

Very pertinent and illuminating was Quinn's conversation at Hammersmith police station in the afternoon of Saturday, 31 October with a woman uniformed officer, Sergeant Elizabeth Neale. His reason for visiting the police station was the bundle in his arms and *not,* he stressed vehemently, to report his partner missing, to have someone take off his hands the baby, who peeped from a blanket, a dummy keeping him quiet. Naturally a statement was taken and this was later to find its way into the ever-swelling 'Nudes' murder file, still retained today in Scotland Yard's archives.

In her report, Sergeant Neale wrote, 'Mr Quinn appeared completely at ease and he did not express any concern regarding the well-being or whereabouts of Brown. His only concern appeared to be for the child. He emphatically denied being the child's father, but stated that he had taken her (Brown) back and made a home for her and the baby because he thought that, with the added responsibility, she would settle down.' This in itself alluded to the rollercoaster ride of both their toxic lives. All very laudable on his behalf, if not exactly plausible.

When pressed as to why he hadn't already filed a missing-person's report on Brown if they were indeed a couple, as he indicated, he brushed it off as 'unnecessary', a waste of his time and that of the police. According to Quinn's unflattering account, particularly of himself, Brown would 'take off for weeks on end', eventually 'crawling back all contrite and pitiful, and would take her beating like a woman should.' Nice. Yet, from many anecdotes – mainly his, it has to be said – 'all' the women fell for his charm! Germane to this narrative is the fact that, in many respects, he was a Freddie Mills lookalike, with black curly hair, blue eyes, several false teeth, cauliflower ears, a boxer's nose, and tattoos, one of a nude woman, on his arms and chest. Mills had been one of Britain's post-war sporting heroes, winning the world light-heavyweight championship of the world. After retiring from the ring, he'd sustained his celebrity status as a TV personality and by making a movie debut. It wasn't long, however, before his phone stopped ringing and show business moved on without him. We shall see later that he has a starring role to play in this book.

Alarm bells weren't sounding in Neale's head. Quinn's Irish blarney was, apparently, superficially believable, if sordid. On her godforsaken patch, Neale was accustomed to hearing about convoluted and outré domestic situations and multiple relationships; they went with the territory, part of the peeling wallpaper and threadbare patchwork. What she didn't know at this stage was that Quinn was married and Frances Brown was a professional prostitute. Add to the mix that Quinn had a police record and was already co-habiting with blonde Beryl Mahood, who had been with Brown on the night she vanished, and you had an imbroglio that was too tangled to begin to unravel, but I shall try.

Quinn gave the impression that he had been looking after the baby single-handedly like a saintly lone parent, but, in fact, all the nappy-changing and baby-feeding had been undertaken by Mahood, while still whoring at night. Nipping back to give the baby his milk, while she was swigging from a whisky bottle, then she'd be off again into the chilly night to milk the punters, with Quinn either in a pub or in the bedroom on top of someone else under his spell.

Mahood had been born Beryl Dickson in Portadown, Co. Armagh. By the age of sixteen, she was pregnant, so she married the father of her baby, Charles Mahood. Within six months of the wedding, the couple separated: he left her to go to prison. Without waiting more than a few hours, she hopped on a ferry to Liverpool and on to Blackburn in Lancashire, where she fell foul of the law, receiving two convictions for larceny. Down the road in Accrington, she was charged with fraud and given a conditional discharge. There was only one hope for survival, she decided. The bright lights of London shone before her defeated eyes. Streets paved with gold. Heard the story before in your childhood? Just insert Beryl for Dick. So she hitch-hiked south, making it safely to Slough, which didn't look much like London to her and it wasn't, of course, much to her dismay. Being homeless, she 'slept around' – make of that what you will – and soon had enough money to travel the final few miles by public transport to her perceived magic city (maybe that's a bit strong). The Shepherd's Bush Hotel was her final destination, where she was soon befriended by Frances Brown and Paul Quinn, who invited her to stay with them. Now she was properly on the game.

Remarkably, 23 October was only her second night on the streets with Brown. It was nothing more than a spin of the coin which of the two cars they chose. Is that what is meant by the lottery of life?

A chance meeting in the Kensington Park Hotel with his estranged wife, Maureen Quinn, led to more upheaval and complications. She was unaccompanied and, after a few drinks together, Paul proposed they tried a reconciliation, probably because he realised that he would require a more permanent and reliable babysitter than Mahood. His wife asked about Frances – there were few secrets on these loveless and forlorn streets – and Quinn explained simply that 'she'd gone'. How true!

However, the entanglement was even more complex. Maureen was living with another man, but, after some cogitation, cajoling and more whisky, she declared, 'Why not?' Anyone who knew Quinn and his habits could have given a thousand reasons *why not*; no one more so than his own wife, who, of her own free will and accord, was prepared to re-enter the snake pit. 'Let's give it a go,' she said, in a drunken whim and deserted her lover (maybe that's too strong a label) for her husband, only to find Mahood a cuckoo in the nest.

Before Maureen could flounce out, Quinn promised to 'sort

it' and promptly kicked out Mahood. As you might expect, the exchange of language was ripe and revengeful. Now it was Maureen's turn to care for another woman's child and that soon led to more emotional pyrotechnics and a quick renewal of their separation vows. Hence Quinn's pained arrival at Hammersmith police station, pleading for assistance, sort of police protection, but for the child's sake, not his, of course. Very noble. He had run out of nursemaids. Don't forget, this was the 1960s when sexual liberation had gone to the nation's head, addling the collective brain, especially in raunchy London town, but even by those dubious standards the bed-hopping merry-go-round of the 'Quinn set' was something extraordinary.

When Neale examined the baby, she was satisfied that the child hadn't been physically neglected or harmed. One issue that continued to gnaw at her was the registered name of the child. Yet Paul Quinn continued adamantly to reject that he was the biological father. 'I did it as a favour to her,' he claimed, referring to Brown and his signature on the birth certificate. He was a Catholic, he explained, and it wasn't right for a child to grow up without both parents' name on the birth certificate. The baby was conceived when Brown had run off with 'another fella', he said, and she returned only so that he (Quinn) could serve as surrogate father to the boy. The moral maze was not for Neale to dwell on or unpick, thankfully for her, so she advised Quinn to consult a child welfare officer in the department's local headquarters on Holland Park Avenue, which he duly did on the following Monday morning.

The welfare officer who interviewed Quinn was Joan Halfacree, to whom he repeated the story, virtually word for word, he had regaled to the female police officer on the Saturday. However, when questioned further, he spiced his story with more colour and incriminating revelations than in the police station. After accusing Brown of being 'a lazy slag', abdicating responsibility for her child, and constantly 'absenting herself' from their home, he confessed that whenever she did 'crawl back with her tail between her legs' he always 'belted her'.

In her later statement to the police, the child welfare officer stated that Quinn boasted he would do so again if he had 'the chance'. Quinn pressed the point that if he took any more time off work he would be fired, so the baby was taken into care and placed with a foster mother, which must have been the right course of action. But still there was no apparent thought of Brown. Quinn was taken at his word that she would frequently 'get drunk and do a runner' without consideration for anyone else, including her baby. 'She's a bad, worthless lot,' he declared. 'I wish to God I'd never got hooked up with her, but she'll turn up like a bad penny.' Correct. But not the way he meant.

The feckless image of Brown was undoubtedly true, but what inducement was there for Brown to return home, apart from her baby? Physical abuse was assured, perhaps a severe, drunken beating. Maybe she even feared for her life... Which was the more dangerous for her – on the streets or indoors, at home? This question had already been resolved, but only two people were privy to the answer. And only one of them was still alive and at large, in fact growing larger than life by the day.

It is not unreasonable to reason that someone in authority should have at least contacted Brown's parents to see if they could shed any light on her whereabouts. After all, she might have run to them, with a very different yarn from Quinn's. But they knew nothing of her latest vanishing escapade, a fact that would be confirmed only after Mr Sutton's search for something else, mere trivia. And there were cruel people, pious and holier than thou, who sermonised that he had uncovered two items of trivia, the dustbin lid of more worth than the other rubbish.

And so the days passed. October slipped seamlessly into November. By the middle of the month, London was already gearing up for Christmas, with the festive mood tiptoeing into offices and stores. Oxford Street, Regent Street and Piccadilly were choking with big spenders. The neon lights were a dazzling shop window of so much gloss and glamour that hid a very different London *down the road* to the west and east, festering and fermenting neighbourhoods that were as much a disgrace to post-war London as the rookeries of St Giles had been in Victorian times.

Frances Brown was forgotten. She was history. Very much so; much more than anyone surmised because she was still, astonishingly, and I believe disgracefully, not an *official* missing person; someone just lost among the flotsam of the rootless *modern* nomads.

Meanwhile, Quinn was living life by the day. His landlord evicted him from the flat in Southerton Road after serious damage to the property during a 'rave'. Quinn had to be out by 9 November and he went quietly enough; just another little hiccup along life's undulating journey. There was always another woman, another bed, another source of income. Not a worry in the world, not for someone enriched with so much blarney.

As if fully aware he would never see Frances Brown again, he gave away all her clothes and binned anything else she had left behind. In his trade, he was known as a jobber, a freelance around building sites, and he heard on his network of mates that a builder was looking for experienced scaffolders in Maidstone, Kent, so off he went and was taken on. But it didn't take him long to tire of living in lodgings and also he was missing his old haunts on his west London stamping ground, so as November began to fizzle out, he told his foreman to 'stick' his job. *Easy come, easy go.*

His last day in Maidstone was Friday, 27 November, when he collected his final pay packet and set sail, flushed, for the White Horse pub in nearby Headcorn, where he splashed out on farewell drinks for his work-gang. And that's when he was shocked 'to the core' to suddenly be reunited with Frances Brown. Not the way he could have ever envisaged, though.

She was lighting a cigarette, seemingly very sophisticated and poised, short-cut thick black hair permed in boyish fashion, wearing a bling necklace, a smart cocktail dress, plenty of décolletage and bare arms, so that the unmistakable tattoos on her lower left arm were vividly visible. There was no mistaking that it was her. The constant runaway. The 'unreliable little fucker'. Come back to haunt him from the front page of the *Daily Express*: 'MURDERED: WARD CASE GIRL: Detectives Quiz Vice Trial Witnesses'.

*Well I never, the little minx!* Quinn mused, suddenly believing that he had something valuable to barter for substantial financial gain.

He had to hotfoot it back to the Smoke. The newspapers would pay 'good money' for his story. Of course he'd have to commiserate with her family, do a bit of that and get drunk with her street-*pals*.

Someone should have reminded him about the truism that liars need good memories because he let slip in the pub that he was the father of Brown's son, a comment overheard by the landlord.

One small detail he forgot: the police in London would be keener to speak with him than even the press.

# CHAPTER 6

# A SCANDAL REVISITED

As soon as I saw the photograph circulated by Scotland Yard of the sixth victim, tagged Margaret McGowan, I knew instantly that it was Frances Brown. I went from the picture desk to my news editor, Ken James, and said, 'The Yard's trying to hoodwink us or at least buy some time.'

Ken, jacket off, the sleeves of his crisp white shirt rolled up, was in his black leather, executive swivel chair, at the centre of his frenetic and abrasive universe; loyal secretary Beth to his right, the foreign editor to her right, the picture editor to Ken's left and the deputy picture editor further left, though not quite as far Left as the paper's politics, though claiming to be independent now that it had morphed from the *Daily Herald,* the bellowing voice of the TUC.

Directly opposite Ken on the long metallic desk that seemed to occupy half the capacious newsroom, was the deputy news editor. Opposite the foreign editor was his deputy. Other factotums completed the court of King James. Throughout the building there seemed to be far more deputies than sheriffs.

'What do you mean?' he said, blinking, face blank, a very restless, insecure monarch.

'This is Frances Brown,' I said, prodding the black and white print I was holding. 'McGowan is her mother's maiden name. Her father is Francis Brown. They live in Glasgow, remember? Frances was a controversial witness in the Stephen Ward trial.'

Suddenly he was as switched-on as the neon advertisements of Piccadilly Circus. 'You *what*!' he exclaimed, eyes jumping like a pair of excited frogs, appreciating, like me, the potential ramifications if what I was saying were true.

'This story's going to run and run,' I said foolishly, as if it hadn't already. I was talking gibberish, drunk on adrenaline, a strong intoxicant. 'There's no telling where it's going to lead us.' That wasn't true. I knew exactly where we were heading: into a completely new ball game.

'Are you sure about this?' he said, with his customary knack for irritating his staff. He wasn't known as 'Cautious Ken' without due cause.

'Ken, I interviewed her outside the Old Bailey last year after she'd testified,' I said wearily. 'She'd been one of Ward's girls, a key defence witness. We have pics of her on file and in cuttings, of course, in the library.' Computer-filing and stories and photographs stored on micro-film were components of science fiction, something that might be available on Mars, but not in Covent Garden in 1964.

'Get out the cuttings,' he said, as if making a decision to press the nuclear button, 'while I have a word with Bob.' *Please* wasn't a word that had yet been introduced into news editors' vocabulary.

Bob Traini was chief crime correspondent. I was another

one of those deputies. Traini wasn't very popular with other journalists. However, I rubbed along with him fine, mainly because we never met and hardly ever talked with one another. His unpopularity in Fleet Street stemmed from his wartime support of Oswald Mosley's Blackshirt fascist fanatics. To Bob, a liberal was anyone to the Left of the Ku Klux Klan. The fact that he had been employed by the *Daily Herald,* the mouthpiece of the Labour Party, demonstrated just how eclectic was the national press. Naturally, he was an ardent supporter of the death penalty – and not just for murder – and believed that all those 'Lefties' vociferously lobbying for the end of capital punishment should be first in line for hanging, perhaps the reason why he enjoyed such a cosy rapport with top brass at the Yard.

Scotland Yard had a special press room for crime correspondents, but Traini often preferred to work from home. He'd ring around the inspectors and superintendents on his 'call list' and then inform me, via the news desk, of anything worth following up. In essence, I was his 'leg-man', a foot soldier on the frontline, doing the digging and chasing, occasionally being decorated but more often left biting the bullet.

One time I was floored in Luton on a quiet Sunday morning by a fifteen-year-old on his parents' doorstep just for politely announcing who I was. I had a staff photographer with me and all he did was dart around snapping shots from different angles. He was delighted as I nursed a bloody nose and split lip on the drive back to Town, enthusing, 'I got some great pics!' The newsroom hacks thought it was hilarious. So did my wife!

The files in our library quickly established beyond all doubt that I was right. The new angle now was: could these murders be linked, however tenuously, to the Profumo/Keeler/Ward sex and spy scandal?

## THE SECRET LIFE OF FREDDIE MILLS

For benefit of the three and a third people in the Western world for whom John Profumo, Christine Keeler and Dr Stephen Ward remain anonymous nonentities, and as a refresher for others, I shall summarise synoptically. Profumo was the Secretary of State for War in Harold Macmillan's ill-fated Conservative Government. Christine Keeler was a 'good-time' girl who has generally been cast in the press as a prostitute, although, in the strict sense, she wasn't. But she was no street-hooker in the grubby image of Frances Brown and all the other hapless conquests of Jack the Stripper. Stephen Ward was an osteopath with a consulting suite in Wimpole Street and high-society clients, such as Lord Bill Astor. Profumo inherited a fortune just after becoming the Member of Parliament for Kettering in Northamptonshire. The most important part of his inheritance elevated him to the fifth baron of the Kingdom of Sardinia and third baron of the United Kingdom of Italy. However, he wisely decided that to exploit his title would be a political impediment.

Here I must divulge a personal connection. My father acted as Profumo's campaign manager in the two parliamentary elections in the Kettering constituency: the first he won, the second he lost. Consequently, Profumo was constantly in and out of our house. On my birthdays, he would always present me with a card and a box of chocolates. Typical of the man, the card would always be a profile photograph of himself, which probably personifies him more than all the millions of words ever written about him and his tawdry life. On the reverse side of the card he would monotonously write, 'Eat the chocolates and always vote Conservative.' I always scoffed the chocolates.

It was alleged that Ward ran a stable of girls whom he leased to 'men about town'; in other words, well-heeled and well-positioned (in society, politics and commerce) punters. No riff-raff. Profumo was married to the snooty British actress Valerie Hobson, who, in turn, was no nun-about-town. Profumo was introduced to Keeler one evening when she was gambolling naked around Lord Astor's open-air swimming-pool in the grounds of his grand Thames-side estate at Cliveden, where Ward rented a cottage and was 'entertaining'.

Ward would converse in code to those to whom he genuflected: *'Oh, Jack, I'd like you to meet so and so, she's French-educated and very knowledgeable about language.'* Translated: she's damned good at oral sex and talking dirty.

Profumo had sex with Keeler at Ward's London apartment. Ward was the conduit. He also brought together Mandy Rice-Davies, who was undoubtedly a whore but rather more astute than Keeler, with Peter Rachman, the lowest form of life in London at the time, worse than the millions of sewer rats partying beneath the streets. In the blink of an eye, Rachman had made his polluted pile through heaping misery on hundreds of the most desperately poor people in west London. He bought hundreds of shabby houses that were already divided into tatty flats and whose tenants' residency was protected by law through statutory rent control. If they couldn't be bribed with derisory inducements to vacate, he'd send in his bruisers with snarling, ill-tempered Alsatians. If that failed, he'd up the ante: rats would be released from sacks into young children's bedrooms and roofs might be removed in the middle of the night, gas and electricity supplies severed. As soon as he'd secured vacant possession, he would re-let at four or times the old rent, particularly to prostitutes and their ponces, or sell. Naturally, he lived in a mansion in the most salubrious corner of leafy Hampstead.

I was interviewing one of his harassed tenants in her structurally unsound flat in the Notting Hill neighbourhood when two of

Rachman's rent-collectors came calling with a couple of anti-social dogs in tow. When I enquired how long it would be before their boss authorised improvements, one of them came up to me very close to say, 'Little fellas with long noses and big mouths don't last long around here.' He even tried to imitate James Cagney, noted for his corny gangster movie roles. I felt sorry for the dogs because they had been trained to snarl on cue and were unnerved when someone laughed in their face.

Rachman was short, though fat, and didn't last long. His heart went on strike at having to work in impossible, cramped conditions under so much ever-mounting blubber and the strenuous pumping in myriad bedrooms. One MP caused crime correspondents many squandered days and nights by declaring in the House of Commons that Rachman wasn't really dead and his body had been switched in Edgware General Hospital's mortuary. My assignment, of course, was to find Rachman, perhaps being sheltered by Ward, Keeler, Mandy-Rice Davies, or even Lord Astor. Why Astor? – heaven knows! The entire affair, with all its strands and tentacles, had become a grotesque circus. Fleet Street was open all hours to any conspiracy theory, the more outrageous, daft and improbable the bigger the bite and swallow. After a couple of weeks searching London, following false trails, for a porky ghost, even the ever-optimistic news editors had to accept the blindingly obvious: the Devil had Rachman tightly in its claws and had no intention of releasing him to the press. His legacy gave us one new word in the *Oxford Dictionary*: Rachmanism, which will assist in keeping his evil alive in the conscience of future generations.

Keeler was also having sex with Eugene Ivanov, a Russian spy, which allowed newspapers to use the potential national security risk as a fabricated pretext for publishing all the sexual gore. Profumo resigned from Parliament, not because of his moronic dalliance with Keeler, but for telling porkies on the floor of the House of Commons, denying newspaper allegations of impropriety, thus establishing just how half-witted he was as a politician.

Ward was charged with numerous absurd offences, including brothel-keeping, living off immoral earnings and procurement (ladies for gents), all trumped-up charges by a scoundrel detective inspector at Scotland Yard, Samuel Herbert, who was as bent as London Underground's Circle Line. Some of the charges were dropped, but only after they had been made public and therefore had softened up potential jurors. Eventually, at the Old Bailey, Ward was found guilty of the lesser offences. However, by then he'd taken a massive overdose of barbiturates and died before he could be sentenced, undoubtedly to gaol in order to appease the baying Establishment, much to the chagrin of the scandalously biased judge, Sir Archie Marshall, a redneck from the Midlands circuit. Keeler was later gaoled for perjury in a different court case.

Ward's show trial was meant to deflect the public gaze and press scrutiny from the political fallout: some chance! In effect, it naturally had the reverse impact and the Macmillan Government was fatally damaged and soon sank. What it demonstrated more than anything was the danger of political machinations affecting the atmosphere in which the police and the judiciary work. Legal experts have unanimously agreed that Ward would have had all convictions overturned on appeal, had he lived, because of the judge's grossly distorted summing-up and misleading directions to the jury. However, in my opinion, that assumption is flawed. It is assuming that the Appeal Court judges would have been immune to the oppressive and overbearing political climate.

An amusing aside: at one juncture during this soap opera, long before the tragic denouement, Profumo went into hiding. Once again news editors were like the masters of hounds, sounding the bugle, crying, 'Tally-ho, off we go! Sniff him out.' Of course I was leader of our pack and I phoned my father, saying, 'You've been inside his head as much as anyone, where might he go to ground, to feel safe and secure from the media at a time like this?'

There was a long, breathy pause, then, 'You know he owns his own plane and he's a qualified pilot. He's probably out of the country. My hunch is that he's flown to a remote part of Italy or Sardinia.'

*Umm,* I thought, *Not much help to me.* It wasn't until months later that I learned Profumo had been standing beside my father at the time of my call. Even worse, he'd been sleeping in *my* bed in the bedroom that had been mine as a child and teenager. I can see the funny side now, but not then. What a scoop that could have been for me, but my father put Profumo before his ambitious son. That's life and politics for you...

Profumo had smelled the hounds closing in and left my parents that day, driving the relatively short distance to Warwickshire, where he holed up with an old friend in the constituency he'd represented since 1950, Stratford-on-Avon, having lost Kettering after the 1945 Labour landslide.

When I next visited my parents for a weekend, my mother commented mischievously, 'Oh, by the way, I'm sure you'll be pleased to know that I've changed the bedding in your room.'

* * *

One thing struck me immediately: whoever murdered Brown had also killed all the other girls in the series, yet none of them, to my knowledge, had been involved, even obliquely, with Profumo, Ward, Ivanov, Keeler, Rachman or Mandy Rice-Davies. *'Jack', where are you? I need you. Is this for real or a red herring?*

First step was to pull the file from the library, take it across the road to the Cross Keys pub, buy a pint and settle in a corner for a quiet catch-up browse. The most sacred rule of the library was that no file should *ever* be taken from the building. That rule was also the most abused of all the office dictums.

Brown had been called by Ward's counsel during the Old Bailey trial to counter evidence for the prosecution provided by another prostitute, Vickie Barrett. Brown and Barrett had shared a flat in Shepherd's Bush and were on the streets together soliciting when 'picked up' in the West End by Ward. Barrett told the jury on oath that Ward drove them in his 'flashy' white Jaguar to his home in Bryanston Mews West, where she was paid to cane another man, charging £1 a stroke, while the others watched.

Brown's version was different. She said that Barrett, a slim, attractive blonde, had been paid to thrash Ward and not another man. Later, when it was too late and Ward was dead, Barrett had amended her story, admitting that Brown's version was the correct one. So why had she perjured herself?

'Under unbearable duress from Herbert,' she'd claimed. Her excuse was that she related the truth to Herbert when originally questioned by him, but he wasn't satisfied, aggressively *suggesting* that it would sound better if she said she'd been paid to beat another man, while Ward was a spectator. She was puzzled and asked what was the point of such a lie. If she can be believed – and there is no reason why she should be, considering her innate duplicity – Herbert answered to the effect that if she didn't comply, he'd ensure that she 'never dare show' her 'face again on the streets of Notting Hill'.

In addition to her convictions for soliciting, Barrett was a notorious liar. However, now that Brown had been murdered and Scotland Yard seemingly was looking at a possible tie-in with the Ward trial, I thought I should at least confirm that Barrett was still alive and in the process might even learn something new and true among the inevitable litany of lies.

The prostitutes of Notting Hill, Shepherd's Bush and Paddington were a colony, tantamount to a large, dysfunctional family. I had an address for Barrett, but, inevitably, she'd moved, so tracing her entailed surfing the tide of her ebbing and flowing network of 'sisters'. When I finally caught up with her, it was dark, she was living in a first-floor flat in a typical old house in the Rachmanised district of shabby and disintegrating west London. There were trees in the street, which qualified it as an avenue, I suppose, but contributed nothing towards genuine gentrification.

The front door was in a crumbling porch. There was a panel of doorbells, from which wires were hanging. There was no knocker, so it was a matter of fist against wood. No one came to the door, but I heard a window at the front being lifted open, followed by a female shouting for all the road to hear, 'Who is it? What the fuck do you want?'

I backed along the path to the road so that I could see the woman. She had her head and most of her torso out of a first-floor window, with her hands gripping the sill for balance. Illuminated by the light in the room, I immediately recognised her as Vickie Barrett.

'Good evening, Vickie,' I called up to her.

'I said what the fuck do you want?' she repeated herself, still shouting, as if drugged or drunk, more than likely a combination of the two.

Before I'd finished introducing myself, she cut in, 'Well you can fuck off. Anyhow, I'm not Vickie Barrett.'

'Yes, you are,' I contradicted her. 'I saw you at the Old Bailey.' Another young woman came to the window and joined the rant. 'Are you calling my fiend a bleedin' liar?'

'Have you heard that Frances Brown's been murdered?' I said, sidestepping the confrontation as much as possible.

'No surprise,' yelled Barrett. 'She was asking for it, the bitch!'

'Why?' I asked. Every question answered was a bonus.

''cus she was nuts, you know that, don't you? Off 'er 'ead, she was. She'd drive any bloke to kill her.'

'So you don't think her death's linked to Ward?'

'Nah! Fiction, that is. She was nothing to any of them. What's the point of topping a nuthead like her? She got her comeuppance for going in cars with blokes. You'd never catch me doing that, no car-jobs for me. That's as low as you can get. No class with them lot.'

'So you haven't been threatened? You're not afraid of being on someone's hit list?'

'Do me a favour, you daft bleeder. Anyone threatens me and they get a stiletto heel in their balls. And you don't go fucking writing that you heard all this from Vickie Barrett because I ain't her.'

'No, she ain't Vickie Barrett, you nosy sod!' chimed the other alley cat. With that, the window crashed down like a guillotine. Fortunately, the two women had remembered to withdraw their heads.

By her criteria, Barrett was probably telling the truth about her name, denying that she was Vickie Barrett. Like all the others in her transient trade, she had her own dictionary of aliases. There was no telling by what moniker she was trading when we had that very public and serrated catechism.

Despite all the aggro and histrionics, I'd elicited more feedback than I'd hoped for and much of it gelled with my own preconceived overview.

These women were very different from Keeler's crowd. I talked with Keeler only once and that was in her first-floor flat in

Devonshire Street, when she was holed up with Paula Hamilton-Marshall, who was usually dressed smartly and conservatively, shrouded with an aura of class, whatever the reality. She had just hopped into a taxi for an address not far from the Palace of Westminster, leaving Keeler 'gasping' for a cigarette. From the other side of her door, she asked if I had a cigarette I could spare her. I didn't, but offered to buy her a packet and she was grateful. I cannot recall the brand she smoked, but when I returned she unhooked the security chain and unbolted the door, allowing me to squeeze in, her jumpy eyes anxious to ensure I wasn't the fugleman for the Fleet Street cavalry. I'm certain this would never have happened if she hadn't been in such need of a nicotine infusion.

She was overtly overwrought and seized the opportunity to pump me about police activity. This was during the interim of Ward's trial and death and the police assembling a case against Keeler for perjury. She was wearing a floppy white jumper, jeans and brown calfskin ankle boots; she wore virtually no makeup but her facial bone structure was perfect. For the duration, she was polite and well-spoken, though hyper-frightened; a cornered animal out of her depth, scared to venture out because of the predatory press gang poised to pounce and just waiting for the rattle of handcuffs outside her door.

I was frank with her, saying that I was as much 'in the dark' about police intentions as she was. It was impossible not to have sympathy for her because, in the context of her social standing and future prospects, she was on Death Row.

She'd had a wretched childhood, brought up in two converted railway carriages, where there was no piped water or electricity, but an overflow of lechery from her stepfather. After leaving home, she'd flitted between numerous jobs to escape seductive overtures from proprietors and managers. She'd never been given credit for her sincere endeavour to swim against the flow of effluence in her fledgeling days in the big, bad city. Eventually, she'd probably said to herself, *Why bother?* And there she was, a pitiful fly in a very large spider's web.

The Establishment was determined to have its pound of flesh, even if it was equivalent to thrusting a bantamweight boxer into the ring with a heavyweight. For the police and press, it had become a game of cats tormenting a mouse, aided and abetted by the Government, a shameful episode in the Establishment's ignominious history.

The morning after my *cosy* chat with Vickie Barrett, I took a call from 'Jack'. 'Thank God!' were my first words, followed by, 'I need you more than a whisky and chaser.'

'I thought you might,' he said dryly.

'Can normal service be resumed?' I hoped.

'As long as we're discreet.'

A rendezvous was arranged for noon in the Salisbury pub in St Martin's Lane, which is situated near the west end of Long Acre, and so was within easy walking distance for me and close to Leicester Square Tube station. However, despite the geographic advantage for me, I thought the Salisbury was a strange choice of venue; an ornate establishment, with mini-chandeliers and brass fittings, it was a honeypot for luvvies, mostly out-of-work actors and actresses who, naturally, were 'just resting between parts.'

This pub always did a roaring lunch-time trade and true to form it was heaving when I jostled my way to the bar, where 'Jack' had pitched his tent and no one was going to dislodge him.

'Not your kind of haunt, is it?' was the way I kicked off the long-overdue get-together.

He explained that he'd chosen it for the very reason that it wasn't a 'copper's pub' and neither could he imagine it frequented by journalists, which he was wrong about. Because of the regular clientele the Salisbury attracted, it was frequented by showbiz reporters; one in particular, from the *Daily Mail,* was a habitué, but I was anxious not to jeopardise the reopening of the pipeline, so I kept shtum.

Detectives knew better than most people that a crowd was the ideal environment in which to retain anonymity. Everyone was so engrossed in their own conversation and making themselves heard that they were oblivious to what was being discussed by others, even those pressed against them.

The issue I wanted to flush out was that of the Stephen Ward association with the 'Nudes' murders. Was it a 'runner' or a 'decoy'?

'The latter,' he said economically.

'But Brown was a player in the trial?' I pushed, playing devil's advocate.

'Forget it. Hers was less than a cameo role.' Good analogy for the Salisbury.

When I pointed out that the leak appeared to have been floated from the guv'nor, Marchant, he grinned slyly into his glass and wet his lips with froth. 'It was tailor-made for you fellas,' he said, a shade smugly. 'Everyone knew you lot wouldn't be able to resist it.'

For the sake of my own integrity I stood my ground and told him pithily that I'd pinpointed all the gaping holes to my news editor. The Yard wasn't interested in disseminating the truth, but was more focused on deceiving Fleet Street, so that the hacks would be running away from the real action.

The danger for a crime correspondent in the thick of a serial-killer investigation is to play armchair detective. I say *danger* because the press are invariably in possession of half-truths – probably much less – and are always off-course with their crystal-ball gazing and guessing. Nevertheless, that's what editors and readers appeared to want, so who could blame the feeding of that appetite if it helped bring about a positive result? If the smokescreen worked, the police were able to proceed at their own pace without reporters and photographers hampering them.

'If the Ward trial connection is a hoax, is *any* progress being made?' I asked, trying not to sound critical.

The breakthrough would come from forensics, he was confident. There were stained markings on several of the bodies that were more than similar; they were identical in chemical content. The paint marks were specific. Not just blobs that came from a domestic tin of paint, the sort used for decorating doors, bedrooms or window frames. 'Industrial paint, with a unique metallic ingredient,' he said, very conspiratorial now.

'Used for what?' was my next obvious question.

'Spraying vehicles.'

'So they've been killed or stored after death in a garage?' Conjecture was taking over.

'Or workshop.'

All the people known to socialise with Brown – men and women – were being interrogated, alibis and backgrounds checked and double-checked, though the murder squad detectives weren't holding their breath over these lines of inquiry in respect of yielding the identification of the killer.

We discussed what Barrett had to say and he strongly advised me not to rely on a word she uttered, denouncing her as a 'pathological liar' who made tantalising statements, only to recant, with the regularity that she went on and off the streets. When I queried if she possibly had 'anything in particular in mind when being scathing about Brown, spitefully calling her nuts,' he nodded solemnly, saying that on the prostitutes' grapevine she'd have been privy to much of Brown's unsavoury history.

The 'nuts' insult undoubtedly alluded to the period Brown

had spent in a psychiatric unit, having been sectioned for twenty-eight days in 1963. From 'Jack's' bleak résumé, it was transparent that after the age of eleven Brown's life had been a precipitous downward spiral, without a sliver of sunshine. Convicted of theft when just turned eleven, she was placed on probation.

In the same year that she finished her schooling, aged fifteen, she secured a job in a shop, only to be sent to an approved school a few months later. This was after Mrs Helen Brown had reported her own daughter as 'beyond control'.

Within two years, Frances was pregnant, giving birth to a daughter, whom she named after her mother, perhaps a subliminal gesture for a reconciliation, reaching out in the hope of being embraced again in the womb of the family, but the father of her child promptly did a runner and so did Frances, though separately, heading for London and leaving mum holding the baby.

Later, after her daughter's murder, Mrs Brown was to say in Glasgow, 'I had a terrible time with her. She was staying out all night and I had no idea where she was. For her sake, I had to report her to the police, an awful step to have to take and I was in tears for days afterwards. I cannot believe what is going on. I *won't* believe! I can't accept she's gone.'

On arriving in London, Frances Brown went straight on the streets and hooked up with Paul Quinn the following year, 1962. The introduction was made by Quinn's wife, Maureen. Paul had served time in prison for theft and shop-breaking. Soon Frances had adopted Quinn's surname. Meanwhile, the Scottish police were seeking her for neglecting her child and another probation order was imposed against her, this time in the Glasgow Sheriff Summary Court.

Soon pregnant again, she sank into depression and overdosed on a concoction of sleeping tablets and purple hearts (amphetamines); in other words, a cocktail of uppers and downers, creating a metabolic tug of war.

In Queen Charlotte Hospital in March 1963, she gave birth to a boy, but wasn't discharged until June, astonishingly with a supply of tranquillisers and sleeping pills. Instead of misusing the medication, she tried gassing herself, but failed. In fact, everything she turned to was a failure, so, in desperation, she tried her hand at theft and attempted to steal a car, failing, of course. At Marylebone Magistrates' Court, she was fined £10 or, alternatively, a month in Holloway Prison. She chose Holloway, but Quinn paid the fine so that she was immediately released.

However, having broken her Glasgow probation order, she was now sent to prison in Scotland for three months. Her son was taken into care by Smethwick Council, an adoption couple came forward, but Quinn wouldn't sign the paperwork, arguing that it was against his Catholic faith. (He'd been adopted and didn't find out until he was eighteen, when he immediately ran away from home, in anger and disbelief.) So the baby, born in April, 1964, was, in fact, Frances's third child and she was still only twenty.

With that topic apparently exhausted, I fast-forwarded the subject to suspects: were there any *promising* ones? 'Nope.' All kerb-crawlers were being 'looked into' along with everyone who had served sentences for sexual offences. Theory had it that sex killers gravitated and graduated from lesser sexual crimes.

Could he 'drop' any names.

Not for publication, but a couple that might 'whet' my 'appetite' and could be 'worth keeping an eye on'.

The first was Lord Longford, who was to make himself unpopular with the public for becoming a confidant of Moors murderer Myra Hindley and lobbying for her release, arguing that she was 'riddled with remorse', quietly pious with a nun's religious devotion, and had embraced Roman Catholicism. Longford hadn't been kerb-crawling in his car, but had been approaching prostitutes, much in the 'manner of Gladstone', a nineteenth-century prime minister who had befriended whores with the worthy intention of converting them and saving their souls. Well, that was Gladstone's story, but it was lucky for him that there was no 'War of the Tabloids' raging then and no outlet for a whore to print her own money by selling a 'kiss-and-tell' steamy series to the highest bidder. Longford, apparently, had been advised in future to be more circumspect when doing God's work and less conspicuous in the red-light districts in view of the tense and sensitive circumstances.

Another high-profile name that was thrown in the mix at that lunchtime rendezvous was the society portrait painter Vasco Lazzolo. 'Don't get too excited, though,' 'Jack' warned, 'but at least it's someone with a racy track-record and you should have him on file.' I vaguely recalled the name and 'Jack' assured me that it would be among the cuttings in my office library. 'In abundance,' he added.

More and more the brass were convinced that forensic evidence would finally nail the perpetrator. 'Something like a speck of dust will lead us to his door.'

At that moment I was reminded of the fabled words of American Detective Sergeant Harry Hansen, who investigated the legendary Black Dahlia murder in Los Angeles in 1947, a crime that has spawned its own library of books, with countless movie spin-offs. Hansen, a cerebral, philosophical cop, said memorably, 'Homicide is a union that never dies. Like marriage, murder is an irreversible act (divorce aside!). It can never be changed or the circumstances altered. The murderer and the victim are tied together in a bond that goes on into infinity.

That's why I say it's sacred and every murder scene has its sacred ground which should not be touched.'

Finding something sacred in this demonic case was a hellish search.

As a footnote, the Black Dahlia sadist was never caught: he bisected Elizabeth Short's body, cut off head and legs, and displayed the remains beside a main residential road like a broken and discarded mannequin. If Hansen had been leading this investigation, which was not a possibility, of course, I'm afraid his poetic approach to solving murders would have found this case devoid of rhyme and rhythm.

# CHAPTER 7

# DENIAL

The Brown family in Glasgow were in paralysed denial. Neither parent, Francis or Helen Brown, would travel with detectives to formally identify their daughter's body. They couldn't come to terms with her brutal death, despite the headache she'd been for them constantly since a scapegrace child.

Mrs Brown even denied that Frances had been embroiled in the Profumo/Keeler international scandal. I say *international*, because a few years later, when I was working in the USA and the Caribbean, the hottest subject of gossip in the cocktail lounges (bars in the UK) was Keeler. Not Profumo. Not Ward. Certainly not Macmillan or Mandy Rice-Davies. Just Keeler, who, while reviled in the UK, had become a cult figure in the States. In Miami, for example, to have known Keeler was always worth a free lunch.

The conservative middle class in the UK symbolically snubbed Keeler because she was pitched as a parvenu. There was also a racist undercurrent in the hostility fired at her: many of her lovers had been black. Britain claimed to be colour-blind; unfortunately, that meant it saw everything in black and white.

In America, however, Keeler was a breath of fresh air; the Brits were not as staid and stuffy as their international persona. She was seen as a racy rascal, a Hollywood siren-type, who had box-office appeal and therefore was high-value currency. The demimonde of US cities envied and admired her in equal proportions, yet another phenomenon of those crazy Swinging Sixties.

When shown photographs of Frances Brown entering and leaving the Old Bailey during the trial of Ward, her mother simply stated that it was a lookalike, a case of mistaken identity or someone posing as her daughter. Not even the police could convince her and sedatives had to be prescribed to avert a mental breakdown. The truth was that the slur on the family name was too much of a burden. 'After all we did for her,' she lamented, a remark that probably unlocked Mrs Brown's psyche – as if Frances had deliberately got herself murdered just to crush her parents further.

Shortly after Frances Brown had set up home in Southerton in west London, she wrote a letter to her parents:

*Well here I am writing to let you know that Paul and I have a great flat, 1 kitchen, 1 living room, 1 big lobby and it has a garden back and front.*

*Paul got a job back with Steven and Carters. He works late nearly every night and he is always tired. Oh, Mammy we have a television and I hope to get a radiogram this week. [The baby] is teething and crying all the time. Paul sends his love to everyone.*

The letter was signed, *Frances and Paul,* plus twenty-six kisses from their infant son.

No hostility or recriminations there. On the contrary, it was optimistic and upbeat, but maybe a shade surreal in view of all that had occurred, plus the emotional and domestic turmoil that the couple had left in their wake when abandoning Glasgow. Frances's two other children, the conflict with the police and other authorities appeared to have been rubbed off the chalkboard of her life.

Maybe she was attempting to ditch her corrosive past, cut the umbilical cord with her squalid history and make a fresh, wholesome start. If that was indeed her mindset, it was stillborn because, almost immediately, she'd gone the way of her inclination, turning tricks. Like so many of her street-clan, she was a dreamer. Tomorrow would bring a new dawn, goodbye to the old, hello the reborn Frances Brown. Unfortunately, most dawns Frances was still hobbling the streets on her stiletto stilts, feet and other body parts sore, and her brain mushy with whisky. Her new dawn would have to wait another day, and so it went on... a runaway train hurtling towards its lurking nemesis. No brake could save her.

A couple of weeks following the letter, Mrs Brown received a picture postcard of Piccadilly Circus, purporting to be from her daughter. On the reverse side, the message read: *Dear Mom, I received your letter OK. Paul, myself and Baby are doing fine and I hope all is the same at home. Lots of love, Frances.*

This postcard gave Mrs Brown 'a funny feeling' and a 'sort of foreboding', a 'bit fishy'. Instead of putting her mind at rest, it did the opposite, unsettling her, as if cockroaches were scuttling around in her head, was a colourful description she saved for me. For a start, the writing did not resemble Frances's 'in the slightest; nothing like.' Secondly, there was no punctuation (I have added some to make it readable) and as seen from her letter above, Frances always included punctuation where she considered it necessary. Thirdly, in the address, the writer had added Scotland after Glasgow. 'That was the final evidence for me that this card wasn't written by Frances,' she told me emphatically on the phone. 'Frances never included Scotland in the address. What was the point? Everyone knows where Glasgow is. You'd only put Scotland if you were writing from abroad.'

The postmark on the picture postcard was legible: Hammersmith, 1 October 1964. So *who* had written the postcard?

'It could only have been that Quinn,' Mrs Brown said disparagingly. 'Who else down there knows our address, except him and the police.'

'Have you informed the police?' I asked.

'Oh, yes. They have the letter and postcard. But I don't think they're taking it seriously.'

This was probably true. The writing and message may have been fraudulent, but the postmark didn't lie. The postcard had been mailed more than three weeks *before* Frances had disappeared. Too many people had seen Frances alive between 1 and 23 October for there to have been a conspiracy to fake the date of her death, Neither could the pathologist have been hoodwinked to that extent. Anyhow, I made a note to raise the issue when I next spoke with 'Jack', which I duly did. I called him late afternoon/early evening that same day from a public phone-box on the ticket-machine concourse at Leicester Square Tube station.

'I haven't heard of anyone this end getting excited about these things,' he said disinterestedly, referring to the letter and postcard. 'Can't see how they can have any bearing. Just fluff. We've got too much else to bother about.'

'Really?' I rejoined. 'Such as?'

'The paint stains. Crucial. And someone well-known.'

'Not Profumo?' I suggested incredulously, upping the stakes.

'Think bigger.'

*Bigger! Bigger than the former Secretary of State for War and husband of one of the most beautiful and celebrated film and stage actresses of the age! Come on!* Surely we weren't descending into risible Jack the Ripper apocryphal yarns, fantasising about princes of darkness and ludicrous machinations of royal culpability? Too absurd! *Stop winding me up, Jack.*

'Just *how* big?' I said soberly, pulse ticking in my ear as I fished for something realistic, a marker, a ballpark figure, figuratively.

Click. He was gone. So, too, any chance of a publishable exclusive. This was the way it was done in the movies – another example of fiction choreographing real life, true crime. The mystery of the postcard and the letter were being handled by the staff of our Scotland office. Time to move on, like vultures: once all the meat was off the bone, there was nothing left to scavenge.

There were lots of debates surrounding the positives and negatives of my writing a feature article about being a suspect in such a heinous series of murders and how circumstantial evidence could impact on an innocent person's life, social, personal and professional, bringing distrust and upheaval in a family and tension to a marriage. *No smoke without fire.* Naturally, I was strongly and vociferously in favour and pushed hard for the go-ahead.

News editor Ken James, as usual, straddled the fence. He recognised the news value of the proposed article and especially its exclusivity, but he had reservations. Therefore, he would have to consult Andrew Mellor, he said. In other words, he wanted to ensure that the bullet stopped with someone else should it backfire. Self-preservation was a common mantra among middle executives in Fleet Street where the casualty rate was war-zone high.

Andrew Mellor was the editorial manager. As self-protective as James, he trotted off to the editor, Sydney Jacobson, who was later to go to the House of Lords, that retirement home for many national newspaper editors and proprietors. The issue, apparently, was the reputation of the newspaper and all the possible ambushes we could stumble into. What would the public make of a reporter discarding confidential information in a public place when sozzled? Politicians and the police might demand an explanation as to how I came by the sensitive information, if only to cause mischief; a proverbial cat among the pigeons. If the truth had to be disclosed that police officers of Scotland Yard, the world's citadel of law enforcement, were on the payroll of newspapers, the whole system could be scuppered. Where would we be then? No more under-the-counter tip-offs. Stymied. Police officers could lose their jobs. There could even be criminal charges, followed by reprisals against the press. Denunciation from the rest of sanctimonious Fleet Street.

The verdict from the three-man jury was unanimous. Too risky. Too much to lose for too little gain. Not a sound commercial proposition. *Sorry, Michael, but hey, it must have been a hoot. Plenty of free drinks to be had regaling that yarn.*

The Scotland Yard hierarchy and most savvy politicians knew about the informal police/press arrangements and had no quarrel with it, as long as it remained underground, out of the public eye and mutually beneficial; after all, it was merely an extension of the Westminster lobby communication network.

With hindsight, I suppose the three wise jurors were right to play safe and, in angling parlance, allow this one to swim away so that something larger might venture into our net without adverse repercussions.

'Jack's' mention of the portrait artist Vasco Lazzolo had to be worth following up in view of the paint marks on the bodies. His name had been dragged into the public domain by Frances Brown during the Ward trial, when she told the jurors that she'd been touting for business in Shaftesbury Avenue with Vickie Barrett when accosted by Lazzolo, without any prior knowledge of his name and fame – even the Queen was among the nobles who had 'sat' for him. That aside, Brown swore that she and Barrett had gone with the artist to his studio, where a threesome sexual frolic had taken place... for money, of course.

Married and with his self-esteem to defend, he appealed for the right to appear in the witness box to rebuff such 'scandalous lies'. In addition to Brown's evidence, Barrett had said that she caned him at Ward's flat for the market price of £1 a stroke.

Not in all his life had Lazzolo been 'so insulted and besmirched,' he said. Both women were liars. 'Why are these degenerates trying to ruin me? How can this be permitted?'

The jurors were unlikely to have known that scandal was not new to him. In 1943, when he would have been in his twenties, much worse accusations had been propelled at him. Arthur Stambois, an inventor of sorts, smeared him publicly as a 'pimp, a diseased pervert, a Portuguese pig and swine.'

Could 'Jack' have been nudging me towards Lazzolo? It didn't seem likely. Wrong kind of paint, for starters. Paint used by artists is very different from all types in the car-spraying industry. The paint stains on Brown and at least two of the other bodies were composed of globules. And how could this portrait painter be considered a bigger fish than Profumo? No, he didn't fit.

Always there was the problem, the stumbling-block, the bedrock of logic, of being able to complete the circle: if Lazzolo killed Brown, he also had to be 'Jack the Stripper', killer of the others, and there was nothing whatsoever to couple him with any of the previous victims.

So who was Mr Big?

## CHAPTER 8

# A FALSE BEGINNING

There was plenty of excitement around the world in 1959. Cuban dictator Batista fled to the Dominican Republic after being overthrown by Fidel Castro and his hot-blooded band of revolutionaries, much to the dismay of the American Mafioso who were the real governors.

In the Pacific, Hawaii became the fiftieth state of the USA, the invasion of Pearl Harbour by the Japanese having taught them the security-comfort of moving in permanently with Big Brother and his nuclear prize collection.

Nearer home, in Paris the President of the Fifth Republic of France was named as De Gaulle, whose pendulous features, exaggerated by his elongated Roman nose, was a dream for cartoonists and their lampooning caricatures.

The British public was continuing to be entertained by the wizardry of James Bond via the Ian Fleming novel *Goldfinger*. People of all ages were tapping their feet to the happy-clappy beat of the pop song, 'He's Got the Whole World in His Hands', something that must have resonated with Prime Minister Harold Macmillan, who would soon be preaching to British citizens that they had 'never had it so good'. Such a sentiment wasn't true for everyone. The fact that the initial section of the M1 had been opened, Britain's first motorway, which would link the capital with Birmingham, the country's 'second city', did little for the millions without cars.

As for the 'working girls', they had never had it so bad, now that there were very few American Servicemen posted in the UK and the Street Offences Act 1959 was introduced by the Government, making it illegal for any man or woman to loiter or solicit in a street for the purpose of prostitution. The Act gave the police the power to make an arrest, without a warrant, if they merely suspected anyone of soliciting. The Act was known colloquially as 'The Street Clean-up Purge'. After a woman's first conviction, she would have no chance of avoiding prosecution and conviction if she was spotted after dark on the streets of a recognised red-light district.

'They're trying to bleedin' starve us to death,' Pauline Mills observed to Elizabeth Figg in the room they shared in Duncombe Road, Archway, north of Islington in London, sandwiched between Golders Green to the west and Haringey to the east. 'Just think of all them toffee-nosed diplomat gits I've been with in the back of their posh cars. What a cheek!'' They were drinking their wake-up cups of tea at almost three in the afternoon.

'One law for the rich and another for us poor sods,' complained Figg, who was known to Mills by the name of Ann Phillips. They were in bed together, just coming round from the night before. Street-whores are nocturnal creatures, pallid and short on vitamin D. Escort agencies and call-girl servicers were to become spin-offs from tightening legislation against prostitute-pollution on the streets, but they hadn't yet come of age. Talking of age, by the time she was nineteen Pauline Mills had racked-up thirty-three convictions for soliciting. She'd joked about becoming a record-breaker and being the pride of the East End. She really believed that East Enders were truly special people.

Escort agencies were an American import, first fashioned in Los Angeles by Brenda Allen, who was 'sponsored' by Bugsy Siegel and Mickey Cohen, of Mafia notoriety. Allen had an 'arrangement' with numerous executives of the major movie studios which might require girls as 'toys' for their male headliners and visiting high-rolling financiers. Gangster actor and real-life Mafia stooge, George Raft, came to London as an underworld emissary, demonstrating how casinos and call-girl rackets should be run in order to circumnavigate hostile legislation.

Figg originated from Cheshire, born in Bebington in 1938. There is a seam of similarity running through the embryonic lives of all the casualties in this book: commonalities such as traumatic childhoods, family feuds, split-ups, an absence of a father-figure or the unwelcome presence of an objectionable one, a lack of continuity, changing accommodation to the tune of the party game musical chairs, spasmodic schooling and frequently, early run-ins with the law. The consequence of ugly divorces when the daughter was at an impressionable and formative age features prominently.

Figg was four when her parents divorced. After the separation, her mother, Elsie, moved to Crewe, but left her daughters behind; Elizabeth had a younger sister, Patricia. When their father, James Figg, departed for Canada, still their mother didn't seek custody of her daughters, instead farming them out to their paternal grandmother.

After returning from Canada, Mr Figg married again, had more children and brought Elizabeth and Patricia into the flock.

This wasn't a happy reunion. They lived in Rhyl, North Wales for a time. Money shortages plagued them. They were evicted and in 1953 Mr Figg was charged with assaulting a county court bailiff. He was convicted and fined the same year.

On returning to Cheshire, the relationship between Elizabeth and her father deteriorated further until it was poisonous. Sewer-language between them was the norm. He regularly called her 'a filthy little slut' and 'unhinged wanton', and likened her scornfully to her mother, 'nothing but a dirty scrubber' who would 'end up in the gutter'. He was almost prophetic. Some morgues were noted for their peripatetic, low-life residents.

At the age of sixteen, she packed her bags, leaving a note on the pillow of her father's bed, 'Goodbye Shitface! I wish you all the harm and bad luck in the world.' Considering the content of their daily slanging matches, these valedictory sentiments were probably reciprocated – in full.

Through a circuitous, southerly job-hopping route, Elizabeth Figg arrived in London and by 1959 she had no other source of income apart from prostitution. Her territory was the Bayswater Road and Holland Park, a very popular and competitive patch for street girls. However, there was sufficient demand to ensure that no girl needed to go hungry. Unfortunately, they didn't have only themselves to feed. They all had ponces – by choice. Men lived off them and the women willingly accommodated them, handing over their takings at the end of the night shift, as if despite their harrowing experiences with their biological dads, they still craved a father-figure in their lives. How Freudian is that?

Summer was starting to strut its stuff. By mid-June, daylight was at its longest. Good news for most people. At ten p.m. you could be drinking in a pub's beer garden with the night sky not yet in place. But for the Figgs of this world, summer could be wintry, when income was at its lowest: obvious really; if you worked under cover of darkness, the lengths of your shifts were determined by the moon and sun and their respective share of the daily cycle.

Hence, on 16 June, Elizabeth Figg didn't begin her beat until well after ten. By eleven forty-five she was in Endymion Road, parallel to Finsbury Park, some way off throbbing Bayswater Road to the south and volatile Holland Park, Rachman-land, and gentrified today beyond recognition.

The one advantage of summer for street sex workers is that they need to wear much less clothing than in winter. Less on, fewer to come off, hence a quicker turnover. Dressing, undressing, redressing were time-consuming components of a 'working-girl's' life and affected nightly takings commensurately. An old-fashioned time-and-motion study expert might have been able to give useful tips on how to further improve output or, in their case, input.

Cynical? Of course. Cold-blooded and clinical? Absolutely. Affection, emotion and passion weren't part of any of these transactions.

As Figg made herself visible near a lamppost, a potential punter was cruising the road in a 1939 black Morris Ten. The driver was a Patrick Forrest and he stopped his car alongside Figg when it was obvious to him that she was on the game. He wound down the window of the nearside front passenger door to enable Figg to poke her face and shoulders inside the car to discuss business and haggle over the price. As soon as a deal was struck, Figg scrambled into the front of the car. Because he was paying for full sexual intercourse, Figg said they'd have to go somewhere secluded and she knew 'just the place', somewhere she used regularly and where she had never been disturbed.

'Show me the way,' said Forrest, initiating low-calibre, chatty conversation. Figg's directions were as precise as any satnav. Not once did they have to stop while she assessed her bearings. Even Forrest, who was reasonably familiar with the area, was impressed by her navigational skills, and the destination, Mount View Road in Hornsey, was reached in a matter of minutes. They pulled up behind a row of private garages, a dimly lit, soulless spread of concrete without anyone about, no pedestrians and no other motorists. For the few minutes they required, they had this urban blot on the landscape to themselves.

Figg was wearing a new blue-and-white striped dress, which had been bought earlier that same day and altered to fit, a pair of black synthetic-leather shoes with steel-tipped stiletto heels, padded bra and knickers, but no stockings or tights. There was no reason to cover the legs in summer. Figg's clients weren't the kind that had to be aroused by saucy lingerie and short skirts that revealed suspenders and exposed a flash of flesh just above stocking-tops. Anyhow, it was too dark for much to be seen and the back of a car was no place for slinky fashion and striptease shows. These men didn't even remove their trousers. Any action was a five-minute – maximum – tawdry, farmyard function, usually requiring some deft manoeuvring and manipulation of the human body.

After they'd hopped into the rear, Forrest popped the buttons of Figg's dress, while she battled to release the bra clip, eventually succeeding but not before she'd also released a few choice expletives. From a box in her handbag, she produced a condom and stretched it on him with an almost sleight of hand technique, and then they were off at a gallop. In the virtual blink of an eye, the ride was over.

*Right, let's get going, luv. You know what you promised.* Forrest had been seeking an all-nighter when they met. Figg dismissed the proposition then relented, but said she had to go to Holland Park first. So Forrest had compromised. He'd have a 'quickie' first, sort of as an aperitif, then drive her to Holland Park and arrange a mutually convenient place to meet her again later, when they could renegotiate a fee for what was left of the night.

When dropping her off at Holland Park Tube station, he asked her how long she'd be and she told him about two hours. As she climbed from the car, Forrest noted that it was one-ten on his wristwatch. He then offered to meet her at that same spot at three-thirty and she agreed. When he enquired how she'd 'get back' to Holland Park, she replied, 'by taxi', giggling that she'd treat the cabbie to a 'free wank' as payment for her fare. Forrest simply laughed and commented, 'Nice one!'

This isn't a *Breakfast at Tiffany's* story by any means, but Figg and all the other disreputable young women were someone's daughter, still redeemable while alive, and so often victims of circumstance before becoming victims of murder. So often the lottery of the womb has a lot to answer for. Princess or pauper, palace or slum, it all depends on a seed sown by someone beyond your control, before your existence: a caution against ever being holier than thou and sanctimoniously judgmental.

From Holland Park, Forrest drove to the West End, making several stops on the way, killing time – nothing else, he later asserted – before returning to Holland Park, arriving there around three-ten. While waiting he smoked a cigarette, but Figg didn't show up, though two uniformed police officers did and moved him on.

Later, according to pathologist Donald Teare, Figg was dead by two a.m., so the most Forrest could have hoped for at three-thirty was a ghost. After the post-mortem, Teare was certain that the prostitute had been dead between midnight and two. It was soon established that at midnight she was in Forrest's car. Forrest was also definite about his timetable. He picked up Figg at eleven forty-five and dropped her off at Holland Park at one-ten, leaving a fifty-minute window in which she encountered her killer. So much rested on Forrest's version. If Forrest was telling the truth, then the importance of Figg being driven to Holland Park grew in stature. Who was she going to meet at that hour? Certainly by arrangement or fateful accident she met her killer and died very soon afterwards. Detectives had just cause in believing that this would be a 'forty-eight-hour wrap'.

The body was under a willow tree on grass in Riverside Lands, Chiswick, a tranquil setting by day two hundred yards west of Barnes Bridge and approximately the same distance from the river – the famous stretch, Putney to Mortlake, along which Oxford and Cambridge crews compete on Boat Race day, a national tradition of the sporting calendar taking place late March or early April. In fact, Barnes Bridge is at most a quarter of a mile from the finish.

This acre of green was called Duke's Meadows on maps of London. However, the women coppers of Chiswick knew it sentimentally as 'Cupids' Corner'. Hardened male cops tagged it more coarsely as 'Fuckers' Field'. Both sobriquets were legitimate. Duke's Meadows was a lovers' lane for couples planning a future together and nature's gift to sex-for-cash girls like Figg. An ideal location, too, for any deranged man with murder on his mind. It was one of those split-personality places: serene and innocent by day, uncouth and ruttish by night, as schizophrenic as some of the people who made use, for various purposes, of the 'meadows'.

The driver of a police car, PC Mills, out of Chiswick police station, was patrolling Riverside Lands when he spotted two white legs on the grass beside a willow tree. He stopped the car. It was five-ten a.m. Daylight was fragmenting the night sky. The River Thames was a sombre, muddy brown python, curling beyond the willows. Mills wasn't alone. He had PC Sparke with him. Until now, they'd had a quiet, boring night shift, made bearable by banter and cigarettes. Mills said he'd 'take a look'. Both of them were thinking of someone in a drunken stupor or KO'd by drugs.

However, the moment Mills saw Figg he had no doubt that they were dealing with a murder. She was lying on her back. Her dress was ripped. Her mouth and eyes were open and her breasts exposed. The hem of her dress was just above her 'knobbly' knees. A white slip was showing. Mills, trained in spontaneous detailed observation, subconsciously hoovered up the gruesome scene in seconds, noticing that her shoes were missing and she wasn't wearing makeup or any accessories such as rings or jewellery. Nevertheless, she did wear the unmistakable marks of murder – bruising to her neck. The pathologist readily identified at the crime scene the bruises as marks made by thumbs and fingers, indicating manual strangulation.

Wasting no time, Teare conducted the PM at Acton mortuary within less than five hours of the body being found. Following normal autopsy procedures, he weighed and measured Figg: she was five feet, five and a half inches tall and weighed eight and a half stones. An examination of her digestive system uncovered a rather large gastric ulcer, but this didn't contribute in any way to her death, though suggested her eating habits had been unhealthy. In fact, the residue of her undigested last meal in her stomach comprised fatty food.

As for the police, what was missing – apart from the clues to the identity of the killer – was anything to ID the victim. The two key players were anonymous. The body had already been cold at just after five that morning. Now it was essential to avoid the other trails going a similar way, thus the following missive was simultaneously circulated to all London police stations:

*Dead body of woman found on bank of Thames at Chiswick at 5am. Today, 17.6.59. Age about 25, height 5ft 2 inches, slim build, hair dark brown, eyes light brown, teeth discoloured, tooth on upper jaw recently extracted, two teeth on right side upper jaw missing. Small circular scar below knee on each leg. Faint scar on right knee. Dressed in summer dress, black and white narrow stripes, white underskirt, no shoes. Please have missing persons' register searched to identify.*

A pity about the dress-colour and height inaccuracies, but it was a rushed job and served its purpose quite adequately.

There was nothing that morning to suggest to the police that Figg was a hooker, especially because her fingerprints weren't on file at Scotland Yard, establishing that she'd never been charged with soliciting. Figg's picture and the sad story appeared on all front pages of the London evening newspapers and in the following morning's nationals, leading to her official identification at midnight, two days after the crime. Elsie King, with her new husband George, went to Chiswick police station and they were escorted to Acton mortuary. Elsie, very sangfroid, almost frostily said, 'Yes, that's my daughter,' then turned and walked grimly from the room.

The following day, thirty-four-year-old Patrick Forrest also walked into Chiswick police station, but for a very different reason. He had information about 'that woman, Figg, isn't it? And things about me and her on the night of the murder.'

Lead officer in the investigation was Detective Superintendent Jim Mitchell, who was pleasantly surprised by the apparent candid cooperation of this witness. Usually men who frequented brothels and paid for sex with street hawkers were secretive about their *addiction,* especially when one of the women he'd recently had sex with on the back seat of his car had been murdered – on the same night and in under an hour of their parting. He must have known that he would be a suspect. In fact, the *only* suspect. Most of the officers at Chiswick police station believed that Forrest had come to hand himself in even though he would almost certainly be hanged for the murder.

Forrest was taken to an interview room and offered a mug of tea, which he readily accepted. Mitchell, a veteran with a wealth of experience in serious crime-detection, functioned on the principle of giving a murder suspect enough rope with which to hang himself, a chilling reality in 1959. So there were smiles and handshakes and a cordial invitation for 'Mr Forrest' to tell them all he knew and how he could be of assistance; kind of him to be so public-spirited in coming forward so punctiliously. It was at this point that he became jittery, not withdrawn, but explaining that he was a Catholic and had only come forward after consulting his parish priest and confessing.

*Confessing!* Mitchell's pulse rate must have been too rapid to count. Calmly, he asked, 'Confessing to what?'

'Going with prostitutes. Doing things contrary to my religion. Breaking the rules.' Smiling nervously, he added, 'I suppose you'd call it being a bad lad.'

Murder was rather more serious than merely *being a bad lad*. And at the age of thirty-four, Forrest hardly qualified as a *lad*. Mitchell sat back. A Scot, known affectionately as 'Gentleman Jim', Mitchell now had all the time in the world. Nothing ever ruffled him. He had a detective sergeant with him; jackets were off, collar-buttons undone, ties loosened. Police station interview rooms could be sweatboxes in summer and freezers in winter. At no time did Forrest sweat. His priest had implored him to 'go straight to the police and tell nothing but the truth', warning that if he delayed it would 'look bad' for him.

Before the police even ran a crime-file check on Forrest, he owned up to convictions in juvenile courts for receiving stolen goods and shopbreaking. 'But I learned my lesson,' he insisted. 'I've gone straight ever since. I've never been in trouble with Old Bill since. I work hard and play hard. Stops Jack being a dull boy, don't it?'

Mitchell was morose by nature but he could play genial when to his advantage and now was the opportunity to show his *human* side, his man-to-man bonding, two men of the world chatting over mugs of tea. *Your dirty little secrets are safe with me.* 'What do you do for a living, Patrick?'

'I'm self-employed,' Forrest answered.

Mitchell waited for Forrest to elaborate, but nothing more was coming voluntarily, so the superintendent had to dig.

'Self-employed doing what, exactly?' He could have been a self-employed plumber, electrician, safe-breaker, burglar or murderer.

'I'm a builder. A brickie. Jobbing for others. When the weather's too bad for outside work, I'll do other things, like decorating or painting.'

Mitchell was eager to hear about his home life, something personal that might give him an insight into the man, and it was soon forthcoming. Was he married? Did he have kids?

'Not married, but I'm going to be soon,' he said cheerily. 'We've been going steady for quite a while now. She's very respectable and likes everything done proper. Sort of old-fashioned in her ways, but that appeals to me. I'm sure she'll be faithful and make a great mother.'

You'll hear it said over and over by detectives that after a couple of years in the job nothing ever surprises them, not even Forrest's next admission. He would be with his girlfriend every evening from five-thirty until eleven, when he would kiss her goodnight, tell her how much he loved her, then immediately go whore-hunting. Nightly. Without fail. He explained that his intended wife-to-be didn't want sex with him until they were married because she was a Catholic, like him, so he had to 'get it' elsewhere. He didn't believe his behaviour was 'much of a sin' nor a betrayal. After all, he still loved *his* girl and there was no fondness or emotional attachment to the women he picked up on the streets. He spoke as if going with prostitutes was simply an extension almost of his business: jobbing, bartering, buying and selling. All this was being noted by the sergeant.

Having softened up the suspect with an almost chummy inquisition so far, it was time for Mitchell to go up a gear and focus forensically on the critical hours. Without reticence, Forrest outlined how he came across Figg in Endymion Road.

'Were you looking for her especially?' Mitchell inquired, with what seemed an innocuous question, but it could have been very defining.

'No, I'd never seen her before.'

'But you were seeking sex?'

'Oh, yes. I knew where to find it. You don't have to cruise those roads for long before you find one.'

'By *one* you mean a prostitute?'

'Yes, and there's normally several to choose from, in just one road.'

He went into detail about the financial negotiations, the agreement, where they drove to, and the drop-off at Holland Park Tube station at eleven-ten, with the understanding that they would rendezvous there at three-thirty for an 'all-nighter'.

Without any badgering or pugnacity from the detectives, Forrest had put himself well and truly into the crucial time frame of the crime. Could he substantiate his movements after they parted? Mitchell probed, believing that this was impossible. In fact, Mitchell admitted later that at this moment he believed, metaphorically, Forrest had put himself on the trapdoor which was already beneath his feet, just waiting for the lever to be pulled.

'Oh, yes,' Forrest said blithely. 'I can account for every minute.'

'Please do so,' Mitchell invited sceptically.

Forrest chronicled his movements thus: he drove southwards along Bayswater Road to Marble Arch, where he saw a mobile hot food and drink stall. After parking, he walked to the stall and ordered a hamburger and a tea. While eating and drinking, he gossiped with the proprietor, who was grumbling about 'almost everyone and everything, but especially about the law and the fact that he'd been charged with obstruction.' 'What am I obstructing?' he was alleged to have said rhetorically to Forrest. 'I'm just providing a public service. Where else can night-workers like you get hot food and hot drink? And do you know what, coppers are some of my best customers. Regulars, they are. I tell you, the law's all against honest working folk, the little fellas. They wouldn't say nothing if I was wearing a pinstriped suit and bowler.' Forrest said he kept agreeing with 'the bloke' just to pacify him and was at the stall for about half an hour or so, 'just chin-wagging'.

'What then?' said Mitchell, gently prodding, in no hurry.

'I went drive-about,' Forrest continued, without visual indication that he was concocting an off-the-cuff yarn.

The *drive-about* in the West End took him along Oxford Street to Tottenham Court Road, Charing Cross Road, Leicester Square, Piccadilly and completing the circle at Marble Arch.

'Were you looking for another pick-up?' Mitchell quizzed.

Forrest shook his head. 'No, like I told you, I was only killing time,' he said adamantly. He was looking forward to another 'session, a longer one' with Figg, though he hadn't known her name at the time.

*And this is a religious man with a respectable girlfriend whom he's planning to marry and dates every evening, before heading for the red-light districts looking for women-of-the-night; match up that,* Mitchell must have been thinking.

## A FALSE BEGINNING

By three-ten he was parked in exactly the same spot that Figg had exited the car. He said he smoked while waiting, but three-thirty came and went. Still no sign of Figg. So, a 'bit pissed-off', he left his car and strolled to the junction ahead, where Holland Park Avenue intersected with Lansdowne Road. He was 'looking up and down', hoping that he might see Figg. In any case, he'd been getting 'brassed off just sitting' in his car, even though it wasn't at all cold.

As he was standing on the corner, 'two coppers came along, looking at me as if I must be up to no-good'. Now Mitchell's ears really pricked up. The sergeant knew exactly what his first task would be as soon as the interview was over.

Forrest had walked back to his car and climbed in, but the two uniformed officers were determined to question him. When they asked him what he was 'up to', Forrest said he explained that he was 'just having a smoke while waiting for a friend'. Not impressed with his answer, he was asked to produce his driving licence and insurance details. One of them wrote down the vehicle's registration number, while Forrest gave his name and address to the other officer and apologised for not having his licence on him, which wasn't an offence. However, the insurance policy was in the glove compartment and everything about it seemed in order. One of the constables shone his torch over the interior, but Forrest wasn't asked to open the boot for inspection.

With nothing apparently to charge him for, the officers instructed him to switch on the car's lights, finish his cigarette quickly and drive off.

Waiting until the officers had continued their beat, Forrest 'hung around' for about another ten minutes, then, cursing, he drove into Holland Park Avenue where there was an all-night filling station. His car was low on petrol and he wasn't sure that he'd make it home to 62 Springdale Road, Stoke Newington before running out of fuel.

As he nosed his Morris Ten into the road from the garage, he saw a woman waving frantically at him, but it wasn't Figg. Nevertheless, he stopped while she hobbled to the car. The encounter he recalled for Mitchell went, 'The flippin' heel's broken off my bleedin' shoe and my ankle's killing me. I can hardly walk. Would you be a love and drive me home? It's not far I'd be very grateful.'

*I'd be very grateful* translated into the offer of a freebie, the currency Figg had mentioned to Forrest when it came to paying for a taxi.

'Where do you live, then?' Forrest had checked.

'Elgin Crescent.'

'Jump in.'

Elgin Crescent was only a couple of minutes' drive away.

'What you doing out this late around these parts, looking for business?' she'd said.

Forrest now knew for sure that he had another prostitute in his car, but he wasn't interest in sex with her, even if it would be free,' he claimed to Mitchell. Instead, he explained to the woman that he was looking for another 'working girl' and described her, hoping perhaps that the woman for who he was doing a favour might have seen Figg, but she hadn't. 'I dropped her off,' Forrest added.

'No sex with her?' Mitchell quizzed, for the record.

'I didn't touch her,' Forrest retorted, as if disgusted by the notion. His night out on the town concluded at around five in the morning.

In his notebook, the detective sergeant inserted bullet points against the immediate follow-ups required from the statement so far: the two officers who had taken details of Forrest and his car's insurance policy and instructed him to move on, the vendor who had served him a hamburger and tea at Marble Arch, the prostitute he gave a lift to from the garage in Holland Park Avenue to Elgin Crescent, and the man on duty at the filling station.

The last part of the statement was probably the most confounding. Forrest claimed that while talking with Figg in his car she 'let on' that she lived at 57 Duncombe Road, a lie, of course, but not an extravagant one. Her flat was, in fact, at number 97. Surprising, perhaps, that she even confided the correct road. Anyhow, having reached his own flat at five in the morning in Stoke Newington, north-east London, Forrest was back in the Holland Park area by noon, continuing his futile search for Figg.

Why had he become so obsessed and besotted with her? After all, she was far from being what male inveterate habitués of London's red-light zones would have called a 'looker'. Nor did she have a unique personality, though she was *blessed* with an arsenal of anecdotes, all fictitious, such as motherly tales about the child she didn't have.

Forrest knocked on the door of number 57 Duncombe Road. The door was opened cautiously by an elderly woman. When he described the person he was looking for, he was told he had the wrong address, no one else lived there. He tried a few more houses either side of number 57 and opposite, but to no avail, obviously. 'So I had to give up,' he told Mitchell.

Both detectives were bemused. What made Figg so special for him if it was true that they had done business together only the once? After all, hundreds of similar women would have given him the same service for a comparative charge, maybe even cheaper. Neither detective had ever heard such an extraordinary yarn before. So farcical that it might even be true, Mitchell had to concede.

Five hours' sleep was the most Forrest could have had and then his priority was to trace the whore who had let him down.

His actions were more compatible with those of a father who was worried about his daughter who hadn't come home from the night before. Certainly in those hours he seemed to have been far more concerned with Figg than the 'respectable' woman he was planning to marry. Bizarre wasn't a strong enough word.

Mitchell asked him what was so captivating about Figg. He replied that he'd enjoyed her company and that she was 'good at *it*'.

'Good at sex, you mean' said Mitchell, for clarification.

'Yes, the best yet,' Forrest said, completely uninhibited. 'She did it like it was enjoyment for her, too, not just closing her eyes and thinking about the washing-up she'd be going home to.'

Still it didn't make sense to the detectives. Didn't he have work to do?

No, not that day. He had spare time on his hands.

Mitchell had another tantalising thought. 'After your failed search, did you still keep your regular five-thirty date with your girlfriend?'

'Oh, yes, that went on as normal,' Forrest answered equably, seemingly oblivious to his aberrant conduct.

Forrest was examined for scratch marks, cuts or bruises. There were none. Had he argued with Figg? – 'No'. Had they fought? – 'No.' Had their sex been rough? – 'No.' Was she into kinky stuff? – 'No.' Were you, is that what you like? – 'Not at all.' Did you tear her dress? – 'No.' Was she wearing shoes when you parted? – 'Of course she was. She didn't go off barefoot into the night.' Did you kill her? – 'Don't be daft. Would I have come into the lion's den if I had?' Could be a clever ploy. 'Would be insane to my way of thinking.'

Mitchell hadn't a clue how Forrest's brain worked.

The two uniformed beat officers who spoke with Forrest were stationed at Notting Hill police station. They verified everything that had occurred, as related by Forrest. The mobile hamburger and beverage vendor at Marble Arch was tracked down and he remembered Forrest without too much prompting. The filling station attendant in Holland Park Avenue recalled Forrest because there was little trade that time of the night and a woman had been flagging down Forrest as he drove off. The elderly woman residing at 59 Duncombe Road said she'd been 'a bit nervous' about opening the door to a 'stranger' because there was 'so much crime about'. But, she went on, 'He was a very polite and cheerful gentleman. I was very sorry I wasn't able to help him. Everything's changed so much around here. Before and during the War, we knew not only our next-door neighbours but everyone in the road. These days people come and go like it's a railway station. I don't know anyone here any more. It's a transit camp.' Mitchell empathised with her, their sentiments coinciding. *Not like it used to be*: something he heard dozens of times a day, including among his own force and family.

Forrest's landlord lived on the premises and wouldn't allow male tenants to entertain women in their rooms, a rule that he applied strictly. 'I make it clear in advance that if the rule is broken, then the tenancy agreement is breached and out he goes,' he told Mitchell. 'From my experience, I've found that men bringing in women, alcohol or fish and chips are the root of all trouble when it comes to renting,' he said, defending his inflexibility.

As for Forrest, he was a 'good tenant, paid his rent on time, never came in drunk or disorderly, but nearly always very late.' However, he never committed the cardinal sin of sneaking in a woman.

When questioned about Forrest's return on Tuesday night/ Wednesday morning, he replied, 'I was already awake because it was light, so he didn't disturb me. That was the latest I've ever known him to be.'

Mitchell sent a detective inspector to Figg's funeral at Chiswick New Cemetery on 5 September 1959. Certain killers were known to be drawn to the scene of their abhorrent crime, in the words of Detective Sergeant Hansen, of the LAPD, 'the sacred place'. Similarly, there were killers who derived a sick frisson from attending the funeral of their victim, mixing with the mourners, playing at paying respect, keeping the murder alive and running. It was a long shot, but Mitchell had little else, apart from Forrest, the enigmatic joker in the pack.

The inspector arrived at the chapel to find that he and the undertakers were the only people at the minimal service, apart from the vicar, who was grateful for living company. Not a single relative put in an appearance, probably distancing themselves from such a *sordid affair,* fearing the presence of the press. They needn't have worried. No newspaper bothered to send a reporter or photographer to record the end of what some crime historians believed was just a beginning.

Forrest's presence would have met with disapproval by both the man of the cloth and the man with the handcuffs. In any case, Forrest had a lot of explaining to do with the 'respectable' woman who must have been wondering whether he could really be trusted to become a one-woman husband. Meanwhile, Figg's ponce was busy *breaking-in* the deceased's replacement and new recruit to his tacky stable. Life had to go on, though some people might have asked why.

Figg's resting place was with five others in a common grave. It's unlikely that even she had ever been involved in a six-some before.

There was considerable pressure on Mitchell to charge Forrest and leave his fate with an Old Bailey jury. He did pass Forrest's file to the Director of Public Prosecutions (DPP), with his own evaluation: unless any new evidence pointed to the contrary, he didn't believe that Forrest was the perpetrator, despite his implausible behaviour. There were those at Scotland Yard who believed that Forrest's own testimony was so outrageous, almost amounting to self-indictment, that a jury would never believe him and the circumstantial evidence would be strong enough to land a conviction. Mitchell was sufficiently canny, though, to appreciate that such a conviction would inevitably be overturned by the Court of Appeal and Forrest would never be able to face a re-trial for the same crime should fresh forensic clues incriminating him surface in the future, as science broke new boundaries. The DPP agreed with him. The hotheads at the Yard and in the media were a liability. Circumstantial evidence could be a dangerous boomerang in the wrong hands, something to which I could vouch.

As alluded to earlier, many criminologists and chroniclers have designated Figg as the inaugural victim in the 'Nudes' serial. This was vigorously disputed by murder squad supremo Detective Superintendent John 'Four-Day Johnny' du Rose, who was to retire as a deputy commander at Scotland Yard, after having taken charge of this investigation in its concluding stages. I am certain he was right. MO and signature are crucial in identifying serial killers. The signature is even more important to the killer than the hunters. Figg was manually strangled; the others were not. Well, at least six of the forthcoming seven weren't, the reason why the exact corpse count attributed to Jack the Stripper has always remained conjecture.

Another critical factor is that if Figg was number one, then it was well over four years before the second strike, unheard of in the history of such impulsive psychopathy, unless *he* had been in prison or abroad, continuing his reign of terror on foreign soil, of which there was no known record.

The most likely debut among the 'Nudes' deadly procession

was Gwynneth Rees (alias Tina Stuart), who was found on 8 November 1963. But even she doesn't make it on to du Rose's 'Nudes' chart, mainly because there remained – and still remains – doubt over the exact methodology of her death. However, she was the start of a chain that added corpse-links at regular intervals through until February 1965. In fact, the intervals became shorter as the momentum increased, consistent with a psychopath's compulsion and inability to restrain his psychological impatience and metabolic craving for the *drug* to which he was addicted, the *high* he doubtlessly experienced from being the most feared predator in the country. Along with the selection process of his quarry, the ritualistic enactment of the execution, the storing of the body as a trophy, a toy even, the exposing of it to the public as a shock exhibit, the headlines, the photographs, the police appeals, the post-mortem report, the inquest, and the realisation that, despite all the chest-beating announcements and upbeat prophecies, the police weren't even close.

The formula was foolproof. It was *his* game. *He* made the rules and the odds were stacked in *his* favour. The *drug* was stronger and more addictive than any other on the black market. However, there was one element of this lore that he'd overlooked: *he* had to be lucky every time, the cops had to get lucky only once.

# CHAPTER 9

# THE DIGGER

**S**hot one: a digger is at work in a landfill or somewhere similar, such as a vehicle-crunching plant. The driver is doing his job robotically, a glazed, bored expression highlighting the monotony. The mechanical shovel digs into the muck and the giant metal claws are clenched by remote control. Another lever is pulled. The elbow of the mechanical arm bends. The high-in-the-sky control cab, like an eyrie, rotates as the driver prepares for the culmination of this segment of the long day's action. The digger's arm looms above the workmen on the site below. The driver prepares to open the claw to release the shovel's contents. Then freeze. The scene is supposed to be suspenseful. But it's not. It's yet another tedious cliché. The jaded viewers know exactly what's coming next. One of the workmen on the ground shouts, 'Hold it! Oh, my God! There's a body!'

**Cut.**

**Shot two:** Police cars circle the digger. From the lead car leaps *Lewis, Frost, Morse, Columbo, Starsky and Hutch, Kojak, Barnaby* of *Midsomer Murders, Wycliffe, Cagney and Lacey,* or any of the cops in the hundreds of gangster movies made since the 1960s.

And this may seem harsh, but I blame poor Gwynneth Rees. Naked, except for one stocking rolled down to her ankle, she was suspended by an arm from the shovel of a mechanical digger, operated by Patrick Dineen. At first, he thought he'd caught some kind of animal, until he had an unobstructed view of the two white hanging legs, whereupon he shouted, 'Bloody hell! I've hooked a body.'

Thereafter, for decades, even now, one episode of every TV crime series had a corpse exposed this way. My theory, and I'm sticking to it, is that this was the moment, at two p.m. on Friday, 8 November 1963, that TV crime series' writers were presented with a formula they couldn't resist. The trouble is that formulae induce laziness and so it has been trotted out ad nauseam, to such an extent that the moment viewers see a digger they know it's safe to pop into the kitchen to brew a cup of tea, confident that they will not be missing anything unexpected. Yawn. Body in the claw. Seen it all before.

If Rees started a clichéd fiction drama trend, she also almost certainly provided the opening sequence in what was to morph into the 'Nudes' serial epic. No other story in the following fifteen months was to gobble up so many column inches in British national newspapers. Du Rose even prophesied that this killer would eclipse Jack the Ripper in the public psyche. That was another issue on which we were in agreement and also jointly mistaken, but for one reason only: the conspiracy between the police mandarins and newspaper editors to censor out the unique murder weapon, which, if made public, would have stunned the world and galvanised Hollywood, long before Watergate's 'Deep

*Left*: Gwynneth Rees, one of the seven victims of a London serial killer nicknamed 'Jack the Stripper', a photograph taken in about 1960. The killings, which remain unsolved, were known collectively as the 'Hammersmith Nudes Murders'. Gwynneth's body was found in a rubbish dump near the Thames on 8 November 1963.

(© *Keystone/Hulton Archive/Getty Images*)

*Below*: A police constable and a group of boys on the Thames towpath, close to where the body of Gwynneth Rees was discovered, November 1963. Rees was probably the first of the seven victims of the serial killer.

(© Evening Standard/*Hulton Archive/Getty Images*)

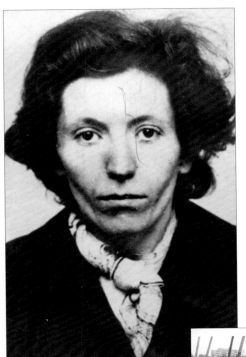

*Left*: Hannah Tailford, aged thirty, whose naked body was found by the river in Hammersmith on 2 February 1964. Although a prostitute like all the other victims, she was untypical for her social mobility.

*(© Bentley Archive/Popperfoto/Getty Images)*

*Right*: Detective Inspector Frank Ridge (centre, in black hat) with other police officers at the murder scene where Hannah Tailford's body was found, with Hammersmith Bridge in the background.

*(© Bentley Archive/Popperfoto/Getty Images)*

*Left*: Irene Lockwood, whose body was found on 4 February 1964 on the foreshore barely 300 yards upstream of where Tailford's had been discovered. This was in fact a double murder, for the autopsy showed that Lockwood was four and a half months pregnant.

*(© Keystone/Hulton Archive/Getty Images)*

*Right*: Helene (sometimes Helen, among other aliases) Barthelemy, a twenty-year-old prostitute, whose naked body was found in a pile of domestic rubbish in Brentford on 24 April 1964, just twenty days after Irene Lockwood's.

*(© Keystone/Hulton Archive/Getty Images)*

*Left*: Detective Superintendent Bill Baldock of 'T' Division CID (centre, with hands in pockets) at the spot, screened by canvas, where the naked body of Helene Barthelemy had been found in an alley at Swyncombe Avenue, off Boston Manor Road in Brentford. The dead woman had been dumped behind the garden of a terraced house.

*(© PA/PA Archive/PA Images)*

*Left*: A police dog handler and a constable searching the area where Helene Barthelemy's body was found.

*(© PA/PA Archive/PA Images)*

*Right*: Frances Brown, whom the police perhaps too quickly named as Margaret McGowan, which was only one of several aliases. The prostitute's naked and badly decomposed body was found in a car park near Kensington High Street on 25 November 1964.

*(© Keystone/Hulton Archive/Getty Images)*

*Left*: Detective Superintendent William Marchant of Scotland Yard holds up an Identikit picture of two men wanted for questioning in connection with Frances Brown's murder, 2 December 1964. Marchant would eventually be superseded as head of the overall investigation into the murders by John Du Rose.

*(© Jim Gray/Keystone/Hulton Archive/ Getty Images)*

*Left*: Bridget 'Bridie' O'Hara, the seventh and last of the victims in the series of killings known as the 'Hammersmith Nudes Murders'.

*(© Keystone/Hulton Archive/Getty Images)*

*Right*: Police at the site in North Acton where Bridie O'Hara's naked body was discovered on 16 February 1965. Unlike the other victims, the twenty-seven-year-old was married, although she had several convictions for soliciting.

*(© J. Wilds/Keystone/Hulton Archive/ Getty Images)*

*Left*: Detective Superintendent Bill Baldock outside Shepherd's Bush police station, 18 February 1965. At the time he was leading the investigation into the murder of seven women, but, to his resentment, would, like Marchant, be eased aside by 'celebrity cop' Du Rose.

*Right*: Detective Chief Superintendent (later Deputy Assistant Commissioner) John Du Rose at Shepherd's Bush Police Station following Bridie O'Hara's murder, 18 February 1965. 'Large, tough and conceited... a flamboyant showman,' Du Rose was 'adept at playing to the gallery, especially the press gallery'.

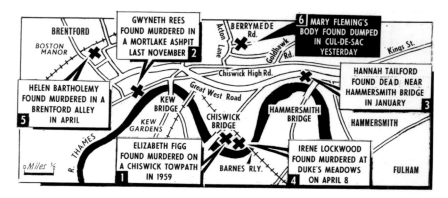

*Above*: A contemporary map of the murders issued in July 1964, showing the close proximity to the River Thames where, at the time, it was thought at least six young women had been found murdered. In fact, Elizabeth Figg's killing was almost certainly not part of the series, and there would be two more such murders before the killer stopped.

*(© Bentley Archive/Popperfoto/Getty Images)*

*Right*: The front page of *The Sun*, 22 March 1965, with the author's bylined story at left (he is on the left in the photograph). The police believed that a girl nicknamed 'Goldie' whom they could not trace was the latest victim in the series of murders. The author found her within hours and brought her to meet Detective Sergeant Bob Berry. In those pre-Murdoch days, *The Sun* was still a broadsheet.

*Above*: British boxer
Freddie Mills celebrates
after his world light-
heavyweight title victory
over US boxer Gus
Lesnevich at White City,
26 July 1948.

*(© Central Press/Getty Images)*

*Left*: American boxer
Joey Maxim from
Cleveland, Ohio, wards
off Freddie Mills's right
arm during their light-
heavyweight title fight at
Earl's Court, 24 January
1950. Maxim knocked
the British fighter out
at the beginning of the
tenth round; Mills retired
soon afterwards and
never fought again.

*(© Getty Images)*

Throat' and Linda Lovelace's enactment of the slogan, her legacy to politics and art, at a stretch.

However, the reason for the retention made sound investigatory sense, because it amounted to what the police in the USA call the 'control question': something known only to the killer and the cream of the investigators – plus, in this case, myself, through a leak, hence such a fuss being made over the remnants of the envelope on the train. A 'control question' is particularly useful for a speedy elimination of the disturbed people who always have a need to confess to high-profile murders, even if execution awaits them, as in numerous states of the USA and in the UK in the early 1960s, if believed. The 'control question' is usually such that the odds would be a million-to-one against a false confessor hitting on it by chance.

If the finding of Rees's body was spectacular by 1963 standards, there was nothing unique about her way of life in London and her method of earning a living. In fact, from beginning to end her lifestyle was something of a bromide. Although the climax wasn't inevitable, it was never likely to have been anything other than tragic. The graph of most people's lives have highs and lows, punctuated by a few plateaux, but hers had flat-lined long before adulthood; in the real definition of living, she was dead long before she died.

On that early Friday afternoon in November 1963, the digger was in use at Barnes Borough Council's household-refuse disposal plant in Townmead Road. One lorry had already been loaded when the discovery was made. A team of three was involved in the dirty work. In addition to Dineen, there was a foreman, Edward Kimpton, and lorry driver Peter Taffurelli. It is easy to understand why so many professional and amateur sleuths are reluctant to exclude Figg from the corpse count of the 'Stripper': *Location, Location, Location.*

This refuse dump was less than fifty yards from the Thames' towpath. From the towpath, one could look across the river directly to peaceful Duke's Meadows, where Figg's body had been displayed beneath a willow tree. So easy to reason that the predator had mapped out this riparian territory of west London as his personal burial ground, another signature, in fact. Very tempting, I admit, but the four-year hiatus and absence of the crucial signature are sufficient for me to dismiss Figg as a one-off, concurring with du Rose.

It was the foreman, Kimpton, who alerted the police. The emergency call went through to Richmond police station. The police posse was led by  Detective Superintendent Frederick Chadburn. The body was still suspended from the shovel by its right arm when Chadburn's team showed up.

Not far behind Chadburn was pathologist Dr Arthur Mant, who made a preliminary examination after Rees's remains were released from the claws. The digger had caused considerable damage. The giant claw had decapitated the corpse and the head had rolled several feet away from the torso into the pit. Major organs were missing, including the brain, which spawned rumours that a belated Jack the Ripper copycat was on the loose. The reality was much more mundane, however: putrefaction was the culprit for eliminating the soft-tissue organs, due to the length of time the body had been buried in the tip, possibly as long as two months, Dr Mant estimated, during the post-mortem in Kingston mortuary on the Saturday morning. Not of great significance at the time, though pertinent to later developments was the fact that four teeth were missing from the skull. Despite so much destruction and natural wastage, the pathologist was able to gauge the woman's age between twenty-two and twenty-five, and her height was calculated at five feet, three inches. Miraculously, in view of the decimated skeleton, he was positive that she took a four and a half-sized shoe. Excellent pathology, but of limited assistance to Chadburn, especially as Dr Mant was unable to confirm how the anonymous woman had died.

The U-shaped bone that supported the tongue had been damaged, but the larynx was missing, adding to Dr Mant's difficulty in establishing the possible cause of death. She could have been strangled, but might have died from a blow, even an injury sustained in a road or river accident. It was also possible that the snapping of the U-shaped tongue bone could have occurred *after* death, quite easily by the rampaging digger. For Chadburn, the outcome of the PM couldn't possibly have been more maddening. Was he investigating murder, manslaughter, misadventure or accidental death? He had no idea, except that the circumstances were suspicious. Instead of enlightening him, the medical findings had obfuscated. Dr Mant had concluded in his official written report that the cause of death was 'unascertainable'.

A coroner's vehicle transported Rees's loose collection of remains to Guy's Hospital, in central London, where Dr Mant lectured in forensic medicine. After more tests, experiments and consultations with Prof. Warwick, his colleague, he was able to be considerably more constructive. With Prof. Warwick's input, Dr Mant was now 'ninety-five per cent certain' that Rees had been strangled; still five bricks short of a full load, though, tantamount to the key to a cell door if anyone was charged with Rees's murder and the jurors were instructed that they had to be certain beyond all reasonable doubt before convicting. Chadburn was happier, but only by about five per cent!

Before thinking about finding the killer – if indeed there was one – the police first had to identify the victim. Just how much did the police know about her? Very little; nothing, in fact, apart from her height, approximate age, the size of her feet and, courtesy of the beheaded skull, that she had long brown hair. From herein, the investigation went into a sort of autopilot mode, with orthodox police procedures from the handbook taking the driving seat. Appeals to the public were made through all media outlets. Every force was requested to scrutinise their missing persons file.

The response was encouraging. Many people came forward, fearing that the deceased could be their daughter or wife, but all to no avail. The breakthrough was to come via the forensic lab, at a time when detective science was being routinely embraced by the more enlightened police forces, though a pocket of obscurantists still existed.

So much of Rees's body had decomposed beyond all recognition, but not the left hand, on which some skin remained in a reasonable condition. This hand was amputated from the skeleton, X-rayed and placed in a forensic lab freezer. Skin from the thumb and forefinger was delicately removed and microscopically analysed, while Chadburn kept his fingers, and much besides, crossed.

Bingo!

Twice!

Not only did the scientists extract a fingerprint, but one that was already on file at Scotland Yard in the name of Gwynneth Rees, alias Tina Smart, aged twenty-two, convicted twelve times for soliciting and once for theft.

Chadburn must have inwardly groaned, though. The good news of identification was qualified by the bad news of Rees's *profession*. The majority of murders were committed by a spouse, a lover, another family member, or certainly within the victim's network of contacts. Not so with prostitutes. The normal rule of thumb didn't apply in the netherworld of the demimonde.

More often than not, the killer would be a random pick-up; more so when the whore was a street girl. At least call girls, nightclub hostesses and escorts on the books of agencies tended to keep diaries of appointments and there were controllers – very different from ponces and pimps – who handled the bookings and were aware of the hotels and apartments used. In stark contrast, street girls were lone-rangers; lone-dangers. They flagged down motorists they'd never seen before; any one of these could be an undiagnosed psycho.

They were driven to remote places, for obvious reasons, including their own protection from the law. Any scream for help would be a silenced one. So where to begin in these daunting situations was always a testing dilemma for the police.

The common approach in such cases was twofold, as adopted by Chadburn: one half of the team would assemble the victim's history, from her first breath, while the other half focused on her street life – girls and ponces she worked and socialised with, until her last breath. Always a Herculean task because, even before setting one foot outside the police station, every officer was aware that he/she would be up against a wall of downright lies, half-truths (if lucky) and slyly doctored recollections, all designed to tamper with the truth.

Chadburn also had the challenge of galvanising his overstretched force. It was not uncommon for the lower-ranking officers to balk at the long hours and foregoing weekends with loved ones: *why all this public expenditure, hours upon hours chasing shadows, shadow-boxing with riff-raff, and our family life compromised for a slag who probably got nothing more than the worst of a spat with her fat ponce?*

'Someone's daughter.' Chadburn would always repeat the sentimental slogan. 'Maybe even someone's mother.' He was right about that this time, without knowing it.

Some of the officers would be spurred on, while others would continue to drag their feet and grumble. Here was a microcosm of the nation, probably an accurate reflection of the divide of public opinion. Life was precious, but some would always be more so than others.

Chadburn was no philosopher. He was old school. If there was a killer at large on his patch, he wanted him caught. To hell with cost and manpower. *Just nab him! Fast!* Before he struck again. The thinking couldn't be faulted, the outcome could.

The records showed that Rees was born in Barry, Glamorgan, South Wales on 6 August 1941. Her father, Gwilyn, was a labourer. Her mother, Amelia, was listed as a housewife. Gwynneth did well at local schools, becoming a prefect in her last year, when fifteen.

Her first employment was in her home town as a machinist in a factory mass-producing lingerie. A year later, when she was only sixteen, her mother died suddenly from brain thrombosis. This was the turning point – tipping point, in fact – in her life. Her father wasn't an emotional or sensitive man. *These things happen. You can't turn back the clock. You just have to get on with it. Tears only make a mess of your face.* He seemed to be completely oblivious to the traumatic impact on Gwynneth, who had four sisters – one older – and a brother who was married. Her oldest sister, Joan, was also married.

After the funeral, Gwilyn reacted as if he'd been jilted, as though his wife had walked out on him. The soil had scarcely settled over the coffin before he was bad-mouthing Amelia. Without preamble, he made it clear that he expected Gwynneth to succeed Amelia as mother to the three younger girls. Gwynneth refused, saying she had no intention of giving up her job to be anchored to the home. There were rows, which grew in intensity and violence. Whenever Gwynneth was physically abused, she hit back, not one for passive submission. The bitterness between father and daughter became explosive.

The house – no longer a home – was a battleground. Gwynneth started staying out all night and not returning in the morning. Twice she was reported missing to the police and twice they discovered her sleeping rough and returned her home, only delaying the inevitable – the Great Escape, to London, the city of flashing neon and nylons, coiffeurs, cologne and condoms, the capital of fun and fantasy, where dreams were realised, where old Father Thames kept its secrets, and spivs loitered at railway stations for runaway female teenagers with all their worldly goods stuffed into a porous shopping-bag. This was Gwynneth's welcome to paradise and freedom. A freedom that would soon see her on the nightly treadmill, sashaying along streets, doing as little as possible for cash in cars, back to padding pavements, and finally *home* to a flat, shared with another prostitute, and handing over much of her takings to her leech, the ponce, who promised her stardom among the sluts: Head Girl one day of London's most lucrative red-light garbage dump, a sort of red carpet of the street-girls' industry. Eat your heart out Hollywood! Sadly, a story as old and current as it was futuristic.

The downhill path wasn't as steep for Rees as for most runaways. There were periods of semi-stability, crossroads at which she paused and pondered, when she still had a choice of direction, a change of course that would have saved her, but the pull of gravity to the gutter and the grave was too great. Her married sister, Joan Oxley, several times gave her shelter at her home in Canvey Island, Essex. Soon, inevitably, they were locked in disagreement. Gwynneth was pregnant and took off for Wales, but not to her father's house, of course.

After giving birth to a daughter, she begged sister Joan to take her back, but this was only a ruse to dump the child. London called to her, pulled at her skirt, and she went running. Her nemesis couldn't be kept waiting. In retrospect, the countdown to the date with the digger had already begun.

During Rees's stay in London while working as a prostitute, the police were able to calculate that she'd resided – perhaps not quite the right word – at twenty-eight different addresses and had given birth to two children; the second was born in the City of London Maternity Hospital on 27 December 1962.

In the first few months of 1963, she even took the baby with her when she went soliciting on the streets late at night and into the early hours of the next cold and frosty January morning. It was gross, but true – she would do business on the back seat of a stranger's car while her son was wrapped in a blanket in the front, often crying for a feed, causing customers to demand cut-price deals because of the noise and nuisance factor.

Cornelius John Whitehead was probably Rees's longest lasting ponce. He was a born and bred East Ender, living in Stepney. By day, he made money by doing as little work as possible as a docker, a protected species in those days. By night, he lived off Rees. Here was a major difference between Rees and all the other women to die violently in this series: the six accepted by du Rose as victims in the 'Nudes' saga all milked the streets of west London, whereas Rees made the East End, Whitechapel, of Jack the Ripper infamy, her hunting-ground.

In du Rose's mind, as he once told me over a pint in a Shepherd's Bush pub, Rees wasn't 'a hundred per cent'. In other words, he had reservations about her right to be included in this cast. No matter: wherever she traded, it all came to an end in the *right* place: west London, near the Thames, opposite Duke's Meadows, immortalised more by our 'Deep Throat' unique murderer than the young gentlemen of Oxbridge who row this stretch of river every spring.

She might have favoured the East End for living, but clearly 'Deep Throat' didn't for killing. All roads led west as far as 'Deep Throat' was concerned.

What attracted Rees to Whitehead? Well, in addition to his twinkling blue eyes, fair hue – including his hair – slim but muscular build and teasing good looks, he was an experienced ponce for his age, twenty-six. There was also much to be said for his street-cred. He had convictions for theft, though they didn't carry much kudos in the East End, rated about the same as raiding a toddler's piggy bank. What hoisted him head and shoulders above the hundreds of petty villains of the East End was his conviction for beating up a police officer; that made him special, a celebrity, in fact. The East End jungle drums beat out the message: *no one messes with Cornelius, not even Old Bill.* Assaulting a police officer earned him respect, bordering on reverence and communal genuflection. Grandees of gangland even began to notice. The gun-slinging, razor-slashing Krays always had their eyes peeled for new *talent*.

Rees doubtlessly saw the benefit in having a *handyman* as a minder. Of course it hadn't occurred to her that all fighters needed sparring-partners and punchbags. She became the punchbag. Her first black eye made her question the wisdom of a working and cohabiting relationship with a thug who believed in settling every difference of opinion with his fists. Whitehead, who was already married, warned Rees that she'd get a beating if her nightly returns fell below a plimsoll line he'd set before she set sail soliciting: this was something he actually boasted about when interviewed by the police.

The last time Rees was seen alive in public she was wearing a tight-fitting black skirt, tan-coloured nylon stockings, a white woollen jumper with a distinctive blue zigzag pattern, a black and white speckled coat with a large collar and patch pockets, and high-heeled navy-blue shoes. This description was given to the police by another street girl, Brenda Meah, Rees's soulmate.

Rees and Meah had been working as a pair in Commercial Road, a rough patch – what other sort was there in the East End then? – in the early hours of Sunday, 29 September 1963, meeting up again later, by arrangement, in Farmer's café, which, despite its incongruous name, had almost certainly never accommodated a rural customer. The not-funny joke was that it was there to service the local cows.

After a cup of tea and feet up for half an hour, they returned to work until four a.m. Having teamed-up again in Commercial Road, they began walking, arms linked sisterly fashion, towards New Road in the hope of finding a trawling taxi to take them to their flat, where, in the tradition of street girls, they never entertained clients. They needed a sanctuary, however much of a tip it was in itself, that was untarnished by the bi-products of their street life.

As they reached New Road, a car passed them, cruising, and stopped. The driver was male, but he didn't turn, so the women saw only the back of his head. Softly the engine ticked over. Headlights remained on. The prostitutes slowed their stride. The driver continued staring ahead. Neither Rees nor Meah wanted any more trade. They were done for the night, well and truly. Suddenly, Rees exclaimed, 'He's all right, I know him.' Breaking from Meah, she ran to the car. Before jumping in, she shouted to her kindred spirit, 'I'll see if he'll take you as well, if you like.'

Meah shook her head, saying, 'No, you go on. I'll make my own way.'

Rees shrugged and climbed in. The car sped off northwards into what was left of the night. Gwynneth Rees was gone. For ever.

# THE DIGGER

Interviewed at length by the police after the body was retrieved from the jaws of the digger and identified, Meah said she couldn't really explain why she had declined the chance of a free lift home. 'It was instinctive, just a gut feeling,' she said. The free ride might have come at the cost of her life, a priceless example of false economy. 'I think he was young,' she added. Is that something that can be gauged from merely the back of a head? Maybe.

Of course, most crucially, Chadburn wanted details of the car. Did she note the registration number? Of course she didn't. Who would have in those circumstances? She scratched and shook her head. 'I'm not good on cars.' She couldn't even recall if it was a saloon, sports or estate model. What colour? Impossible to tell at night in street lighting. After more rumination, she reduced the possibilities of make to a shortlist of three, after being shown photographs: a Zodiac, Consul or Zephyr.

Cornelius Whitehead drove a Ford Zephyr.

Within hours, Whitehead was arrested. He admitted knowing Rees, having regular sex with her 'over a period of time' and giving her 'quite a few whackings', which 'the lazy cow fully deserved'. What's that saying about not speaking ill of the dead? However, he denied being her ponce because it would have been 'a poor business investment' as she was 'such a bloody useless earner'. And to think that some woman had actually married him and he was a couple's son-in-law! What a duff hand they'd been dealt.

Scrubbed bloodstains were detected in Whitehead's car and on his clothes. Analysis proved of little help. Both Rees and Whitehead had the same blood group, O, the most common. DNA profiling and other high-tech forensic techniques were mere embryos and a long way off hatching. Whitehead readily accepted the bloodstains could have come from Rees, when receiving one of the punishment 'whackings'. With utter disrespect and scorn, he said, 'But I guess she won't be pressing any charges against me.' Chadburn was too much of a veteran to be incited into doing something silly that he would regret.

During the two days that Whitehead was detained at Richmond police station, several East End prostitutes gave statements, testifying how scared they were of him because of his propensity for unprovoked, savage violence, out of all proportion. 'Someone to stay well clear of,' said one. Whitehead asked Chadburn, 'Where the fuck is Mortlake, anyway; in Yorkshire?'

Unamused, Chadburn quizzed Whitehead about when he was last in the Mortlake area. Whitehead's response was predictable. 'If I don't know where the fucking place is, how can I have been there, except by accident, like passing through, unaware.'

The more Chadburn garnered evidence of Whitehead's reputation, the less he became a suspect. 'He's all right, I know him,' Rees had said to Meah, before running to the car. If she'd known it was Whitehead, surely she'd have run the other way – jet-propelled. The litmus test of logic was steadily but inexorably ruling out Whitehead. Chadburn was right to have groaned when Rees's occupation was made known to him. The investigation had become a nightmare, bogged down in a maze of dead ends.

Two inquests into Rees's death were adjourned. The third and final one was held with a jury on 4 March 1964 at Kingston Coroner's Court. The outcome was a formality: the jurors returned an 'open verdict', confirming that the cause of death was 'not ascertainable', exactly what the pathologist had concluded months earlier. One week later, Rees was buried in the ancient graveyard of St Katherine's Church, Canvey Island. A simple aluminium cross marked her final resting place, but not where her life had ended, something still eluding

Chadburn, which it would continue to do throughout the year, and not just him, but all those who followed in his despairing footsteps.[1]

Whitehead was an East End boy to the core. West was for the toffs. And Mortlake was in a foreign land. In 1964, Chadburn was sure that Whitehead was guilty of many crimes, but not the murder of Rees. He was not 'Deep Throat'. But Chadburn was philosophical, if not a philosopher. Whitehead would keep. Time was against him. And in 1964, the Old Bailey and 1969 were not far off. Not if you had the patience of Scotland Yard.

---

[1] On 7 January 1969 Whitehead stood in the dock of the famous Number One court at the Old Bailey. Alongside him were Ronnie Kray, Reggie Kray, Charlie Kray, John Barrie, Ronald Bender, Anthony Barry, Christopher Lambrianou, Anthony Lambrianou and Freddie Foreman. Whitehead was now in the big league, among a gallery of gangsters who for years had terrorised London from east to west. All were charged in connection with the murders of George Cornell, Jack McVitie and Frank Mitchell. Found guilty of being an accessory to the murder of Jack Mitchell, Whitehead was sentenced to seven years in prison. Few people among the public would have remembered him as a suspect in the 'Nudes' murders. The police remembered, though, and no doubt wondered...

# CHAPTER 10

# ALL WASHED UP

B ack to the river Thames, such a central feature in all these crimes, as if the main artery of the story, choreographing all the twists and turns. A tidal river, ebbing and flowing, once the lifeblood of the metropolis, now just another of its myriad, murky attractions, like the Tower of London, where heads once rolled off the chopping block. As the Thames ebbs each day, so it deposits its flotsam, even the human detritus, on its muddy foreshores. The river police are always looking for floaters. The sinuous stretch of river through the capital has always been a temptation for those with suicidal ambitions. The Thames has also been the watery grave of people who have died by the hands of others, using the river as a convenient repository. Certainly, if the Thames could talk and write, it would have the best story in town to tell. But kiss and tell isn't Father Thames's style; it keeps its dark secrets buried in its sediment until prised out.

Sunday, 2 February 1964 was no day of rest for Chadburn and

his overworked team. They were busy preparing for the inquest into Gwynneth Rees's death, while continuing to garner evidence in the forlorn hope that a denouement might be delivered by a magic spell, otherwise known as unbelievable luck.

Not far away from Richmond police station, just a few miles east along the Thames on the sweeping bend before Hammersmith Bridge on the Surrey side, members of the London Corinthian Sailing Club were preparing for a dinghy race. Most of them were in the comparative warmth of the forty-year-old clubhouse, but brothers George and Douglas Capon were messing with a rubber craft on the foreshore, near a pontoon. Casually casting his eyes around the area, Douglas spied an object beached further along the foreshore that bore 'a remarkable resemblance' to a human body, so he wandered off to explore. Moments later, he was shouting to his brother, 'George, come here quickly!' The mysterious object wasn't a 'resemblance' to a human body but a real one. Female, dead and naked, apart from a pair of nylon stockings around her ankles and knickers stuffed in her mouth.

Douglas guarded the body while George scampered breathlessly into the clubhouse to raise the alarm and make an emergency phone call. Naturally enough, there was soon a ghoulish gathering around the bloated discovery. If there is such a phenomenon as telepathy, Chadburn's antenna should have been twitching as it received the foreboding signal.

Joshua Stein, the divisional surgeon and one of the first officials on the scene, reckoned that the dead woman must have been in the river for 'quite a few days'. The tide was rising and the Thames was preparing to reclaim its current star attraction, so she was hastily transferred to the Hammersmith mortuary, a manoeuvre urged by renowned coroner Gavin Thurston. The 'Nudes' series was gathering momentum, driven almost by a kinetic energy, though this was something that could be grasped only with hindsight.

By six-thirty that evening, pathologist Dr Donald Teare was conducting the post-mortem and making routine notes, such as height, five feet, two inches; brown eyes; dark brown hair; abdominal scar indicating Caesarean surgery; slender build but age difficult to assess; pronounced stretch marks on lower stomach; several teeth missing. Body weight was immaterial because of water-absorption. In fact, the corpse was totally waterlogged, proof that it had been immersed in water for between two and seven days. The lungs had 'ballooned', consistent with death by drowning, which was the pathologist's knee-jerk conclusion that day.

Not so *routine* for recording in Teare's notebook were the knickers filling the deceased's mouth, bulging her cheeks and puckering her lips, plus the fact that they were heavily stained with semen, unwashed by the discerning Thames.

In her stomach was a fatty meal, mostly undigested. Identification was uncomplicated this time. Fingerprints gave her an immediate name: Hannah Tailford, aged thirty, born in Heddon-on-the-Wall, Northumberland, more recently of a number of London addresses; a prostitute with a colourful track record. She was highly unusual because of her social mobility. She traded relatively upmarket as well as unequivocally downmarket. Tinker, tailor, soldier, sailor, rich man, poor man, she straddled the spectrum: a unique accomplishment.

But let's not race ahead of ourselves. Despite the perfunctory findings of the pathologist, the police quickly abandoned any notion of suicide or accidental death. What woman would strip naked in mid-winter and ram a pair of soiled, semen-soaked knickers so far down her throat as to induce choking just prior to leaping into the river? Who would bother to consume a hearty meal if, in a few minutes, they intended to leap towards watery oblivion? As for an accident, how absurd! Logic, logic.

Consequently, by the Monday, a fresh murder squad had been scrambled, headed by Detective Chief Inspector Benjamin Devonald, who was stationed at Shepherd's Bush, which immediately demonstrated an administrative and organisational weakness. As we know, less than three months earlier prostitute Gwynneth Rees's murdered body had been found a little to the west of where Tailford was washed up. Yet there were two different murder squads at work, with separate chiefs and Indians, one tribe encamped at Richmond and the other in nearby Shepherd's Bush. The only common links between the two encampments were pathologist Dr Teare and coroner Gavin Thurston.

It was going to be several months before a Scotland Yard commander took an overview role and introduced joined-up thinking and an all-inclusive Yard appraisal and approach. Even then there would remain different leaders of the individual investigations, which inevitably triggered friction and rivalry instead of cohesion and harmonisation of effort. However, it would be remiss to take these crimes out of the context of their era and judge the police response and performance by today's standards and investigation methodology. Serial killers were still rare beasts and unexplored. Understanding them was limited. Forces worked as individual firms. Information was only grudgingly shared. Brawn still outweighed brain when it came to policing.

Admittedly there had been John Haig, the 'Acid Bath Vampire', who murdered six people – men and women – then drank their blood, disposing of the bodies in vast, sizzling vats: the 'Blackout Ripper', who killed four women in war-ravaged London. Of the latter, Chief Supt Fred Cherrill wrote, rather hysterically for a normally measured senior cop:

# ALL WASHED UP

*Not since the panic-ridden days in 1888, when Jack the Ripper was abroad in the East End, had London known such a reign of terror as that which existed in this war-time February (1942) when, night after night, death – fiendish, revolting and gruesome – came to four unsuspecting women in the heart of the metropolis.*

Hyperbole, perhaps, considering the *reign of terror* of the Blitz, which Londoners were still in shock from, but there was something phantom-like about a killer who stalked the street under the cover of darkness, perhaps shrouded by fog, and striking at random prey. Perhaps such a killer was indeed spookier than a silently falling bomb or the sudden engine-cut of a V1 or V2 remote-controlled missile.

Haig's crimes, although spine-chilling, had a conventional motive – money and greed. The 'Blackout Ripper' was dismissed as a vagary of war. Airman Gordon Frederick Cummins was quickly arrested and hanged, aged twenty-eight, in Wandsworth Prison. Nothing to be learned from him because the police had been so proficient, though their task had been made easy by such an artless perpetrator who left so many clues, like confetti at a wedding; detection would have been a snip for any armchair sleuth.

The 'Nudes' killer was in a completely different category. It would be misleading to suggest that he didn't leave clues, but they always seemed calculated ones, not mistakes; frustrating clues because they led nowhere, except to sleepless nights and frayed tempers for the pursuers.

The knickers in Tailford's mouth were some kind of message, but any attempt at deciphering could only be clumsy conjecture, squandering valuable time. Yet the deliberate desecration was so deliberate and taunting that it couldn't be ignored. Was 'Deep

Throat' highlighting his disgust, portraying Tailford as a dustbin, a vessel for trash, nothing but garbage, like herself? Maybe he was revealing what he'd done to her, how he liked his sex, giving away something as a tease, a sort of, *now let's see how clever you are. Game on!* Or was the message more sinister, sort of Mafia-styled. A warning to certain people to keep shut about events that could cause embarrassment – even ruin – in high places if made public? This would have been a risible theory with Rees or Figg, but not in the case of Tailford who seemed to lead a schizophrenic working life, criss-crossing social boundaries. High and low. Variety. The spice of life. Poison, too.

Hannah Tailford was formerly identified by her sister, Mrs Elsie Youngman, on 5 February. Hannah was the second daughter of coal miner John Tailford and mother Elsie. By the age of fifteen, her life was already in meltdown.

Most of her teenage years were a shameful catalogue of thefts, care and protection orders, approved schools, absconding, probation, breaching probation, running riot and finally borstal, from which she also escaped; she was obsessed with delinquency and had a dog-of-war tenacity against authority. What a beginning! She managed to break through every safety net. Nothing would impede her fall.

Soon she was in London, soliciting in Hyde Park, opposite and parallel with Park Lane, emulating the Victorian courtesans, many of who would parade on horseback or in carriages. Tailford kept her feet on the ground, if not her delusions.

Within a few months she was pregnant, resulting in her conceiving a crazy scheme which exemplified her depravity and the moral depths to which she'd plummeted. She placed an advert in a shop window in south London, offering to sell her baby to a 'good home'. Although not yet born, she promised that the child would be on the market in April. Of course this was illegal, but had years ago ceased to be an impediment to Tailford's impulses. What were laws for it not to be bent and broken had long been her anarchic philosophy.

When confronted by a reporter from the *Sunday Pictorial*, she assumed the alias Theresa Foster and her sob story (a litany of lies, of course) was related by her with all the aplomb of a RADA-trained ingénue. 'I know it's shameful and wicked of me,' she simpered. But I was forced to make this terrible offer to attract attention to my plight. I met my husband, John, a merchant seaman, five years ago at a fairground in Manchester. We married eighteen months later. He seemed to like the idea of becoming a father. But when I told him the baby was on the way, it started a terrific row. Next day he left to join a ship. I haven't heard from him since and I don't know where he is. I cry at nights wondering what to do. Now I know it's illegal, I have withdrawn my advert. But my baby must have a good home. I shall be broken-hearted parting with it, but I'm only doing my best.'

What a tear-jerker! What an inventive mind! All of it was fantasy, of course. She wasn't married, there was no seaman in her tacky life and all her penury was self-induced. The only truth in her pitiful plea of mitigation was her pregnancy.

On 22 May she gave birth in St Stephen's Hospital, Fulham to a boy. Despite now aware that selling a child was illegal and a serious criminal offence, she went ahead with negotiating a deal with a couple who were desperate for a baby of their own, but the wife was unable to conceive. Instead of going through the proper channels and being vetted as a suitable couple to adopt, they met Tailford surreptitiously on the premises of the hospital on 5 June, the day she was being discharged with the baby. The couple had drawn up an agreement, which Tailford readily signed because it meant she pocketed twenty pounds in cash immediately for handing over the newborn.

Rather than heartbroken, Tailford was cock-a-hoop. Of course in such a busy environment, it was inevitable that the transaction failed to pass unnoticed and it was reported. Hospital officials were rightly disgusted and the crime was left to London County Council's legal department to implement legal proceedings, but after considerable internal soul-searching a decision was taken to ignore the transgression. The one person who would have suffered most from court proceedings would have been the baby. Not only would Tailford have been charged, but also the couple. The baby would either have been returned to his biological mother, a lawless street girl, or taken into care at public expense, though with the possibility of going to a decent home through a recognised adoption agency, repeating a process already consummated but without the underhand exchange of money. Occasionally the inertia of bureaucracy could be the wisest and most humane course of action.

From the late 1950s, Tailford cohabitated with a man known as Allan Lynch, although he'd been born William Ewing. Wherever they lived – too many different addresses to count and document – they posed as husband and wife, although they never married. Hannah gave birth to a daughter in April 1961, and a boy in May the following year. The son went the way of his half-brother, hawked for adoption in a blackmarket auction. What made Tailford keep the daughter is another of this narrative's mysteries. Much of the time  the little girl was farmed out to babysitters. Of Tailford's three children, the boys were undoubtedly the lucky ones.

By the beginning of January 1964, Tailford and Lynch were living in West Norwood at 37 Thurlby Road. Virtually every afternoon, when Lynch was at work in a billiards' hall, Tailford would be visited by a stocky 'woman', with dark hair, an aquiline nose, and about five feet, eight inches tall, always arriving in a van. Tailford's flat was on the top of three floors. She told her neighbours that her visitor was 'Auntie Gwen'.

As soon as 'Auntie Gwen' was inside Tailford's three-room flat, off would come the wig, dress and high heels and there would be the recently retired Thomas Trice, an odd-job and handyman, who lived in the Victoria area of London. Certainly he was odd and also very handy, especially with Tailford. In return for doing all the chores, Tailford would service him in the bedroom. Usually he was made to clean the flat naked, which was to his liking.

After an hour or two scrubbing and polishing, he would have to stand to attention in the bedroom while Tailford inspected his housework. If she found as much as a speck of dust, she would thrash him with a cane, which she kept hidden under the mattress. Apparently, 'Gwen' was disappointed if he failed to displease.

Tailford's very personal drag artiste would often drive her in the evenings to her various patrol zones. Like many of the street girls, she would have breaks during the night shift, stopping at one of the numerous mobile snack bars around central London. Her favourite was on the Charing Cross Embankment. One client she met there was a chauffeur, William Sales, who drove his employer's Bentley, which really impressed Tailford, who had never had sex in such a 'classy' car. They drove all the way to Epping Forest to do business, and there was enough room in the front, on the soft, lush leather upholstery, so they didn't have to clamber into the back. 'She came cheap,' Sales was to tell the police ungraciously.

On other nights, along the Bayswater Road, which could become congested with hookers in the sex 'rush hours', she was 'collected' by a car bearing diplomatic plates and driven to a mansion in 'Millionaires' Row', alongside Kensington Palace Gardens, for an orgy, in which there might be at least twenty participants, reminiscent of Sir Francis Dashwood's eighteenth-century Hellfire Club. All very 'civilised' and polite, and so very different from her normal trade.

At first this may seem improbable. Why choose from the lowest end of the market when women like Mandy Rice-Davies, and enthusiastic 'amateurs' from the courtesan higher echelons, might well be willing and available? There are several plausible answers. Most importantly, women such as Mandy Rice-Davies would have recognised a politician or many of the peers, such as the lecherous Lord Boothby, for example, or a sporting personality. Street girls rarely read newspapers. If they watched TV, it wouldn't be the News, so the men they would be *performing* with would most likely be unknown to them. *Bon viveurs* and entertaining conversationalists weren't required. The 'parties', as they were billed euphemistically, were for men with kinky tastes who also liked a bit of rough, hence the Tailfords. The women had to be prepared to dominate whipping and bondage sessions and also acquiesce when oral and anal sex were requested.

Most times the men would be dressed in dinner suits and black bow ties. The 'party' wouldn't begin until after the men had dined, smoked cigars and downed vintage port. Only then would the toastmaster rap his gavel and declare, 'Gentlemen, the girls are ready to be served!'

The women would be seated in a drawing room, drinks and cigarettes in hands. The men would bow, mix, circulate and choose. All rooms were available. Another reason for its plausibility was the ease with which a dozen street girls could be corralled. These weren't women residing miles apart in suburbia who were slaves to a social calendar and their diary, having to juggle Ascot with Henley Royal Regatta and Wimbledon, Glyndebourne and weekends in Nice or Cannes. The chauffeur 'collectors' could drive to one square-mile of streets in west London and round up a dozen tarted-up women, game for anything, within twenty minutes. By the time they were deposited back on the streets where plucked from, they would be legless from drink, drugs and exhaustion, with only a hazy memory of where they had been. However, the money in their handbags would have reassured them in the morning that it had been a worthwhile night's work.

If those anecdotes had come from prostitutes, ponces, a woman trying to sell her story or creative hacks, then I would, of course, have treated them as apocryphal. Those sorts of stories immediately build a wall of suspicion around discerning researchers. My sources were of a very different calibre. The facts were validated by the police. MI5 and the Special Branch were concerned about how the foreign *diplomats,* some of them spies, were using 'honey traps' to compromise UK politicians and influential donors to political parties.

Of course, at the time of Tailford's death, none of this was known to me. Along the way, however, 'Jack', my informant, drip-fed me with mouth-watering titbits, later endorsed by Deputy Assistant Commissioner of Scotland Yard John du Rose: 'There were indications that Hannah had attended "kinky"' parties arranged by a foreign diplomat, who employed an agent to recruit women willing to take part in perverted sexual practices,' he wrote in his autobiography, *Murder Was My Business,* published by W.H. Allen in 1971.

Tailford was a really bad lot; to depict her as evil is no exaggeration. 'Auntie Gwen' was also far more devious than an eccentric cross-dresser, chauffeur and factotum for Tailford. They had their own little racket going, a blackmailing cottage industry, but this wasn't even uncovered by the police until considerably later. Facts to emerge leant weight to the theory that the gloating, silent message to Tailford with her knickers rammed in her mouth was: *Now you're the one who's stuffed!* Oh, what a picture! (A big clue there.) Clarification will follow.

Detectives questioned more than seven hundred people as they compiled a documentary of her life, then men and women with whom she'd been acquainted, and her last hours, a tedious and yet at times illuminating insight into her dark, deep and labyrinthine psyche and daily habits – almost intrusive if it hadn't been for the commendable motives – and yet the breakthrough remained tantalisingly elusive.

Tailford last left home for the streets on the evening of Friday, 24 January. She was dressed in a flame-coloured frilly nylon blouse, a black cardigan and matching skirt, a dark blue winter overcoat, light blue pixie hat and black leather court shoes. She also had on a wristwatch with a black leather strap and a wedding ring. In her black leather patent handbag was a wallet containing notes and coins, a vanity mirror, brown plastic purse, a key to the flat, tissues, a diary, cheap ballpoint pen and a packet of Benson and Hedges cigarettes. There were vague reports of sightings of her right until the end of January, but these were dismissed as unreliable and misleading by the police. One person said he'd seen her 'stoned on uppers' on 31 January, but there was no trace of amphetamines in her blood at the autopsy.

Before daylight on 19 February, Sergeant John Towes was navigating his police launch on the Thames near the Festival Hall Pier, quite close to the King's Reach shore, when the boat shook, shuddered and spluttered. One of his crew of two constables called out that something had become 'caught up in the works'. Towes cut the engine and managed to drift the launch to the Waterloo Pier police station.

Later, Sergeant Ronald Wills soon located the problem – a blue woman's overcoat, now considerably shredded by the launch, but sufficiently intact to be identified as the one worn by Tailford on the last evening she was seen alive.

After two adjournments, the inquest into Tailford's death

was finally concluded on 28 April. Despite the medical evidence that still pointed to her having died from drowning, there were bruises to her chin, which could have come from blows, maybe fists, prior to her death, Dr Teare conceded. Before entering the water, she could have been rendered unconscious by a couple of professional, knockout punches. As in the case of Rees, the jury returned an 'open' verdict. Certainly no one now was thinking any more of suicide or accidental death, especially as Scotland Yard – already twenty days into yet another 'Nudes' episode.

# CHAPTER 11

# MOTHER AND BABY

The tide was rippling in. The River Thames was swelling, inching up its banks, creeping inland wherever the land lay low. Spring was bringing lukewarm sunshine to the capital. Sergeant Robert Powell was humming as he steered his police launch along Corney Reach, Chiswick. Eyes peeled, the pale sun behind him, he saw the human body on the foreshore.

It wasn't yet eight a.m. and Powell had been looking forward to his breakfast after mooring. Now his appetite was crushed. Even before landing his boat against the stony bank, he could tell that the body was of a naked woman, lying facedown and spread out. Of course Powell knew that it was imperative, if possible, not to move a body at a potential crime scene, but this presented a problem: within an hour, he estimated that the river would have risen enough to cover the woman and become a body-snatcher, carrying her away again.

Divisional surgeon Joshua Stein arrived just in time to examine the body in situ. There was a gash, between six and eight inches long from the right breast to the middle of her chest. Her mouth was slightly open. A police photographer was able to take shots just as the water was beginning to lap against the corpse. Removal of the body was authorised by Detective Inspector Reuben Ridge, yet another team leader.

On this occasion the body went to Acton mortuary, but it was the ubiquitous pathologist Dr Donald Teare who conducted the post-mortem, starting mid-morning that day. Sergeant Powell had skipped breakfast. Spring, the budding and bursting of new life, wasn't all that it was cracked up to be, he could be forgiven for thinking.

This death was a double tragedy because the victim was about four and a half months pregnant and the unborn child was a girl. Curiously, the knife-wound to the breast and chest had been inflicted *after* death, but no viscera had been removed. Someone in a rage? Someone suffering a sexual paroxysm? Someone hell-bent on desecration because of such hatred for the woman? None of these possibilities seemed a persuasive fit. No other injuries appeared to have been inflicted. There was no damage, for example, to the vagina or the pubic region.

How long had this one been in the Thames? Not more than forty-eight hours, said Teare, which was promising news for the detectives because it meant that she would be fresher in the minds of witnesses.

But what would she have looked like before becoming bloated by the murky river? Teare's recordings showed that the woman had been a mere five feet tall, a little on the plump side, hair dyed a strawberry blonde, although it was naturally straw-coloured, and she was tattooed: a cross and flower on the right forearm, with the words 'John' and above that 'In Memory'. Although Teare believed she had died from drowning, he was equally convinced that she had been unconscious when dropped into the river.

This body had been recovered barely three hundred yards upstream from where Tailford had been washed up. There was no possibility of suicide or accidental death this time. Dr Teare and the police could no longer keep from the public the indisputable fact that there was a serial killer at large using the Thames and its surroundings as a depository. The detectives knew that the latest delivery by the Thames was a case of murder and put together with all the similarities, the nudity and vicinities of the findings, this was homicide in the plural. But who was the latest one? That question would soon be answered – beyond dispute, in fact – within a couple of days.

On 10 April, after having seen photographs and descriptions in the newspapers, Mrs Pamela Edwards, of 16 Denbigh Road, Notting Hill, hurried to the mortuary at Acton and identified the dead woman as Sandra Russell, a recent tenant of hers who she believed had done a 'midnight flit', owing two weeks' rent that she apparently couldn't pay. Now she knew where her ex-tenant had gone. She also knew that she was to remain out of pocket.

Of course, Sandra Russell wasn't the victim's real name. She was Irene Lockwood. Detective Superintendent Frank Davies, soon to become a commander at the Yard and head of the Flying Squad, now took charge, demonstrating the Commissioner's determination to assuage both the public and the politicians, who were beginning to snap at his heels, particularly the Home Secretary. The press were inevitably feeding like vultures off the pickings of these murders. The police were coming under fire. A gentle breeze of panic was wafting across the streets of west London after dark. A result was essential, and needed fast.

Davies made his headquarters at Shepherd's Bush police station, which was rapidly becoming awash with different teams of murder squads. But were they talking to one another? Astonishingly, it was only just beginning to dawn on the parallel teams that there could be a crossover between the nude victims and just a single perpetrator.

Once again the Davies team followed the formula of attacking on two fronts: Irene Lockwood's early life and the days prior to her disappearance and death.

She was born in 'Little Holland', Lincolnshire, the flatlands, celebrated for their fields of vibrant tulips in spring that lit up East Anglia. Gainsborough was her home town. She was an only child and both her parents were killed during the Second World War. Her grandfather was a farmer and it was on his farm that she lived during her years at secondary school. Between the age of fifteen and sixteen she worked for her grandfather on his land and then one day 'just took off', she told two police officers when arrested for soliciting in Kensington's Church Street in January 1964, neither she nor those cops privy to the script of fate that already placed her with one foot in the grave.

From the solitude of Lincolnshire she had 'escaped' to manic Babylon, where 'wealth, glamour, opportunity and rich husbands-to-be grew on trees'. She had her dreams like any other teenager, but for her they came at an exorbitant price. In the 1960s, fantasy was about the most that the majority of teenagers could afford. But if you could buy a ticket to London, then there would be a red carpet awaiting you, so the fantasy went in Lockwood's daydreaming head. She, like so many of her peers, hadn't thought beyond stepping off the train at Liverpool Street.

For two years she survived as a waitress in Islington, which wasn't then the fashionable area it is today. Disillusioned but too stubborn to admit her mistake and return to the farm and a quiet country life, she headed for the city of Nottingham, where she found employment as a cinema usherette. More relevant to her future, she found a man to live with, John Russell. They were together in Nottingham for five years in a stable relationship, during which time she gave birth to a boy who was later taken into care, an indication of the nosedive that was beginning again.

Restless and bored, she parted from Russell, travelled south as far as Northampton, hooked up with another partner, this a short-lived relationship, before once more seduced by the pull of London's bright lights and all they represented in her dizzy head. The flashing neon of the West End has been an irresistible drug to so many young dreamers, the good and bad. Russell somehow tracked her down; there was undoubtedly some kind of adhesive between them and life together began anew – until he was arrested for handling stolen goods and was sentenced to a year's imprisonment.

The press statements coming out of the Yard parrot-fashion comprised the usual anodyne stonewalling: lots of words, little information... *Several avenues of exploration are underway... There are people of interest to be located and eliminated* [not literally!]... *It's too early to say if there is a prime suspect, but as soon as we have someone in custody a press release will be issued... There is no reason for respectable women to be afraid, though red-light districts should be avoided after dark by lone females who could be mistaken for promenading with immoral intent... It would be wise for prostitutes to stay off the streets at night...* And so on.

I needed a meet with 'Jack' urgently to try to discover what was *really* going on. This was before a moratorium had been imposed, of course, so we rendezvoused at the Jack of Clubs in Soho's Brewer Street at eleven-thirty.

The band was playing and the velvet tones of Jo Marney were soothing away the rough edges of the day, but little else was happening. We were the only customers; hardly big spenders, we both ordered pints of beer. If the manager had known 'Jack' was a cop with Scotland Yard, even the beers would have been 'on the house': that's the way Soho worked, better to have the cops on your side than the Krays on your back. The 'hostesses' were there in their finery, of course, at their usual table near the band, rather glum because the night had all the makings of being a washout for business.

Very early into our meet, I said to 'Jack' bluntly, 'What the hell's going on now?'

Frank as ever, he replied, 'Nobody knows. Everything's up in the bloody air. If it was Christmas it would make a bloody good panto for the Palladium. But Frankie [Frank Davies] might have turned up trumps.'

'You mean he's on the brink of cracking it?'

Immediately he could see that headlines were flashing in my head.

'Don't you go writing that... that's not what I'm saying. He's got a lead, you can put it that way.'

'A *strong* lead?' I urged.

'Early days, Mike. Early days,' he repeated whimsically.

*Early days!* I thought. *How many more bodies do they need to get beyond the beginning?*

Every line of inquiry was always in its *early days*.

A few customers began trickling in, all drunk from pubbing, but no trouble. Out-of-towners, up for a conference or sales seminar, just the sort to bring avaricious smiles to the hostesses.

'So what's Frankie hit on?'

'Jack's' glass was already empty. *Early days* of a murder hunt was thirsty work. I nodded to Mr Pino, who was hovering nearby, ever attentive, just having seated the new arrivals. He nodded to a waiter, pointing at our table. Messages among staff were passed by their own semaphore. The service ran like a well-oiled machine.

Sufficiently lubricated, 'Jack' was all set to deliver. Leaning closer to me conspiratorially, he explained that Lockwood had not only been a friend of Vicki Pender but had worked with her in a scam. The name Vicki Pender meant nothing to me and this must have shown on my face. 'Surely you must remember the Pender case?' he said incredulously, as if I must have been in a coma or on a desert island for the past year or two. Here I should explain that I was very much a new kid on the block of Fleet Street's crime beat, the youngest reporter on a national newspaper and, in the argot of actors on TV chat shows, the 'Nudes' was my *big break*. So I huffed and bluffed to the effect that of course I'd heard of Pender but I'd been working 'undercover' on something else at the time, giving myself the chance to play catch-up.

'You might remember Vicki by her real name, Veronica Walsh,' he suggested, still finding it hard to accept that I was ignorant of a case that had been a headliner.

'Of course, now it's all coming back,' I lied.

Everything about this Lockwood twilight world was an alias. It was all far less true than virtual reality. True crime involving prostitutes inevitably flirts with fiction. The players change names on a whim. Their life stories are revised to suit the company they're keeping. They're remarkable human chameleons, fabricating so fluently that they fool themselves, to such an extent that the embroidery is the *honest to God truth* in their own belief. Like the very best actresses, they live the role they're playing. Often their lies ring with such echoes of validity that even professional psychologists and police profilers are cheated by them. The cliché in the blurb of so many crime novels – *nothing is ever as it seems* – could be an encapsulation of London's underbelly in the 1960s.

Lockwood and Pender had worked together in surreptitiously filmed porno movies, *starring* with their unwary clients, some of them wealthy and married, plus a few celebrities. The scam had been blatant blackmail. Pender had shown the 'targets' still photo frames from a home-made movie, claiming to have been duped as much as the punters, but she would be able to get possession of the complete film roll in return for a sizeable payment.

Pender had received a few severe beatings and death threats. Both women were habitués of the drinking clubs at the lower end of the market in Soho, the Bayswater Road and Notting Hill.

'Did they make any money from blackmail?' I asked.

'Well, Vicki was skint when she was snuffed in her two-room flat in Adelphus Road, Finsbury Park.' North London. Near Highbury, then the Arsenal football stadium. A far cry from the glamour of the West End. To me there was something skewed about this; well at least an awful lot of beef missing from the bone and too many wrinkles that needed ironing out.

Anyhow, after the murder, fingerprints in Pender's flat led the police to the home of ex-paratrooper Colin Welt Fisher, of Leverstock Green, Hemel Hempstead, Hertfordshire, where he lived with his wife and two children. Pender's fingerprints were lifted from the front and back of the interior of his car. She had died from strangulation after taking a beating. When interrogated, Fisher boasted that he had a 'cast-iron' alibi for the night of the murder. Who could vouch for his movements and whereabouts at the material time? None other than another prostitute, Irene Lockwood, which still didn't do a lot to cushion the relationship with his wife.

When he picked up Lockwood from a street in west London, she claimed her name was Sandra, which was plausible enough. They'd gone drinking before spending the remainder of the night together in a hotel, the name of which he couldn't recall because they'd been so drunk, but it was in the King's Cross area. Neither was he sure what name he'd used when signing in, except that it was 'Mr and Mrs something'. Going to hotels with clients wasn't Lockwood's style, of which Scotland Yard was well aware, of course. When shown a rogues' gallery of London street prostitutes, he'd immediately fingered Lockwood, which fitted with the two women being in cahoots.

The prosecution had a very different version to present to the jury at the Old Bailey. The accused, Fisher, had met Pender in the Nucleus Club in Monmouth Street, Soho. Before entering the club, he'd bought a packet of reefers and purple hearts from a street-corner dealer. There followed a 'weekend bender', when they were both 'high' on drink and drugs. The partying continued at Pender's flat, where she was murdered in the morning. Pender's body lay there undetected for four days. Fisher was convicted and received a life sentence. Lockwood had not betrayed her erstwhile work partner by lying for Fisher.

'I can see which way Frank is going with this,' I remarked. 'Is there a suggestion that Pender was attempting to blackmail Fisher?'

'Jack' said that Davies would be interviewing Fisher in prison and 'blackmail' would be 'high on the agenda'.

I had to test him with my scepticism. 'Hidden cameras, lighting issues and getting exact angles, regardless of working the machinery, just doesn't seem to fit with scatterbrain, scapegrace street girls who traditionally trade in cars,' I said. 'Just think of the cost of all that equipment. They wouldn't invest in that. If they did, they'd have no idea about setting it up. The cameras would have to be the kinds that are activated by movement and sound, a job for professional photographic technicians.'

'Jack' pointed out that the prostitutes would be just the pawns in the operation. They would solicit, as normal, take the 'catch' to a pre-arranged address that was all set up and provide the sex that was required. More loose ends. 'How could they know the real identity of the punter?'

'They'd note the car reg.'

'But to get a name and address from that they'd need a bent cop?'

'Let's not go down that dark alley,' advised 'Jack'.

The home of Thomas Trice, 'Auntie Gwen', in Welling, Kent had been raided. In a shed, the police came across a box that was filled to the brim with women's clothing that had been worn. Among the clothing was a pair of women's shoes with mud-splatter. Forensics had tried to match the mud on the shoes with that on the foreshore where Tailford had been beached.

'With what result?' I asked.

'Neither negative nor positive. Not enough to rule either way; a stalemate on that one.'

'Were the shoes Tailford's?'

'Right size.'

Something else was awry here. Tailford had been stripped before being thrown into the river. She hadn't been killed on the foreshore where found, so how could the mud on her shoes possibly have come from there? The forensics exercise seemed pointless in the context of the foreshore and the murderer. It was probably another piece of Scotland Yard propaganda, keeping the pot boiling, so I left it, recalling the words of wisdom f rom a veteran news editor, 'One too many questions can spoil a good story.'

However, from the bottom of a wardrobe in Trice's bedroom they'd bagged a cache of spyware equipment, including cameras and voice-recording devices of high quality, but no film, prints or tapes. Further inquiries indicated that he rented a room, on an ad hoc basis in Pimlico, near Victoria, which explained his frequent meetings in that area with Tailford. Because Trice and Tailford had often been seen breakfasting in the Victoria station cafeteria, there was speculation that these meals together were the culmination of a night of 'naughty tricks' in 'Auntie Gwen's' one-room pad, a lair for suckers. The room had been completely bare, without even one item of furniture, when searched.

Trice had denied all knowledge of a blackmailing sting. In his statement, he said he 'got a buzz' from being taken for a woman in public and he enjoyed shopping for 'fancy underwear' with Tailford. He'd last seen Tailford on the night of 23vJanuary, when she'd left the snack bar on the Charing Cross Embankment with a French diplomat. He assumed she was being driven to a 'party' at one of the embassies or a Belgravia residence that accommodated orgies. He didn't know any of the addresses and had never been to the parties. He wasn't the least jealous of Tailford 'screwing around' because he didn't 'screw women'. He claimed to be a keen photographer of 'wildlife' (ha! ha!), hence the cameras and the voice-recording equipment, which was for the sounds of 'birds' (no laughs, please). 'In other words, he was taking the piss out of us,' said 'Jack'. Despite extensive searches, no diary had been uncovered to show that Trice was keeping a record of 'targets', their addresses and phone numbers, plus any personal details, such as marital status and employment. Nevertheless, his bank statements revealed some large cash injections, not regular and not of the same amount. His explanation had been the stock reply: lucky on the horses, knew a trainer who gave him hot tips.

Was he a suspect?

'Has to be.'

But did he know the other victims, essential if he was the 'Nudes' killer.

'Ah! That's the problem, you see... No known communal connection. Still working on that one.'

I took that as a no. *More early days!*

'Frank's tearing out his hair in frustration.'

A feat of magic, that, because Davies was bald, though he did sport a snazzy moustache.

Suddenly 'Mad' Frankie Fraser appeared like an apparition at the foot of the stairs, brimful with boisterous *bonhomie* for Mr Pino, who shook his hand, almost bowing in courtly fashion, as if greeting royalty, and saying, 'How nice to see you again, Mr Fraser.'

'*Mr Fraser!*' Frankie guffawed. 'I ain't been called that since I was last nicked. Old Bill are the only buggers who call me *Mr Fraser* in this fucking town.'

'We're in for trouble,' 'Jack' whispered. 'Time for me to slope off.'

'Typical copout!' I said, which wasn't very funny, but a passable pun for that time of night and the occasion.

At least 'Jack' accepted the crack in good humour and, squeezing my arm, said, 'I think you've got enough from me for a decent story. Don't forget, lobby rules. Nothing came from me.'

He tapped the end of his nose before saying as a valediction and double entendre, 'Enjoy the cabaret!' As he spoke he was staring at Fraser, who was swaying across the dance floor towards a table near the kitchen's swing-doors. Before he was even seated, he said, loudly enough for everyone in the club to hear, 'I want all the hostesses to myself tonight. I'll have 'em lined up to be banged one at a time later on. All six! Bring 'em on!'

At a stroke the hostesses were silenced, all optimism for the night guillotined.

I decided to stay for the 'fun', which could be dangerous for bystanders, but there was always the chance of an exclusive crime story; being on the right or wrong spot at the right or wrong time was the credo.

'Bring on the bubbly! Make it magnums.' This was Frankie again, in an expansive mood, playing to the gallery, but he could change in a split second, like the flick of a switch, a real-life Jekyll and Hyde, joker to throat-slasher.

Two tables were pushed together for all the hostesses to encircle their crazy host. The cabaret act was introduced: it was pop pianist Russ Conway, an international star, who had only just begun playing his signature tune when Fraser pulled him from his stool and started thumping the keys, not the right notes and not in any melodic order, to desecrate a Morecambe and Wise joke. The out-of-towners were suitably entertained, believing it was all part of the knockabout cabaret routine.

Mr Pino scampered up the stairs, while Conway looked nonplussed, a spare part on the dance floor. Even the hard-nosed hostesses were giggling. Finally, Mr Pino reappeared, with doorman 'Nosher' Powell towering behind him. By then, Fraser had decided that he couldn't be parted from his champagne any longer, so he abandoned the piano, nudging Conway's shoulder, saying, 'It's all yours, mate. Be a sport and tap out a few oldies we can do a knees-up to.'

With order restored, the show continued, but Nosher remained like a colossal sentinel on the periphery of the proceedings, expressionless, arms crossing his barrel chest, as motionless as a stone statue.

I stayed to see the ending and it was well worth the wait. When the bill was presented to Fraser at around three a.m., he screwed it up into a ball and tossed it towards the feet of the waiter, with the taunting instruction, 'Send it to Ronnie and Reg [the Kray twins], they owe me.'

The hapless waiter looked appealingly to Mr Pino for help, but it was Nosher who crossed the dance floor like a tank rolling into battle. Before he'd even reached the table, Fraser shouted threateningly, 'If you don't want a razor taking off your fat head, stay out of this, Nosher, old son.'

In one deft, almost balletic movement, belying his bulk, Nosher lifted Fraser out of his seat by his ears and held him within a couple of inches of his face. 'Now, Frankie, you're going to be a good little boy and pay up just like all the other customers do, then no one gets hurt,' he said steadily, as the hostesses made themselves scarce. 'If you've any problem with that, tell me now.'

Fraser's little legs were flailing like a man doing the dance of death when hanged with a short drop, being strangled rather having his neck snapped.

'Put me down, you big ape,' Fraser growled. 'How can I get to my dosh like this?'

Nosher let go as if dropping him into a sewer. Still grumbling, Fraser fished out a stocky wad of notes and peeled off a bundle, as if it was merely Mickey Mouse money to him.

'And settle with the ladies,' said Nosher, keeping up the pressure.

'They ain't done nothing yet,' Fraser balked.

'They've put up with you for three hours; that should be worth a pension for each of them.'

Fraser swore again, but coughed-up. Then Nosher caught everyone by surprise. With unimaginable dexterity and strength, he ripped Fraser's tie from his neck and pushed it into his own dinner-jacket pocket, saying, with a crafty smile, 'Now you're barred until further notice, Frankie, for being improperly dressed. You're in good company,' he added, a reference to the Krays.

Fraser departed in an apoplectic rage, kicking chairs and tables as he went. Humiliating in public someone as deranged as Fraser was tantamount to mishandling dynamite, but Nosher was immune to fear. He recognised that only the strong survived in Soho, while the weak were trampled on. Even so, he was walking a high-wire tightrope, with the Krays and many others either side just waiting for a slip. Nosher knew better than most, through his tough military training, that a bullet was a great equaliser. What that night proved to me was that Nosher, the doorman and cloakroom attendant, was the real boss and powerhouse of the club and the Isows – father and son – had staked their lives and livelihood on his reputation. I was still scribbling notes when the cleaners were moving in around me...

\* \* \*

Towards the end of the month, I was at my desk when I took a call from 'Jack', who, from his breathless tone, was obviously hyper. 'It looks like we've got him,' he said with semi-restrained excitement.

'Who?' I said, somewhat vacantly.

Instead of answering, he said, 'Stick around. Don't go out of town. There'll be a statement about a charge.'

'Charged with the *lot*?'

Other reporters around the newsroom were cocking their ears in my direction, sensing that whatever stories they were working on were about to be upstaged.

'Full confession,' 'Jack' enthused.

'Trice?' I ventured. Now news editor Ken James's ears pricked up across the room.

'No. A new face. Out of the blue. Can't tell you any more. When it's official it has to come from the top. There'll be a statement, probably a press conference for the crime-beat pack. I can't begin to tell you the relief being felt. Just sit tight.' Then he was gone.

By then James was at my side. Without a word we wandered to a quiet corner by the sub-editors' desks. The subs, as they are known in the trade, didn't begin their shifts until the afternoon. I briefed James and he said he'd call Bob Traini, the chief crime correspondent, who was at home. A little later James beckoned to me. We sloped off again for another tê*te*-à-tête, where he told me that Trani had heard on the grapevine that 'something sensational was up' on the 'Nudes' front.

**169**

## THE SECRET LIFE OF FREDDIE MILLS

That evening, Kenneth Archibald, aged fifty-five, the partially deaf caretaker of a lawn tennis club in west London, was charged with the murder of Irene Lockwood.

Everyone was wrong-footed.

Especially the police.

But I'm getting ahead of myself. Something else of importance had occurred in between.

# CHAPTER 12

# TRAPEZE ARTISTE'S DEADLY FALL

A mere twenty days after the murder of Irene Lockwood, another nude victim was waiting to be found, this time in a pile of rubbish and not beside the Thames. This grisly discovery was made by Clark May at seven-fifteen a.m. on Friday, 24 April in Brentford, west London. Mr May, who lived at 199 Boston Manor Road, had gone to dispose of domestic garbage at a dump-site in adjoining Swyncombe Avenue.

'Here we go again!' was the melancholy mood around the police stations of west London that morning as the bleak news filtered through.

Demonstrating the Yard's mounting impatience and a certain amount of unbridled frustration, the 'heavy mob' was deployed: Deputy Commander Ernest Millen, Detective Chief Superintendent Jack Manning and Detective Superintendent William Baldock, supported by a whole range of lowerranking detectives. This was equivalent to sending in the SAS on a *do-or-die* mission, with failure not an option.

Pathologist Dr Donald Teare was torn from his breakfast. The body was transported in a black coroner's vehicle to Acton mortuary, where Teare undertook the post-mortem, in something of a dark, brooding mood. I was enlightened by 'Jack' that Teare enjoyed lingering over breakfast while mentally tussling with *The Times* crossword puzzle and wasn't kindly disposed towards interruptions.

In purely clinical, professional terms this new corpse had promise. For a start, it hadn't been immersed in water. Secondly, she'd been dead for no longer than three days, possibly even only twenty hours. Not only was this a great boost for the pathologist in determining cause of death, but also a bonus for the detectives because the trail should be fresh. Even though the unknown (not for long) victim was dead, the last hours of her life should still be very much alive.

Indicatively, she was missing four teeth, which didn't seem to have been professionally extracted nor punched out of her mouth, even though half of a tooth was lodged in her throat. These findings were to become pivotal within a few months, but their significance was not readily recognised. Had she been in a fight? A fight for her life? There were marks and abrasions on her face and a slightly swollen cheek, but nothing to signify a brawl sufficient to result in the loss of four teeth, let alone her life.

Teare was also able to tell that the body hadn't been stripped of underwear – pants and bra – until at least eight hours after death, due to imprints left. In all, she'd been on her back for at least twenty hours. She had not died where found; the Thames was within easy reach, but this time no wet ending. Another conundrum. No disfiguration of the vagina. Definitely no rape. Just murder. Apparently motiveless, although there was no such thing. However absurd and demented, the killer always had his own reason.

'Jack' called me at ten. He knew I was never in the office any earlier and I hadn't even had time to collect a wake-up coffee when the red light on my phone was flashing.

'Brentford's the place to be for today's action,' he said, delighting in the subterfuge. Unknown to me, the news desk had already been tipped off about a huge police presence in Brentford and there being a large area cordoned off by a reader. Not yet apparent was the reason for the cop circus camping in dreary old Brentford.

'What's up?' I asked.

'Another one.' All very cryptic, cloak-and-dagger, low-budget gangster-movie dialogue. Why couldn't anyone speak plain English; no intrigue embedded in mundanity, I suppose.

'Another what?' My brain wasn't in the right gear for circuitous teasers.

'Nude,' he replied starkly.

'Oh, shit!' That's what *he* should have been exclaiming, not me. 'Where? Who?' Finally I was posing the right questions.

'No ID yet.'

'But where?'

'Swyncombe Avenue, off Boston Manor Road, but you didn't get that from me. Anyhow, it'll soon be on the wires, but at least you'll have a head start.'

'Thanks.'

I was talking to myself.

After a staccato conversation with James, I was on my way to Brentford with a photographer in a chauffeur-driven office car; no expense spared in those heady days. The thrill of the chase was a drug that never ceased to accelerate the pulse. By the time we reached Brentford, not exactly one of London's beauty spots, the body had been moved to Acton mortuary and was being dissected by Teare.

Death was due to asphyxiation, but the pathologist wasn't able to say whether she'd been throttled by hands or strangled with a garment, such as one of her stockings, a possibility mentioned by Teare because there was no normal ligature mark around her neck, such as left by flex, string, tie or narrow belt. Swabs were taken and were 'negative', according to one report, and 'inconclusive' in another statement; it was all very vague and unsatisfactory. Something *was* known and being withheld within an exclusive cabal; well, that was my reading of the situation and I was to be proved right, fairly soon.

The small dump area where the corpse had mingled with the rubbish had been sealed off, allowing the forensic clue-pickers to work undisturbed. Any witnesses had already been collared by the police and taken away for interviewing and statement processing.

Now the main outstanding inevitable question was: who *is* she? If she was a prostitute, like the others, then almost certainly she'd have *form* and her fingerprints would be on file. In fact, the police probably already knew her identity, I reasoned, in view of the fact that the body had been so well preserved, apart from being rather dirty. While the photographer merrily snapped everything moveable and immoveable, I looked for a pub, not an exacting challenge in London.

Within minutes I was phoning 'Jack' from a coin box just inside the entrance to a pub that was as instantly forgettable as the rest of Brentford. Unsurprisingly, 'Jack' was out on an assignment but would I 'like to leave a message?' No, I didn't like, but I was polite about it and promised to call later. 'Can I help you?' the desk-shackled officer pressed. 'Sorry, it's personal.'

My next call was to the office. 'Any messages for me?'

'Yes, that Jack fella called, said he'd be in touch later.' That was all I needed to know. 'On my way back,' I said.

The snapper was still using up film.

Identification of the deceased was straightforward and, of course, it was to the benefit of the police to have the name broadcast as far and wide as possible in the public domain. Helene Barthelemy was the name. She rented a single, furnished room on the ground floor at 34 Talbot Road, Harlesden. But that was the end. Where was the beginning? What was her story? Did she begin life in the gutter or was it an inexorable gravitation? Having an excellent contact embedded in the core of the detection operation certainly cut a lot of corners for me in piecing together the jagged jigsaw of her truncated but turbulent life, which sizzled with more variety and adventure than all the lurid lives of the others sewn together.

She had been educated in a convent until the age of sixteen. Her mother and stepfather were devout Catholics and Helene attended church enthusiastically every Sunday from an early age, seemingly mesmerised by the Latin litany.

When she was fourteen, she even talked animatedly about becoming a nun, joining a silent order or perhaps in a teaching or nursing capacity. Within a year, however, she *found* boys and the prospect of a life of seclusion and celibacy began to wane. Her parents were quietly relieved because they believed she was capable of carving out a constructive, secular career for herself in a more conventional and worldly environment, and hoped one day they'd be doting grandparents.

What they weren't prepared for was her taking off for Blackpool, when she was still just sixteen, to join a circus. According to her friends, she craved excitement. She was bored by the relative stability and predictability of provincial life. She always said that it was her father's blood that fuelled her thirst for cliff-edge adventure. Her biological father, Maurice Barthelemy, had served with the Free French Navy during the Second World War, but had been deserted by his wife before D-Day. After divorce, Helene's mother had married again, becoming Mrs Mary Thomson and living in Cleethorpes, Lincolnshire.

By the time Helene was fifteen, her quarrels with her stepdad became daily contests and stand-offs, neither conceding. Whenever he gave her advice, she dismissed him disdainfully as 'dull' and nothing like her *real* father and she couldn't understand what her mother had 'ever seen in such a dodo'. Of course this was designed to be hurtful and was unfounded because she'd never really known her biological father; he'd only come alive in her psyche from the spiced-up bedtime stories of her mum, which had generously been embellished to make him a hero to her daughter; it was, in effect, a backlash. Helene's own vivid imagination enlarged her dad's status in her life, while further belittling her stepdad and increasingly alienating the two. Mother had created her own monster.

In the circus, Helene was trained as a trapeze artiste; she had the figure and agility for it, slim, light-framed, dexterous, and she was fearless of heights. Fearless of anything; all the ingredients for someone who would be risking life and limb nightly, high in the dome of the Big Top, the magic arena for children and, indeed, their parents. She literally thrived on the gasps of the neck-craning audience a long way beneath her as she entrusted herself to 'The Catcher', who had to snatch her wrists as they swung towards one another in mid-air and she let go; the precision had to be split-second perfect or disaster. Here was yet another drug, as addictive as any on sale in seedy Soho.

Blackpool's 'Golden Mile' was as seductive as Las Vegas's neon 'Strip'. In summer, it was teeming with hustlers. All had something to sell, especially dreams. Flattery, cajoling and some high-octane booze and pearly promises were enough to entice Helene away from the dazzle of the circus; a crack of fickleness was beginning to show in her character.

She was now a stripper, having lecherous men throw coins and notes at her feet, as provocatively she removed each item of scanty clothing to the slinky rhythm of appropriate music. Never before had she been such a focus of attention, except in the Big Top, but there she had heard the muffled applause but never seen the faces. This was different, so close up and personal; seduction and sex by proxy. Men queued to offer her literally the world in return for a date. And men were dated mechanically, as if on a factory assembly line.

The excitement evaporated when, aged nineteen, she gave birth to a son. Now the feckless 'Golden Mile' turned its back on her. So she became a waitress in a café. No disgrace in that, but it wasn't what she'd left home for. There remained the option of returning home to Cleethorpes, but to someone as free-spirited as Helene that would have represented defeat and a complete climb down, doomed and damned for ever. If she ever had a motto, it was probably *Ever Onwards*, though that wasn't the same as *Ever Upwards*.

Instead of seeking respectability in tune with her upbringing and education, she instead gravitated downwards in free fall: one-night stands rather than steady relationships and a gradual shift into really bad company, culminating with being charged with unlawful wounding and aggravated robbery. Her trial was held at Liverpool Assizes on 8 October 1962.

She pleaded not guilty, but the evidence against her illustrated the speed of her decline. The prosecution alleged that one evening, after dark, she lured a holidaymaker to a remote part of the beach, among sand dunes, where three thugs were waiting undercover to attack him. His face was slashed and he was repeatedly kicked. His wallet was stolen and his face wound required eighteen stitches.

Barthelemy vehemently denied the charges, although she'd been picked out by the victim in an identity parade. She did confess, however, to prostitution and owned up to having been fined for helping to run a brothel. So much for becoming a nun! Upon conviction, she was sentenced to four years in prison. The flame of her fighting spirit extinguished, she collapsed in the dock.

Helen Paul, Barthelemy's landlady in Blackpool, couldn't believe what she read in her local newspaper. 'She was the most lovely girl you could ever wish to meet,' she said. 'So kind and full of life. She'd do anything for anybody.' So she did! 'I really do believe there must be a mistake and I hope and pray it's quickly sorted out. Prison is no place for such a sensitive young woman from her background and breeding, and with such prospects. She was so bubbly and ablaze with ideas. Anyone should have been proud to have her as a daughter.'

Four months later, her prayers were answered. Helene was out on the streets again, *bubbly* and *ablaze* with ideas, no doubt, though it didn't mean that she was innocent of the serious and callous charges, simply that the prosecution hadn't done its homework or had wilfully deceived the jury. Her legal team had stumbled on an escape route for her. They exposed the 'innocent victim' of assault and robbery as an inveterate liar and pickpocket who had twice served substantial prison sentences. Accordingly, Barthelemy's convictions were overturned on appeal.

She must have begun to feel that her life really was charmed. Fate could be so cruel with its devious and veiled acts of *good fortune*. If she hadn't appealed against her sentence and won, she wouldn't have been on the streets of west London in April 1964 and presumably it would have been another prostitute whose nude body made headlines. The reward for winning was to lose everything.

Six months after discharge from prison, Barthelemy had hit the streets of London running, a fully fledged whore by now, conducting her business in cars and prepared to do pretty much anything, if the price was right. Fellatio was her speciality and most probably contributed in no small measure to her death.

One of her common aliases was Helen Paul; obviously her landlady in Blackpool had made a lasting impact on her. Helene was to confide that Mrs Paul was the 'only mother' she'd ever really had, which was rather unfair because she had been loved and cared for in Cleethorpes. Neither was her stepfather the *problem*. The complication was his presence in their lives, which she resented. She wanted the dad of her dreams, the romantic Frenchman and freedom fighter, a dashing Pimpernel character, a figure of fiction, hatched by a well-meaning mum.

Detectives soon established that one of her favourite places for vehicle business was Duke's Meadows, which fitted perfectly within the geographic pattern that had emerged. Nevertheless, it had no bearing on the perpetrator's whereabouts; it related only to the prostitutes' choice of venue for sex. The punters were directed to those sites by the girls. The detectives were learning almost everything about the prostitutes' modus operandi but next to zilch about the killer.

Transparently evident was the fact that there was nothing one-dimensional about this latest victim. She merrily criss-crossed London to trade: the fashionable West End haunts, Bayswater Road, Queensway, Notting Hill, Shepherd's Bush, Maida Vale, Kilburn and even Cricklewood Broadway, which was noted for its boisterous Irish colony. She avoided the East End ('too rough') and south of the river ('too quiet and suburban'), regions of the capital that held no appeal to her.

It was an education for the police to see how a stranger to London could so quickly and uncannily hit on the hotspots for prostitution, as if she had some inbuilt navigational system or antenna that was on a special sexual high-frequency wavelength.

For entertainment, Helene was a habitué of The Roaring Twenties club in busy, throbbing Carnaby Street. This popular club among the demimonde, a basement joint for all kinds of mischief, especially the purchase of reefers and purple hearts; a place you could go on a 'trip' by merely inhaling the smoky fog. Every species of human cockroach gravitated there, from hoodlums to sneaky, shifty ponces, who counted living off the earnings of street girls as a career choice.

During her short period in London, Helene had several 'boyfriends', the last being in reality her ponce. All the men with whom she was known to be acquainted were interviewed at length. 'Jack's' assessment to me was that the 'whole load of excrement was a dead loss' and couldn't be 'flushed down a bog fast enough'. Not a single statement tallied. They were all certain when they'd last seen Helene and they were all certainly wrong. Not lying necessarily, but just bombed out of their skulls by the daily mix of drugs and drink which they were on perpetually, a brain-blitzing cycle of self-destruction.

There was also an element of resignation by now creeping into the inquiries. The hierarchy kept returning to fundamentals: if there was a possible suspect in *this* solo killing, he would have to be eliminated unless he could be related to the crimes against the other 'Nudes'. It was for this reason that the senior detectives increasingly theorised that the serial killer had to be a casual pick-up, someone almost certainly unknown to all the acquaintances of the victims. He was an *outsider*, someone unconnected with the circle except on death-nights. He could be a clergyman, a judge, barrister, doctor, salesman, TV personality or whatever, but not a ponce, pimp or vagabond. In other words, all their interviews so far amounted to nothing more than going through the motions, filling cabinets with crap. The statements were junk, not worth the paper...

The most the detectives could do for the time being was to get a fix on the last time Helene was seen alive by a *reliable witness,* a tall order. Helene's neighbour at 34 Talbot Road, Harlesden, auxiliary nurse Nellie Manhertz, who rented a room next to Barthelemy on the ground floor, recalled seeing her at around seven-thirty p.m. on Monday, 20 April. Another tenant, Purgy Dennis, recounted seeing her the following day, when Helene was ambling between her room and the communal kitchen – just three days before being found and quite possibly her last day on earth.

Through a process of elimination of the clothes she was known to own, it was guessed that when meeting her killer she was wearing a black jumper, long sleeves, high neck, a thigh-hugging black skirt, a brown overcoat with a black leather collar and black leather calf-length boots. She was also likely to have been carrying a black or red leather purse.

Shortly after six a.m. on 24 April, a little more than an hour before the alarm was raised in Brentford, a Buckinghamshire farmer, Alfred Harrow, was driving his Bedford van along Boston Manor Road. He was on his way to Brentford Market, a round-journey he made regularly once a week. Visibility was adequate and the sun was breaking up the night sky. Just as he came to the junction with Swyncombe Avenue, a grey Hillman swung out in front of him from the side road. It had sped from Swyncombe Avenue so unexpectedly and without warning that Mr Harrow had to break sharply. Despite the early hour of the morning and with many residents probably still asleep, he was so angry that he sounded the horn for several seconds. The driver of the Hillman's only response was to accelerate even faster, quickly drawing clear of Mr Harrow's vehicle.

In a statement to the police, Mr Harrow said he'd juddered to an almost complete halt or there would have been a major collision. 'This vehicle then carried on in the direction of the Bath Road, without even slowing or stopping. There was only one person in that vehicle, a man, but I could not identify him.' The Hillman had been driven away so fast that he hadn't managed to note a single letter or number of the registration plate.

Scotland Yard's senior detectives calculated that the driver of the Hillman was 'their man'. All they had to do was find *the* Hillman and *the* driver. Of course, the driver might not have been the owner of the car, but it was a breakthrough. Of sorts. Just a few thousand drivers and vehicles to locate before the next nude awakening!

And then, in a stroke, it was over. Closure as docile and undramatic as a thriller without a thrill.

'Jack's' voice on the line: someone was going to be charged. A full confession had been made. Suddenly there was an air of bathos. The thrill of every chase inevitably had to end in anti-climax. Sometimes, though, an anti-climax could be premature. Occasionally, there *could* be more to come.

# CHAPTER 13

# A BLOODY NUISANCE

Kenneth Archibald, caretaker of the Holland Park Lawn Tennis Club, had a crafty, money-making idea. He'd turn his rent-free basement flat on the tennis club premises into an all-night drinking den. All that was required was a record player and a bar, which he could construct himself. After all, he was the resident DIY factotum. This was duly completed at the start of 1964 and he circulated the news on the underground grapevine that his private little club would be open for drinking and dancing all through the night, and the pavilion and courts, conveniently hidden from the public, could be utilised for 'all kinds of pleasures'. He reckoned that he'd tapped into a real nice little earner. And so it was for about six or eight weeks, until the night of the fracas and the call to the police.

Archibald, who hailed from Sunderland, tried to blag his way out of the predicament. It had been a private party, he argued, no drinks were sold, and there was so much convivial noise and gambolling that he hadn't noticed the disturbance or the damage to the property. One of the constables who had gone to the club at 1 Addison Road, Kensington said he'd have to report the incident to the secretary.

Piqued, Archibald said, 'Do you have to?'

'Yes, I do... I have a public duty,' replied the constable.

'But I'm in charge here when the club isn't open,' Archibald protested.

'But you're not part of the management, are you.' This wasn't a question but simply meant to put Archibald in his place.

'You realise I could be fired,' said Archibald, playing the sympathy card as a last resort.

'Then that's something you'll have to deal with.' Heads have no chance against a brick wall.

From questioning people who had attended the alleged 'private party', the constables quickly sussed that it was no such thing and Archibald was guilty of running an unlicensed drinking club, used by many prostitutes to find punters. These officers had no sympathy for Archibald whatsoever.

Archibald didn't lose his job but was told he would have to make good the damage out of his own pocket and that there would be no more 'parties' or else...

On the 27th of that month, Archibald phoned Notting Hill police station to report a break-in. He was informed that the matter would be 'looked into', but that afternoon he walked into Notting Hill police station, where he introduced himself to the front-desk officer and said starkly, 'I've come to give myself up.'

A detective constable, standing behind the desk-officer, knew about Archibald's report that morning and stepped forward, a little perplexed, saying, 'What, the break-in job at the tennis club?'

With a complete blank look, Archibald said, 'No, I pushed the girl in the river.'

Further bemused, the detective struggled for clarification. 'Girl? What girl are you talking about?'

'You know, the blonde Lockwood at Chiswick. It was me. I did it. I'm the bloke you're looking for. Do you want me or not?'

Nonplussed, the detective said, much more shakily than Archibald, 'Are you serious? You're not tossing me off?'

'I tell you, it was me,' Archibald repeated, his face pained with sincerity. 'I want to get it off my chest.'

Archibald was taken into custody. The murder squad at Shepherd's Bush was alerted. The news spread through the ranks like a bushfire. At first the CID at Notting Hill were told to 'hold on to him. Lock him up.' Minutes later, the order changed. 'Bring him to us. Quick as you can. No press statement. A complete publicity blackout.'

In under ten minutes, the partially deaf and semi-disabled Archibald, a former merchant seaman and soldier before that, was on his way to notoriety. If it was recognition he was seeking, he would soon be fully rewarded.

Frank Davies was still compering the 'Irene Lockwood Show', so he cautioned Archibald and oversaw the taking of his confession, which went: 'I finished work at the Holland Park Lawn Tennis Club at between eight-thirty and nine p.m. on 7 April this year, 1964. After that, I went on a pub crawl. I can't remember how many or which ones I went in, but they were my regulars and the last one was definitely the Windmill in Chiswick High Road.

'I got chatting with a blonde at the bar, a customer – she wasn't working there – and after a while I realised from things she said that she was on the game. It wasn't long before she asked me straight out, brazen as you like, if I fancied a quickie with her.

'She was drinking gin and tonic, which I'd bought her. I was on beer, a pint of draught. All the booze had made me pretty randy, so I said yes to her proposition and asked her where she wanted to go. "I'll show you, just follow me," she said. So we left the Windmill together.'

At that stage he asked the interviewing detectives if he could have a cup of tea because he was thirsty and also needed an intake of caffeine to 'bring him round' because he had a 'belter' of a hangover. Accordingly, the interview was suspended while one of the three officers in the interview room fetched Archibald a mug of tea.

Anyhow, Lockwood had steered him to the Thames, which was nearby. 'She kept pestering me for the money,' he continued. 'All she would talk about was the money, demanding it before she was prepared to do anything. She was getting on my nerves, probably more so than she would have normally because I was drunk. Finally, my nerves snapped and I grabbed her throat. We grappled for a few seconds. She was swearing like a trooper and kicked me in the balls. I really went mad then and gave her a mighty shove, with all my strength.

'There was a wall behind her and she cracked the back of her head, then fell to the ground. She was out cold. That's when I started stripping her. When I'd got all her clothes off I rolled her over and over, like a barrel, down a ramp until she splashed into the river. I thought the cold water might revive her, but she didn't make a sound. It was the first time she'd been quiet all night. I just stood there a few minutes waiting and watching, but she was gone. I couldn't see her. The Thames took her.'

Then came the questions. *Did you intend to kill her?* – 'I just wanted to shut her up.'

*What did you do with the clothes?* – 'I took them home in a bundle and burned the lot. They stank to high heaven.'

*Did you have sex with her?* – 'No. We never got that far. It all went wrong before that. I didn't give her any money. I would have done, though, if she'd just shut up and waited until we'd come to an arrangement. I'd no intention of trying to rape her, nothing like that.'

*Are you absolutely sure about not having any form of sex with her?* – 'One hundred per cent. My flies stayed done up the whole time.'

*Had you seen Miss Lockwood before that night?* – 'No, never.'

*Do you make a habit of going with prostitutes?* – 'No, I'm too old for that game generally.'

*But not too old when it came to Miss Lockwood?* – 'I'd had too much to drink that night. I didn't know really what I was doing.'

*Did you mean to kill her?* (A repeat question) – 'She'd made me so mad, I just wanted to shut her up.' (A repeat answer.)

*You must have been aware that by rolling her into the river she could easily drown?* – 'I suppose so.'

*Have you attacked women before?* – 'No, never. Only cowards hit women'.

*Are you a regular drinker?* – 'I like my tipple.'

*Do you drink every day?* – 'Most days.'

*So you can handle drink?* – 'Usually. When you've been in the army and merchant navy, you're not likely to be teetotal, and especially coming from the north-east. We can really drink, not like the soft-bellied southerners around these parts.'

He was shown mug shots of Tailford and Rees: *Were these women known to you?* – 'I think I've seen them before.'

*Where?* – 'Round about. Weren't they the ones in the 'papers? They were done in recently, weren't they?'

*Were you responsible?* – 'Not to my knowledge.'

*What does that mean?* – 'Well, if I did. I must have been so skunked because I can't remember a thing about it.'

*So you could have?* – 'I don't think so. I'm not confessing to it.'

*You fully understand what we're saying?* – 'Yes.'

He was taken to a cell while his statement was typed in triplicate. Later he was returned to the interviewroom and was asked to read the typed version.

*Is that a fair and accurate record of what you've told us?* – 'Yes.'

*Do you wish to make any changes or add to it in any way?* – 'No. Nothing.'

With those formalities completed, he was then asked to sign the bottom of each page of the top copy, which he did. Tape-recorded interviews were not then a part of the interviewing process of suspects.

Archibald wasn't legally represented and hadn't been offered a lawyer to protect his legal interests. At least one of the detectives believed that Archibald was drunk or suffering a severe hangover when he gave himself up.

On 30 April, at 6.45 p.m., Archibald was charged with the murder of Irene Lockwood. Hence the forewarning call to me from 'Jack'. Of course, from the moment Archibald was charged the entire case became *sub judice*. Newspapers could report nothing more than the name of the accused and the charge, so that the case for prosecution and defence could not be compromised. This didn't mean that journalists or the police were required to stop investigating. On the contrary, for the media, the tempo was racked up a couple of notches. More than ever there was an insatiable appetite within the press for background material, not confined to evidence related to the charge but a comprehensive history of the defendant who would be in the dock in the coliseum of British courts, the Old Bailey. 'Jack' was going to be a more essential conduit for me than ever.

So to the Jack of Clubs and its subdued lighting and an atmosphere that swathed this archetypal nightclub of the Sixties with a suffusion of decadence, a melting-pot of cultures, where vicars and villains could put away dog-collars and weapons (usually): was Archibald, this short, tubby, limping, semi-alcoholic really the 'Stripper Ripper'?

'Jack' was in a dilemma, so was Scotland Yard. Archibald was inflexible about his guilt, but he'd lied in his confession. Rudimentary detective plodding had uncovered incontrovertible proof that Lockwood and Archibald had known one another long before that alleged fateful meeting in the Windmill pub. She had been a regular at Archibald's illegal drinking club. Furthermore, she'd visited him several times at his basement flat in the daytime for sex, with no quarrels over price and payment in advance, the way it's done the world over. This information had come from friends of Lockwood and a couple of men who did some shady business with the tennis-club caretaker. Archibald wouldn't have balked at paying upfront for sex because it was the norm.

Archibald's lie about not being acquainted with Lockwood didn't make sense. This untruth didn't add to his guilt or point to his innocence: a pointless lie. What it did demonstrate, though, was erratic behaviour and a Walter Mitty aberration. The pathologist's report hadn't mentioned anything about a bump to the back of Lockwood's skull, which would have been substantial if she'd been knocked unconscious when hurled against a wall. Throughout, the confession lacked the ring of truth.

'To be honest, all we have is his confession,' 'Jack' said gloomily, comfortable in the knowledge that none of our conversation could be published.

Which brought me to the crunch question: 'Did he kill the others? And if he didn't, then he didn't kill Lockwood, right?'

'Jack' was silenced. I'd pinpointed the flaw, the *dilemma,* the festering sore for which there was only one cure and that salve seemed further than ever away from Archibald.

'You know what,' I said, 'I don't reckon he's your man. I think you've got a waster.'

'And a wanker!' he retorted, as instant as a ricochet. It was a considerable time before he spoke again, more content drinking, and when he did I had to admire his frankness. 'It's another classic cock-up. Just clutching at straws. No name, but one of our top dogs is even starting to think about witchcraft being at the root of the killings. He's been consulting the weather forecasters about the type of moon on the nights of the murders. I tell you, it's got us all going gaga. There are some great detectives who are just burying their heads in the sand. There are too many chiefs all doing a sort of tribal dance and hoping magic will save their reputations.'

'Will they allow this to run all the way to a trial?' I asked.

'Looks like it,' he said morosely. 'Buying time; dangerous strategy, though. Scary!'

'Because the real killer of Lockwood and others is still among us, on the streets, having a laugh?' I suggested.

'At our expense and just waiting to make bloody fools of us. He'll probably strike again the day after Archibald's convicted or freed. What will that make us in the public eye?'

'As mad as he is,' I said, hoping not to endanger our symbiotic friendship.

'He should have been bailed pending further investigations and kept under twenty-four-hour surveillance.' After another hiatus, he stated what was the fear among many murder squad detectives, including himself: 'We've taken our feet off the pedal. Everything's gone on hold. So much precious time's being wasted. We should be pushing on, trying to prove that prick Archibald is guilty, regardless of his confession, and also involved in the deaths of the others, or just another nutter and boot him out. As it stands, there's nothing to tie him to Tailford or Rees.'

We were both right.

## A BLOODY NUISANCE

On 23 June at the Old Bailey and after a six-day flimsy trial, the jury took a mere fifty-five minutes to clear Archibald of murder, after he'd withdrawn his confession in a late legal manoeuvre and pleaded not guilty. Standing at the rear of the court, red-faced and cringing with embarrassment, were some of Scotland Yard's finest, now with egg all over their ego. This was yet another nadir for the Yard, the self-proclaimed citadel to all other police forces around the globe. Worse, far worse, was still to come...

Meanwhile, the idiot Archibald was holding his own court on the pavement outside the Old Bailey, with a captive audience of reporters, photographers and TV cameramen. 'Phew! That's the last time I'll confess to anything, especially to a murder I never committed. Thank heavens I retracted my false statement in time.'

Of course the question coming from all corners was why did he concoct that absurd confession that no one, except apparently the police, believed for a second.

'Well, I was fed up, depressed, confused [not the only one]. I felt I'd let my friends down at the tennis club, what with one thing and another. I saw myself losing my flat [which he now had], my job [which he now had, too] and my army pension [which he kept]. And somehow my imagination – yes, you can say it's a highly lively one – just ran away with me. I'm turning my back on London. It's no good for me. I've always led a normal life. [Questionable!]

'I should never have had all that beer, then I wouldn't have shouted my mouth off in that ridiculous way. I just kept talking, thinking up the story as I went along and, by amazing coincidence, certain details fitted in with what the police knew. I was confused and depressed, although I'll never really know why I said what I did. I have been really silly.' The truth at last!

However, the most disgraceful *confession* came years later when one of Scotland Yard's most senior officers, Deputy Assistant

Commissioner John du Rose, admitted that the detectives in charge of the Lockwood case knew all along that Archibald was innocent of the crime and was just another nuisance factor.

Du Rose said, 'We had no reason to believe that Archibald had anything to do with the murder, but he had to be charged and a jury had to decide the case because he had repeated his false confession twice before eventually retracting it.' Pompous rubbish! Cynical deceit!

As explored earlier in the book, detectives heading high-profile murder investigations always have a 'control question' retained from the public domain for the sole purpose of weeding out time-wasters, the hundreds of people, slightly deranged and for perverse reasons, who have a compulsion to confess. They are rooted out and never charged. Implicit for a successful conviction is the necessity for the police to *verify* with irrefutable *evidence* a defendant's guilt, independent of a confession. All confessions have to be meticulously tested, sort of calibrated forensically, long before a case reaches court.

The 'A6 Murder' was a typical example. James Hanratty was charged, convicted, and executed in Bedford Prison in the early 1960s. Before he was even charged, throughout the trial, and long after the hanging, another man persisted with his claim that he was the killer and was the one who should have gone to the gallows.

Respected writer and TV presenter Ludovic Kennedy was even hoodwinked. He wrote virulently about the miscarriage of justice and vociferously led a campaign for Hanratty's posthumous pardon. And then... along came the dawning of DNA science and profiling which ended the argument as firmly as a door slammed in the face of the campaigners: the state had hanged the correct man. All the critics of the investigation were silenced by a single lab technician. The detectives had refused to be deflected by a confession they conceived as a tissue of lies told by an unbalanced nuisance. As an irrelevant footnote, I never understood why the media immortalised this crime as the 'A6 Murder' when it was committed on Deadman's Hill: surely a gift for all headline writers.

Exactly three weeks after Archibald walked from the Old Bailey a free man, another nude victim was awaiting collection in west London.

The police may have taken their feet off the pedal, but this serial killer wasn't slowing down. And Archibald had kept his word and gone north, so he wasn't around to confess to this one.

# CHAPTER 14

# SOME DUMMY!

G eorge Heard yawned and stretched. It was not yet five a.m.,
  but being mid-summer the day dawned early. Mr Heard
was a chauffeur and he was eager to see if the weather was going to
match up to expectations for that season of the year, so he padded
from his bed to the window and opened the curtains. The date
was 14 July 1964.

*That's funny,* he thought, rubbing his eyes, hoping for clearer
vision. Slumped outside a neighbour's garage was a tailor's
dummy; well, that's what it looked like in the half-light and from
the elevated angle. But as his eyes cleared, he said to himself,
*Blimey! I reckon that's a body, not a dummy.* So he scrambled into
some clothes and went to inspect close up.

First impression had been wrong. Second impression had been
right. Mary Fleming was no dummy, but she was as lifeless as
one. Number five had turned up, but not courtesy of the River
Thames. This had been a straightforward dump-and-dash job.

Mr Heard lived at 52 Berrymede Road, Chiswick. He was up with the crow of the cock because one of his daughters was going to France on a day trip and he was to drive her to Acton in his employer's car; he drove for a City of London banker. His crowing cock had been a pre-booked phone alarm call. The body was outside number 48. 'Just squatting there,' he told police and press. 'You can imagine my shock. Nearly had a heart attack. Enough to put me off my food for a week. I scarpered indoors and dialled nine-nine-nine. I was told not to move or touch anything. I was too spooked for that, anyhow. It gave me the creeps. I told them I took one look and just ran indoors.'

Just before five-thirty, two uniformed constables, Houston and Braddock, arrived from Shepherd's Bush police station. One of them radioed a report to their HQ while the other taped off the crime scene. Sightseers, some in dressing gowns and even less, were beginning to fill the cul-de-sac. By seven o'clock, there were five detective superintendents there, one of them from the murder squad, Maurice Osborn, who was to take charge. They had to wait another hour and a half for the overworked pathologist, Dr Teare. 'Here we go again,' he was heard to murmur, as he commenced his preliminary examination.

Through markings on the body, Teare was able to state categorically that Mary Fleming had been stripped after death. Grease stains on her back and buttocks hinted at her having been transported on the floor of a vehicle, such as a van that was used for work. Distinctive imprints on her back were also consistent with her having lain for a while on a patterned carpet or rough-haired rug. A massive bruise on her left breast, directly above her heart, bore the shape of a fist and the blow appeared to have been delivered with the force and precision of someone exceedingly strong and probably quite heavy, such as a man with boxing skills. At only just over five feet tall and weighing barely eight stone,

## SOME DUMMY!

Fleming would have had no chance of defending herself against a man of even average build, even though she was believed to be armed with a knife, never mind perhaps a professional pugilist. If taken by surprise, she would have been helpless, whatever precautions she had taken.

Bill Marchant quickly assembled a team of door-knockers. Someone must have seen or heard something worthwhile. Of something the police were already certain: the killer wasn't local. This criminal didn't mess on – or near – his own doorstep.

Several residents of Berrymede Road had been woken by a noisy, revving vehicle between one and two a.m. All agreed that the engine seemed high-powered and had been driven into the road and then away at speed. Another resident had returned home at just after ten-thirty p.m. on the previous evening from watching greyhounds racing at Wembley Stadium and the body wasn't there then. So a time frame was beginning to emerge. All the evidence pointed to the drop having been made between one and two, which, on its own, helped the police not one jot.

Dirt was scraped from Fleming's body at the mortuary and despatched to the Metropolitan Police Forensic Laboratory for examination, marked 'urgent'. The outcome was promising. Minute particles, visible only under a microscope, were isolated from the rest of the dirt and were an identical match with those from Barthelemy's body: dust from coal or coke, and red, black and blue paint. Not only had these two women been murdered by the same man, but unquestionably had been stored in the same place. Find that place and you may have found the serial killer, though not necessarily: always a caveat. If the storage venue was some sort of commercial garage, for example, it could be used quite legitimately by scores of people. Never mind, this was a major development, probably the only significant one so far.

So what did the police know about the latest deceased, apart from the fact that she was a prostitute and had lost twelve teeth during the night, ten from the upper deck. She drank a lot; whisky was her favourite tipple. She smoked even more, around forty cigarettes a day. 'Could stop but don't want to; enjoy fags too much.' Just like the other victims, she stalked the streets around the Kensington Park Hotel, the Warwick Castle pub and the Jazz Club, all paradises for ponces, prostitutes and pimps, the three Ps of west London vice.

Foot-slogging detective probing established that on the night of Friday, 10 July she was at the 'gym', not doing press-ups but scotch knock-backs. The Gym was a euphemism for an illegal drinking club at 32a Powis Square, run by a monumental Jamaican who made extra money from appearing in movies and TV documentaries as a slave. He would joke, 'I get whipped for a living.' Fleming had been dancing there and 'called it a night' at around five a.m. and was in bed soon afterwards with her lover at 44 Lancaster Road. She was also there at six o'clock that evening, 11 July, because she returned from shopping to relieve her regular babysitter; Fleming had two young children.

After putting the children to bed, she dressed in lace G-panties, a red suspender-belt, dark nylon stockings, black padded bra, a green-grey blouse, matching jacket and tight woollen skirt, made from heavy material. To finish off, she put on a pair of white plastic sling-back shoes. Her babysitter for that night was an Irishman.

As detectives continued to piece together the final hours in Fleming's life, it became apparent that she was still alive on the streets at three a.m. after being recognised by a Transport Police officer turning from the Bayswater Road into Leinster Terrace. Earlier, she'd spoken to other prostitutes, complaining bitterly that she hadn't turned 'one trick' and was 'fed up' by the lack of trade. It seems that before admitting defeat and knocking-off for the night empty-handed, she was in the mood to do *anything* with a punter to clinch a sale. That was the last sighting of her, halfway through the night of Friday/Saturday, until she reappeared on the forthcoming Tuesday naked and dead, all those teeth missing and death due to asphyxia; something blocked her airways, but was removed from her throat or neck.

House calls were proving a waste of energy and valuable hours. Most promising was the scientific progress that continued to increase in value. The particles of paint on the body were globular, so they hadn't come from a brush, but much more likely from a spraygun. Industrial premises, warehouses, garages, boathouses, boatyards, riverside huts and lockups were raided within a six-mile radius of where the bodies of Fleming and Barthelemy had surfaced, with nothing but recurring, monotonous negative results. One hundred and five officers were commandeered for this fruitless operation and more than one hundred and fifty premises were searched. Dust was meticulously collected from stone floors and sent to the lab. Dust was also settling on yet another abortive investigation. After hours of scrutiny under microscopes the response from the boffins was always the same: 'Sorry, no match.' Back to 'Go'. Throw the dice again. Begin another circuit. This was soul-destroying, bad for morale, and even worse for Scotland Yard's worldwide cred.

As Marchant rightly observed, 'Just because the bodies turned up in this area, why should we assume that the killing was carried out here or indeed anywhere nearby? The ploy could be to throw us off the scent, to send us on a wild goose-chase.' If that was the ruse, it was working. The detectives also had to accept that anyone could be using a paint spray at home in a private garage or workshop. Never had so much forensic detail been of so little use.

Referring to the paint particles, 'Big John' du Rose commented that 'the general picture of the colours seemed to fit the pattern of motor cars being currently produced by certain manufacturers and it became that these two bodies [Fleming and Barthelemy] had been in or near premises in which cars were spray-painted during repairs. But where were the premises?'

He hadn't a clue. Nor had any other detective, top of the ladder or on the bottom rung.

Du Rose added, 'We had a double headache. We had to find a killer and we had to ensure, as far as humanly possible, that nobody else fell victim to him. But such were the difficulties that existed from the very beginning that the tempo of the investigation, involving countless inquiries, could not be quickened enough to prevent the deaths of yet two more women.' However one massaged the facts and tried for an upbeat spin, the overriding message was one of abject failure.

He continued, 'Already the manpower engaged on these murders was affecting the work of the Metropolitan Police, and particularly the CID. Sir Ranulph Bacon, the Assistant Commissioner for Crime, had allocated a far larger number of men and women to the investigation than is customary in a murder inquiry.'

Scarce inspiration came from that little homily.

The weeks passed, then the months, summer turned to autumn and winter, finally November. Even more finally for Frances Brown, where we came in.

# CHAPTER 15

# FEET FIRST

M y meeting with 'Jack' on Wednesday, 13 January 1964 was, as usual, at my instigation. I was seeking a progress report, which normally turned out to be an oxymoron. *Progress* wasn't something readily associated with this stumbling, bumbling, pitiful investigation. But this evening was different – or so it seemed.

'I think we're getting there.' Oblique but definitely stimulating. Not another Archibald, I hoped.

I gulped on my beer. We were in Milo's drinking club. Two detectives from Bow Street police station were chatting-up the one and only 'hostess', who had seen better days. She was probably someone's grandmother. There were only a couple other customers, Covent Garden workers of some kind, one of whom was steadily feeding the jukebox. 'King of the Road' was playing. The lighting was very low, probably for the benefit of the hostess, giving her a chance.

'Jack' didn't know the two middle-aged Bow Street detectives, who resembled a couple of bookmakers' clerks, he told me with a smattering of snobbery. Scotland Yard, especially the murder squad, represented the elite, a cut above the staff of the neighbourhood stations, mimicking the clash in the US between the FBI and regional police forces. The riposte from the Bow Street Boys would have been that smart-arse Scotland Yard wasn't proving its elitism when it came to catching 'Deep Throat'. Fifteen-love to Bow Street. And how about Jack the Ripper? Thirty-love to Bow Street.

So what did 'Jack' mean by *we're getting there?*

'Not for publication,' he prefaced what was to follow. *Not for publication* was worse to the ears of a journalist than *this is off the record,* which at least left room for bargaining and nifty manoeuvring.

'OK,' I said pragmatically, but *what exactly* isn't for publication?'

'"Top Gun" believes we've got our man nailed.'

*Top Gun!* I'd never heard that one. 'Who the hell's "Top Gun"?'

'I can't tell you that, either.'

This was becoming more ludicrous than a scene from *Spooks.*

'I assume it's Osborn or Marchant?' I fished.

'Or above.'

How high was this going? 'Well, is he senior or not?'

'It's immaterial because no names, OK? You know the drill.'

I wasn't sure that I did.

'King of the Road' ended. Someone else took his place. Sound and rhythm a carbon copy. The volume was high, pleasing 'Jack', who was pre-empting any Bow Street earwigging. Time to drill for oil.

'You're near to making an arrest, is that it?' I avoided any sarcasm alluding to Archibald.

'Nearer than ever before.'

That wasn't saying much.

Had all the scientific evidence come good in terms of a final resolution?

'Yes and no,' he said enigmatically. Here we go again, I thought, just like those mysterious crop circles in the West Country.

'Is there about to be an arrest?'

'Could very well be.'

Definitely time for another drink. Milo recognised my strafed expression and pleading gesture towards our empty pint glasses. Replacements came by express delivery.

'He lives in south London.' This was offered before I'd even asked another question. Alcohol had the magic quality of opening doors, but south London was a big area, something I pointed out, devoid of pugnacity. He then asked me if Beulah Hill meant anything to me. It didn't; not immediately.

'Keep an eye on south London,' he urged me. 'That's where all the action's going to be. We're closing in. It's all rather complicated. There are known vintage villains connected to this.'

South London, *known vintage villains,* that could only mean the Richardson mob, surely, who were into organised fraud and torture, for kicks, as a pastime when life was tedious. So I said, 'Must be the Richardsons, right?'

Slowly, 'Jack' shook his head. 'Wrong name.'

It couldn't be the Krays; they ruled east and west. South of the river was a foreign country to them.

Finally, I tired of this guessing game. Two pints had lubricated the tongue a little more. 'I don't want you to be fooled, Mike,' he said earnestly. 'This will be a decoy, to lure someone out of his lair by turning the spotlight in the wrong direction.'

It didn't seem to me that 'Deep Throat' needed *luring from his lair;* he'd already murdered at least six young women, the last only a few weeks previously, but I had no wish to dissent and ruffle the symbiosis.

'Jack' then reminded me of something he'd said to me at a previous rendezvous. *Think big.* Did he mean a big man in size, reputation, authority or notoriety. I posed the question.

'Three out of four,' was all that he'd say on that subject.

Suddenly Beulah Hill in Upper Norwood, south London, near Crystal Palace, registered with me. 'Not Jimmy Evans, the safe-blower?' I said incredulously.

'Jack' just grinned impishly and said,' Now there's a name to conjure with.'

'But is he the decoy or the real deal?'

'He'd blow the tarts' heads off, not just mangle their tonsils,' he answered irreverently.

Evans had already castrated with a shotgun George Foreman, brother of gang mobster Freddie. 'So Evans is just the dupe?' I pushed.

'Use your noddle,' he said. Eliciting a straight 'yes' or 'no' was tantamount to Oliver Twist with his bowl asking for more.

If Evans was just the distraction, then who was the real fox that the hounds were after? This I put to 'Jack'.

'That's something that has to be firmed-up,' was all he would say.

'Does this have anything to do with what happened last week in the House of Peacocks?' I wondered aloud.

'Forget it. Nothing at all, but it will spice-up the background material for you when you're able to write something.' This was harder than trying to push a juggernaut uphill single-handed.

Jimmy Evans lived in a mansion-sized house he called The House of Peacocks. The previous Wednesday it had been raided by armed police. Evans wasn't there at the time. In fact, the house was empty. But next day the national newspapers had a carnival with the story, describing a 'siege' that wasn't one.

*The Sun,* my newspaper, was no exception, but I wasn't the guilty party. A *Daily Mirror* reporter wrote:

> Swarms of police raided the House of Peacocks yesterday in the search for Ginger Marks who is believed to have been shot in a London street. Since two a.m. hidden detectives had kept watch on the big corner house where two pet peacocks strut in the back garden. At lunchtime fifty police – some with dogs – suddenly surrounded the house. One detective climbed to an upstairs window and tried to get in. Others went to the back and broke a window... Police had been given a phone tip that Ginger Marks had been taken to the house, badly hurt.

The *Daily Sketch* really went over the top: *Revolver-carrying detectives moved in... the message was clear: whoever lived in the House of Peacocks had shot and abducted Marks.*

If they'd carried out the raid a few days earlier, they would have encountered Evans and thirty of his gunmen, but no Ginger Marks. They were armed with every conceivable weapon from revolvers and shot guns to semi-automatics, not expecting the police but Freddie Foreman and his gang with firebombs, retaliating against the shooting of brother George by Evans. This swashbuckling yarn is told in much fuller detail by Evans in his autobiography, with Martin Short, entitled *The Survivor* (Mainstream Publishing, 2001). Marks was a small-time crook who was presumed kidnapped and murdered: his body was never recovered.

Around noon the day following my drinking session with 'Jack', I received an anonymous call. The man said something to the effect of, 'Prepare for the arrest of Jimmy Evans. Not for robbery, but murder. Not Marks but mass murder. All in west

London. Follow my drift?' Then click, he was gone: the tried and tested format of seasoned troublemakers. I tried to ID the voice because it was familiar. I phoned 'Jack'. He was out. I called again after a liquid lunch. Now he was at his desk. I told him about the call. His explanation was given in one pithy word before hanging up just like the tipster: 'Decoy.'

Stupidly and irresponsibly, the *South London Advertiser,* a weekly local newspaper that subsequently went out of business, took the bait and fell for the hoax. The day after my call to 'Jack', this newspaper splashed on the canard, without verification or tracing the source: 'Has the House of Peacocks a Link with the Thames Nude Murders?' The text went:

> On Tuesday an *Advertiser* reporter passed on to a senior Scotland Yard detective information linking an Anerley man with the Beulah House of Peacocks raid, the disappearance of Ginger Marks and the Thames Nude Murders.
>
> The information came during three telephone conversations between the reporter and a mystery voice who was an underworld tipster. He explained that the man in question is believed to have controlled the activities of three of the murdered prostitutes – Hannah Tailford, Margaret McGowan [Frances Brown] and Gwynneth Rees. He was detained in Kensington police station by detectives inquiring into the murders, but later released.
>
> The name cropped up again after last week's Flying Squad raid on the House of Peacocks during the massive London hunt for the missing East End car-dealer, Ginger Marks.
>
> The 'grass' or 'tipster' said that the name of the man

owning the House of Peacocks was known to criminals as an alias of the man questioned about the Nude murders. The 'grass' also said that the man had done some crooked car deals with Ginger Marks.

In a third conversation, the 'grass' cast further light on what might have happened to two of the prostitutes the night they died. Gwynneth Rees died of an abortion – not as the result of a sexual assault as such, one of the others died in a bath in a house in Marylebone Road before being dumped in the Thames.

The 'grass' then alleged that the man bossed a chain of brothels and call girls, and held the lease of house in Curzon Street, Mayfair, formerly owned by the notorious Messina brothers. [They controlled brothels and street-prostitutes in the West End for many years previously.] He gave this reporter names of two South London prostitutes, the addresses in in Notting Hill Gate and Bloomsbury used by prostitutes and the name of a south London public house used by an unnamed prostitute – she arranged to meet the man in the House of Peacocks – all the women were controlled by the same man.

The 'grass' said the man, knowing he was known to the police, had provided himself with an escape route to Dublin. The 'grass' then said that the underworld generally believed that the man was in hiding abroad. 'But,' said the 'grass', I know that he is living at Number ... ....... Road, Anerley.' He added, 'My underworld friends tell me that 'Ginger' Marks is not dead but seriously wounded.

One of the two cars standing in the driveway of the House of Peacocks – the blood-red Ford Classic – belongs to the man. The other, an American convertible, is known to criminals as belonging to an associate of the man.

## THE SECRET LIFE OF FREDDIE MILLS

The astonishing aspect of this wildly inaccurate and libellous story was how it ever got into print without credible backup and authentication. Solicitor Jimmy Fellowes wasted no time in issuing the newspaper with a writ for libel on behalf of Evans, who was understandably incandescent. Despite his criminal record, Evans won a small fortune that in today's money would amount to about £250,000.

It was years after the 'Nudes' murders had become mothballed, and following my reading Evans's account of his life, that the identity dawned on me of the man who had phoned me anonymously forewarning me of the notorious safe-blower about to be arrested as a serial killer. It was Tommy Butler, one-time head of the Flying Squad, whose obsession had been rounding up all the Great Train Robbers, perhaps for more than purely professional reasons. It became proven – not merely *known* – in police circles that when recovering stolen loot he would squirrel away a percentage for himself and a few of his cronies; one of those cronies was Detective Chief Inspector Frank Williams, of the Kennington police station, south London. Evans had good reason to know and detest him because he traded with the Foremans. So, too, did Butler. In his book, Evans went on to accuse Butler of being the 'Nudes' serial killer. Now that was carrying a grudge a step too far. Butler may have been severely 'bent', but he was no killer; well, perhaps that's vindication without proof, but he definitely *wasn't* 'Deep Throat', who was indeed much bigger than he in both physique and celebrity status. Evans's only justification, apparently, for naming Butler as the serial killer was that he lived within a mile of most of the cast-out bodies, was single, and as we saw earlier, not only lived with his mother, but had strange habits. Yet the only really *strange* habit of his for a policeman, that I can see, was his propensity for stealing cash from burglars.

Of course it was shocking that a coterie of senior officers

of Scotland Yard, the mecca of policing, was undoubtedly corrupt, but that shouldn't be confused with being surprised; it was an almost inevitable gravitation. Fleet Street reporters, for instance, were earning more than GPs, surgeons, Scotland Yard commanders, airline pilots and even the Prime Minister. As Sir James Anderton, the former Chief Constable of Greater Manchester, said, nearly all police officers throughout the nation came from a 'working-class' background. Nationally there was a large economic imbalance, and there still is.

In the 1960s, the police considered themselves the poor relations of the services. Egalitarianism had gathered momentum after the war as a political and social issue. Crime, especially white-collar crime, was seen as acceptable and a proportion of the police, all from CID, started helping themselves to some of the spoils, not seeing themselves as criminals but exploiting their own influence and clout to create a fairer society. They were merely joining the *every man for himself* culture and redistributing wealth: there was no evidence of women officers being admitted to the dubious magic circle.

Long has been the assumption that any trend starting in the USA would soon be imported to the UK, and so it was with police corruption. The evergreen 'Black Dahlia' case in Los Angeles more than any other demonstrated the depth of corruption within the LAPD, embracing the police chief and political administrators, right up to governor level. Elizabeth Short had followed the well-worn trail to tinsel town in search of stardom – America's take on Dick Whittington – which she found dramatically but not in the image of her dreams. As briefly described earlier, she was carved in two, decapitated, her face slashed from ear-to-ear, viscera including her womb removed, then deposited beside a residential road; all the parts were laid out like the pieces of a jigsaw puzzle, there for a pathologist to try to reassemble. Grisly, right?

What emerged from 'Good Cop' Harry Hansen, who was leading for much of the time, was a day-to-day working relationship between police, City Hall, movie studio bosses and gangsters, mostly the Mafia. Hansen deduced that Short had been disembowelled and further butchered following a botched abortion, which was then still illegal, by an 'eminent' gynaecologist who regularly carried out these procedures for the stars, such as Marilyn Monroe and Ava Gardner. A cabal of gynaecologists of high rank in their profession, equivalent to Britain's Harley Street professionals, would perform the illegal procedure, if the money was right. But for every thousand dollars they took, fifty per cent went to the police to keep them out of gaol. Short's body had been so professionally dissected that Detective Hansen recorded that this could only have been performed by a qualified surgeon.

Donald Wolfe revealed in *The Black Dahlia Files* (Time Warner Books, 2006):

> When the Gangster Squad came under scrutiny by the Grand Jury in 1949 and was found to be enforcing pay-offs from the Syndicate [the Mafia], the name of the Squad reverted back to the 'Intelligence Unit', under the regime of Chief William Parker. However, when the Intelligence Unit was put under investigation by the Police Commission in 1974, it was learned that once again only the name had changed.

So no one should be the least surprised by corruption among London's police in the 1960s. They were simply behaving like police forces the world over. No excuse, but a reality check nonetheless. We have to understand without condoning.

# CHAPTER 16

# NO DUMMY

February 1965: Leonard Beauchamp stopped abruptly. Two bare feet came into view. They were partly covered by the undergrowth. He was to say later, 'I first noticed a pair of feet and I could see them up to the ankles. My first reaction was that I was looking at a dummy.' Even though the toenails were painted.

Unperturbed, he ambled to the main shed on the industrial estate in Acton to tell the store man, Maurice Chester, of his find. 'I told him there was a woman's body behind the stores. I was half joking. We had a laugh and a joke about it.'

Minutes later, Beauchamp crossed the compound to the admin office where he made a report to production manager Gerald Marshall. Consequently, a small investigation party marched to the appropriate spot of undergrowth, where all kinds of rubbish was discharged. Marshall concluded that they were looking at a dummy, but 'to be on the safe side' he would phone Acton police.

Body number seven was just about to be unveiled.

Showtime again. Curtain up. The troupe would be on stage within the hour. The same old routine, dancing to the tune of the police manual. The same morgue humour. Synchronised shaking of heads. Scripted blasphemy. Jack the Ripper was well and truly eclipsed. London was under siege from a new kind of Blitz, bodies dropping like bombs. There was a distinct smugness among the *clean living*. This Blitz killed only whores. It was selective, leaving alone the gentrified. No cause for alarm, then, among the *good girls,* such as those who went to bed for a diamond necklace rather than a paltry fiver. Still someone's daughter, though; I'm not sure that epitaph entered many heads.

Bridget 'Bridie' O'Hara was completely naked. 'Wrong time of year for sunbathing,' quipped Detective Superintendent Bill Baldock who took charge. Yet another leader. Scotland Yard was rapidly running out of murder squads.

Enter a new pathologist, Dr David Bowen. Dr Teare, probably much to his relief, was already carving up someone else. Dr Bowen arrived at the Surgical Equipment Supplies Ltd. depot in Westfields Road, Acton at a few minutes after one p.m. and within three hours he was conducting the PM in the Acton mortuary.

O'Hara was five feet and one inch tall, weighing nine stone. Clearly this serial killer liked them short – and undoubtedly submissive. Not one had given him a fight. Never any blood under the victims' fingernails, few marks except the occasional bruise from a blow to subdue them. *A big man.* A big name: that's what 'Jack' had said. 'Jack' knew his stuff. He was there at PMs, heard the pathologists, and was in the confidence of every team leader. He crossed boundaries, drank with different chiefs, and was privy to every latest development, even when it was nothing more than another head bashing against a brick wall

Apart from being dead, O'Hara was reasonably healthy. The state of her aorta testified to her addiction to booze and fast, fatty food. She wasn't pregnant and no damage had been inflicted on her vagina. However, some male fluid was found in her airways. Death was due to asphyxia. The interior of her mouth and throat were extensively swollen and there was some bleeding in the tonsils region. Her tongue had been forced down below the lower level of her teeth, of which several were missing, including a plate. There was no sign of strangulation; no ligature or hands had squeezed the life from her lungs. The only clues of asphyxia were in the mucous membranes of the face and lungs. Neither the larynx nor neck had been injured. X-rays established beyond all doubt that there wasn't a single fracture in the whole of her body.

Giving away the definitive conclusion one lab technician remarked sardonically, 'It was as if she'd been *lovingly* robbed of air' (the italicisation is mine). But when had she been killed? Dr Bowen calculated that she'd been deceased for two or three weeks, plenty of leeway there. She'd been lying in the undergrowth on the industrial estate for a week and had been stripped *after* death, something the pathologist could determine from the lividity and tell-tale discolouration on various parts of the body: another repetitive signature.

That same evening she was identified by her husband, Michael Joseph O'Hara, aged twenty-eight. He had eleven convictions for robbery, assault, theft and shoplifting. They were well-matched. He was also his wife's ponce. Naturally enough, the police went to work on him, if only for show, but anyone with a toy marble for a brain would have known that, despite his criminal record for violence, he couldn't be implicated in this murder unless he could be tethered to all the other victims; the ultimate litmus test.

Mr O'Hara maintained that he hadn't seen Bridie since the evening of 11 January and she'd been last seen alive leaving the Shepherd's Bush Hotel at closing time that day. She had been wearing a loose-fitting, grey herringbone tweed coat, with a black-fringed scarf, a fawn cardigan over a red and black speckled blouse, a black skirt and the same coloured, calf-length boots. She was also known to be carrying a small black plastic purse. On one finger was an octagonal wedding ring. She also wore a white metal eternity ring. The missing plate from her upper jaw had been fitted with six teeth.

So what was Bridie O'Hara's story?

Born in Dublin on 2 March 1937, she was the sixth child in a Roman Catholic family. Her father, Matthew Moore, was a plasterer by trade; honest, hard-working and devoted to his wife and children. Her mother had little time for anything beyond caring for her ever-expanding entourage of children. Money was severely limited, but they were proud folk. All the children went to school and church clean, tidy and well fed. Although devout Christians and resolutely God-fearing, there was no ascetic extremism to their faith.

Bridie left school at the age of fourteen and secured work immediately as a cleaner, firstly in a hospital and then in factories, where the wages were slightly better. When she turned eighteen, restless and stifled, she waved goodbye to her tearful parents and headed for London, that neon magnet for the young, settling in Acton. It's hard to imagine the attraction of drab, unfashionable Acton, except that it was probably affordable, a place where there was a bed.

Work as a cleaner was easy to come by. The pay was peanuts, but that was something to which she was accustomed. It was a launch pad, but in which direction? It was not long before she was living with labourer Michael 'Mick' O'Hara in Shepherd's Bush. It was also not long before Mick was arrested for robbery and sentenced to three years' imprisonment. Two of Bridie's brothers were despatched from Ireland to 'save' their sister from sin and the Devil. They found her drunk in a pub. A few hours later, all three were drunk and arrested for disorderly conduct. There was a certain Irish inevitability to this segment of the story, albeit it mirthless in truth. Bridie already had convictions for soliciting. The die was cast. When news reached Bridie's mother, it is said that Mary Moore stayed on her knees in church for two continuous hours and worked her way through her rosary even during her fitful hours of semi-sleep.

Despite all this, Bridie and Mick were finally married in Dublin in the neighbourhood Catholic church on 17 September 1962. The night before the wedding, both had attended confession and were forgiven all their sins. It is not known how many Hail Marys they were *sentenced* to, but by rights it should have kept them up all night and through the honeymoon, which comprised nothing more than a trip to the pub. Her parents seemed reconciled to her attachment to Mick; at least he was a Catholic, even if a villainous one and an inveterate layabout.

Everyone got merrily drunk at the reception, including the parish priest, and it was noteworthy for not having one single fight as entertainment. After the hangover, Bridie had to return to London; there was a living to be made, customers to be serviced.

As the turbulent end approached, the rowing, fighting, brawling, occasionally affectionate, semi-civilised couple were living at 41 Agate Road, Hammersmith, a few roads from top cop Tommy Butler; another teasing red-herring.

By 21 February, the man at the helm of the serial killer investigation was the celebrity cop, Detective Superintendent John du Rose: large, tough, conceited and always surrounded by an aura of invincibility and a pack of sycophants. Baldock had been ruthlessly usurped by this flamboyant showman, who was adept at playing to the gallery, especially the press gallery. Baldock resented the way he had been eased aside as if a disposable nonentity, a mere prop on this stage where du Rose had arrived as the saviour.

These two men had never rubbed along. Baldock decried du Rose as a glory hunter and publicity stuntman. This wasn't now a harmonious team. Baldock also despised du Rose's deference to some of his Masonic pals in and out of the force. However, under the frenetic orchestration of 'Four-Day Johnny', the tempo reached a feverish high. Detectives descended on Wimpey Autos, a grubby, lock-up sort of commercial garage at 1a Barb Mews, Hammersmith, owned by a William Chissell.

Forensic pickers swept up dirt from the stone floor, bagged it and took it to the lab. After extensive tests, the head of the lab was able to inform du Rose categorically that the globular paint stains on several of the bodies, now revealed as including Frances Brown, were 'very similar' to those separated from the dust retrieved from the floor at Wimpey Autos.

'We're there!' Baldock exclaimed. Not quite. As usual in this case, there was yet another stumbling-block: the globular paint was more or less the same as the spray used in *all* garages that specialised in spraying. The detectives were confronted and confounded by the recurring obstacle: Cresswell or an employee had to have had a provable sexual adventure with not only Brown, but also all the others. Back to genesis.

Other items were lifted from the garage, including a Luger pistol. Great, except no one had been shot. Du Rose was far more interested in a ledger that listed clients and jobs done for them. 'Big John' burned the midnight oil in an office in Shepherd's Bush police station, sifting through the pages alone. Three insertions caught his eye, one for a spray and two for servicing. The name of the client merely read 'Citroen Freddie', plus the explanation, *paid in cash*. Freddie *who*? He would have to ask. One thing was certain: the answer wasn't long coming. How do I know that?

'Jack' told me, of course. Not immediately, but within a few weeks, while he was salivating over sultry Jo Marney, whose voice that night was as beguiling and seductive as ever, though I could have spoiled 'Jack's' evening by telling him that she was accounted for. But she was certainly a convenient distraction.

Three men worked at Wimpey Autos garage. All denied knowledge of the pistol and of ever encountering Frances Brown. Soon, like so many other suspects, they were eliminated from the murder investigation. But du Rose was harbouring a secret. He knew a Freddie who drove a Citroen Cadillac, a fellow Freemason. Now he was in a dilemma. He would have to tread carefully, which was against his nature because, by instinct, he was a cross between a bulldozer and a bulldog.

Fear and paranoia on the streets of west London mimicked the terrifying days of Jack the Ripper. Even the night fogs and smogs were as bad, adding atmospheric creepiness to the build-up to each disappearance and death, occurring almost on a three-monthly cycle, enabling the police and press to bang on endlessly about another murder being due or overdue. Everything about these serial killings was spooky and haunting.

The hookers kept a keen, twitchy eye on the calendar. Some refused to venture out when the date for a death approached, even if they were behind with the rent or it meant a beating from their ponce.

One of du Rose's first initiatives was to flood west London streets with decoy 'whores', all fearless policewomen volunteers from across London. Working in twos, the brief was to allow themselves to be propositioned by kerb-crawlers. Looking the part, dressed and painted as tarts, they discussed terms and conditions. They haggled, encouraging punters to discuss in detail their proclivities. 'Don't be shy, luv, just tell me *exactly* what you're looking for. Don't worry, I've heard everything before, so give it to me straight.' The patter had been rehearsed before they were sent forth to ferret. The men they were targeting were 'Deep Throat' bandits.

While the negotiating proceeded, one of the officers would casually wander to the rear of the vehicle, 'clocking' the registration number. Finally, they'd make an excuse not to chance a joyride and walk off, strutting their stuff once more.

One of the registration numbers of interest that popped up several times was a Citroen and the driver was readily recognisable.

'Want my autograph, sweetie? What am I doing? – Just soaking up the scenery. Girls, girls, girls.'

'Citroen Freddie'. Du Rose now knew a big fish had been caught in the net, a headache for him on a personal level.

# CHAPTER 17

# FREDDIE ENTERS THE RING

Most readers of this book, I suspect, will never have heard of Freddie Mills. He was a British boxer who punched above his weight. As a protagonist in this book, he also punches above his weight in the thickening plot. He is no lightweight among the cast of characters.

Britain wasn't noted for its pugilists, a sport monopolised at the top by Americans. Although big-hearted, our fighters tended to be big losers, especially in the ring of the world stage. However, in 1948 Mills became the world light-heavyweight champion of the world, defeating Gus Lesnevich. So home-bred Freddie was a world-conquering hero just at a time when Britain desperately needed an infusion of sporting cheer in the wake of a debilitating world war that had left the country on its knees, not buckling or in genuflection, from exhaustion and an economic haemorrhage.

Freddie was a national treasure long before this eulogy had

become a tired, meaningless cliché of a country running on tabloid hype. He had tousled, ruffled black hair, a craggy, trampled-over face, the crouched posture and freestyle action of a fairground prize fighter, and he was fearless to the point of recklessness.

'Fearless Freddie' dominated the back-page headlines during the days when he was mismatched by greedy promoters, who often upgraded him to the heavyweight division, having him brawl with opponents much heavier than he, by as much as four or five stones on some occasions. I say *brawl* consciously because Freddie *was* a brawler, a street fighter. He would dance from his corner, intent on attack and with contempt for defence; a charging warrior who would never retreat, even in the face of a machinegun-fire of punches. For Freddie, boxing was trench warfare: *over the top* and into the cannon's mouth, whatever the cost. Consequently, he absorbed an abundance of punishment, especially to his head, but took it with the resolve of a masochist. Some weeks he was overdosing on painkillers, combined with neat whisky, which resulted in his even forgetting where he lived while out and about in London.

The year he was crowned world champion coincided with his marriage to Chrissie McCorkindale. Chrissie, a divorcee, had been married to another boxer, Don McCorkindale, so she was used to sleeping beside a bruised and battered husband. Freddie was twenty-nine and had enough sense still left in his head to accept that his career in the ring wouldn't last much longer, if he wanted to retire while at the top and in command of most of his faculties; cauliflower ears couldn't be avoided, but a brain of mashed potatoes, hopefully, could still be thwarted.

So he invested in a Chinese restaurant at 143 Charing Cross Road in London; it was only a basement place, but so what? Much of London was underground. He had partners: Andrew Chin Guan Ho, manager; George Riley, a pet food merchant; and

Charles Luck, a civil engineer in Northamptonshire. Luck was the restaurant's licensee.

Very few champion sports personalities – especially boxers – know when to hang up their gloves: correction, they *know* when they *should* walk away from it, but common sense has been knocked out of them. The heat of the spotlight, the clang of the bell, the popping of photographers' flash-bulbs ringside, the sweat, the blood, the roar of the crowd, the referee holding up their arm in a victory salute, the exultation – it's another drug, such a variety of them about, as this book unmasks. Purple hearts feeding a lot of black hearts.

So Freddie decided on just one more fight. It was always *just one more*, one for the road, the one that can turn a fun night into a fiasco. Even the astute and highly intellectual Muhammad Ali duped himself with that *just one more* delusional mantra.

Freddie's biggest payday would be 24 January 1950; it would set him up for the rest of his life. He was to defend his world light-heavyweight crown at Earl's Court against the Italian/American Joey Maxim, who had honed his skills on the streets of a ghetto in Cleveland, Ohio, a neighbourhood of poor immigrants, where his opponents often had knives and he was armed only with knuckles. Always the knuckles won. In many ways this was to be a clash of similar styles: both men were sluggers. Maxim was only a year younger than Freddie and was considered the underdog, but only by the partisan British press.

Joey Maxim was an off-the-shelf name, so much more American than Giuseppe Antonio Berardinelli. Maxim was the name of a prototype machine-gun and aptly reflected Joey's speciality, a left jab that was unleashed with the repetitive speed of such a weapon. Nevertheless, the biased British predicted that 'Fearless Freddie' would be bathed in more glory; that's what he was brainwashed into believing by not only the media but his manager, an avaricious promoter, his sycophantic pals and the blinkered public.

The result: he was murdered: perhaps *murdered,* in the context of this narrative, isn't an appropriate description, but I'm sure it leaves the reader in no doubt of the nature of the contest. Freddie was floored, down and out, in the tenth round. At least he was alive and had a future, albeit a rollercoaster one and far from as planned, and with three of his teeth left embedded in one of Maxim's gloves. Missing teeth seem to have become a feature of this book, one way or another.

Right from the launch, it was obvious that the restaurant was never going to be a money-spinner, but Mills was undaunted in those everything-to-play-for days. Although he'd retired from the ring, he was still a marketable sports star, a celebrity, who was constantly appearing on TV chat shows and other variety programmes, plus as a pundit for newspapers when there was a big fight coming up on the sporting calendar. He was the ideal B-list celeb to open fêtes, new sports arenas, carnivals and commercial enterprises.

'Always friendly that Freddie,' was typical of the compliments you'd hear wherever he'd undertaken a public engagement. 'Always grinning. Always got a gag to tell.' It was true too; even if he had a humdinger of a headache – and he was haunted by those – he would still manage to retain the *cheerful chappie* public persona that made him so popular. In fact, most people assumed he was a cockney, especially when he began hanging out with the disreputable Kray twins, Ronnie and Reggie, but nothing could have been further from the truth. He was born and raised in sedate and stuffy Bournemouth, an image that this south-coast resort shed years ago.

After a few years following sporting retirement, the name Freddie Mills ceased to be such a marketable brand and he wasn't a natural entrepreneur. TV viewers began drawing producers' attention to Freddie's slur and mental sluggishness – not a result of over-indulging in alcohol, but punch-drunkenness. In that era, the damage that could be caused by incessant blows to the head that didn't result in concussion or unconsciousness was still not fully appreciated, even by neurologists. In layman's language, he'd been incrementally beaten batty.

The Kray family was collectively very fond of Freddie. In view of their record for sadism and thuggery, it's hard to imagine fondness as having a place in the Krays' makeup, but they were a boxing fraternity, it was in their blood. Although they respected – yes, *respected* – all boxers, Freddie was special to them. He was their kind of fighter. In other words, he was a bit 'mad'. The more he was hurt, the more he attacked. The more he was hit, the more he slugged back. Pain was painless to him. That doesn't make sense? Of course not, but it demonstrates the loveable side of his 'madness' and his affinity with the Krays.

So when the restaurant was floundering, the twins paid Freddie a visit, took him to one of the nearby snooker halls, and advised him to turn the basement premises into a nightclub. Now, *advice* from the Krays usually meant do it or you're dead, but this really was an example of their being solicitous; protective without demanding money for it – a freebie from those villains really was something special. Freddie vacillated. He knew nothing about running a nightclub. Not ones for pulling punches, just like Freddie, they told him that it seemed as if he knew even less about running a restaurant. He saw another obstacle. Didn't nightclubs become targets for the protection racket sharks?

'Yeah and that's us!' Ronnie laughed, with Reggie slapping his twin's back; what a breeze! 'That's the beauty of it for you, Freddie. You've nothing to fear from us. We'd never hurt you. And when others hear you have us for pals, then you're armour-plated.' This was an anecdote Freddie often repeated to friends, frequently the same ones, forgetting he'd already recounted it to them several times before. That head of his was leading him into trouble.

Freddie discussed the proposition in his south London home with wife Chrissie. She was diffident. The very nature of the business would mean that Freddie would inevitably be out all hours. Freddie countered that objection with the reasonable argument that he would be no more hands-on than with the management of the restaurant. He explained that he'd employ specialists at operating nightclubs in London's West End and he'd just be *The Name.* He was still delusional, though encouraged by hangers-on and spongers such as the Krays, in believing that the name Freddie Mills remained a seller and that it would put bums on seats and hands in pockets.

In his defence, Freddie wasn't a conceited man. On the contrary, he was practical, thankful for his good luck, and had invested in several properties in south London, faithful to the credo that bricks and mortar would always rise in value, but the downside was that he had no innate commercial acumen. As a boxer, he'd always been managed. Now he was a boss, he still needed managing. He was vulnerable and it was a role in which he was uneasy. In the ring, he never felt exposed, even when he dropped his guard. But to drop your guard in the predatory West End, especially in London's nightclubs racket of the 1960s, was a death wish.

Of one thing Mills was aware: the worst enemy you could have was the Krays. The best friend you could have, for personal and business protection, was also the Krays. So 'The Firm', as the Kray brothers were known in their territory, which spanned London east to west, had the final vote, after also applying considerable verbal pressure on Andy Ho, one of the partners in Freddie's restaurant.

## FREDDIE ENTERS THE RING

On the opening night of the Freddie Mills Nite Spot, the Krays were at the centre of a photocall, smart-suited as ever, and later they circulated, glad-handing like slick politicians. Not on view were the girls. They would be wheeled out later for the paying customers, the bread and butter. No West End nightclub had a chance of survival without a stable of 'hostesses'. As mentioned earlier, by tradition, they received no salary, so they were no liability to the club, but they demanded a fee from a customer for sitting with him, then haggled over bedroom rights. This was an issue between Freddie and his wife, who wasn't a West End kindred spirit, although she was au fait with London's nightlife.

Chrissie was also under no illusion about her rugged and no-frills husband. She loved him but not his foibles, of which there were many: the positive and negatives to his character were finely balanced. While working in TV, he'd had a number of affairs, most of them not much more than one-night trysts. Now, though, he was no longer a trophy. Any woman bragging that she'd *had* Freddie Mills, would be asked curiously, 'Freddie *who?*' He was yesterday's mutton. And so he'd started paying for it, doing the club circuit, purchasing his sexual pleasure off the shelf, arriving home at dawn in summer and end of the night in winter, lying that he'd been carousing with pals, playing snooker or poker. But sex has its own aroma and its smell was not lost of Chrissie. All wives are finely tuned to another woman's perfume.

Chrissie began checking up on him, in addition to her alternate Saturday nights, when she would meet Freddie at the club around eleven o'clock. At other times, she'd drive over Waterloo Bridge to the Nite Spot around midnight, but mostly he wasn't there. Ho would cover for him, telling Chrissie that he was 'down the road' at an 'all-male' billiards and snooker saloon. Of course she wasn't fooled. She might stay for a drink or two, hoping for Freddie to show up, but by one or two o'clock she'd slink off dejectedly, hearing the hostesses sniggering, and, perhaps paranoid, though with ample justification, suspect they were laughing at her, the wife who was futilely trying to rein-in her husband.

There were a plethora of rumours in orbit and Chrissie couldn't have missed many of them: Freddie was bi-sexual (correct), he was Ronnie Kray's lover (untrue), he had a homosexual affair with the crooner Michael Holliday, who had two number-one hit singles (true), he had sex numerous times with a girl young enough to be his daughter (correct), he was a mug punter, haemorrhaging money by the truck-load at cards, on the horses and dogs, two cockroaches scuttling across his club's kitchen (true, encouraged by his Chinese associates), and his favourite party trick was to flash his penis and invite all women present to 'wrap a big smile around that' (apparently also true).

Mandy Rice-Davies, of Christine Keeler/John Profumo infamy, was heard to say, 'It was huge enough to choke a woman!' Very prophetic.

Mandy had been booked at Freddie's Nite Spot as cabaret singer for a week. Unfortunately, the titillating event turned both farcical and sour when an advertisement in the London *Evening News* announced her as *Mangy* Rice-Davies. I interviewed Mandy for the *Sunday Express,* when this very right-wing newspaper was edited by the eccentric John Junor. The feature article was commissioned by a middle-ranking editorial executive for the 'Meeting People' regular column. Junor was extremely bigoted and wouldn't have anyone featured in his columns if he disliked them, such as gays and socialists and social agitators, no matter how newsworthy or famous. Unknown to the commissioning editor, Junor despised Mandy Rice-Davies and didn't want his readers corrupted by her free-spirited adventures, though he was perfectly content to give room and a warm handshake to 'poor, victimised Profumo', though he would have kicked Stephen Ward into the gutter.

Anyhow, I met Mandy in the clubby bar – soft leather armchairs and sofas – of the Waldorf Hotel in the Aldwych, where I'd booked a table for lunch. She drank a couple of whisky sours on the rocks and thereafter champagne, all of this before eating. Of course the interview wasn't especially about Freddie Mills, but she mentioned him while gossiping about men in general who had made an impression with her.

'There was definitely something sinister and even frightening about Freddie, in addition to his being a rather loveable rogue,' she trilled mischievously during her second whisky sour. 'In fact, I'd go further; he was dangerous and that appeals to women – well, *me!*' Did she fall for him? 'Depends what you mean by that. Did we have an affair? – No. Did we fuck? – No. Did we have sex? – Yes. Well, let's say *he* did. It didn't happen many times because he was so one-dimensional and gave me no satisfaction whatsoever. Same as Peter (Rachman), but he was much richer, of course, so he was worth tolerating.

'I should have asked Freddie for payment, boredom money. He got off on oral sex, over and over. He didn't want to give me anything in return; I mean physically. He was also pretty rough with it, too. I know it's bad form to speak ill of the dead, but it's better than speaking ill of the living, which is the cross I bear quite happily. Towards the end each time he got a wee bit too out of control, gripping my head with both hands, shuddering like he was having some kind of spasm, and not letting me go. I ended up gasping for air and the third occasion was enough for me, but he did have a certain animal magnetism, reminding me of Tarzan the Ape Man and I think I'd have enjoyed normal sex – whatever that is! – with him, but he must have reserved that just for his wife. I mean, he did have kids.

'When I was pissed one night, I did mention to him the rumour of his liking for men and he told me to "shut my dirty bitch mouth", so I said he could wank himself in future. I just have no control over my mouth; it runs on its own momentum and whims. I just listen in horror sometimes, so I was expecting a left jab to my big mouth, but he just burst out laughing, saying, "I might just do that as a cabaret act at the club if you promise to watch." I'll never just roll over and be an easy ride.'

Relevant to this book, though perhaps not readily apparent, was her opinion of the police, particularly as her father was a country copper. 'I hate their rotten guts, especially those bent bastards Herbert (Detective Chief Inspector Samuel Herbert) and his batman Burrows (Detective Sergeant John Burrows). Scotland Yard is a mafia. They're very different from provincial coppers; two different breeds. Scotland Yard detectives have fashioned themselves on New York cops.' Bear in mind that this was more than forty years ago.

Mills was very friendly with comedian Bob Monkhouse. There is a very telling quote in James Morton's book, *Gangland Soho* (Piatkus, 2008), in which Monkhouse, talking of Freddie, says to the author, 'I heard he was less interested in penetration, more in a Clinton-Lewinsky type of activity,' a reference, of course, to the US President Bill Clinton having oral sex in the White House with luscious-lipped Monica, an intern at the time.

There is a very convincing reason why Monkhouse's insight into Freddie's personality and habits should be taken very seriously, which I shall highlight shortly. He further told Morton, 'Freddie had a very dark side. Freddie had male companions and he also consorted with a number of ladies on a casual basis. He'd try anything. With some people when they become famous they feel the right to have anything they want.

'I didn't see him do it, but the story was that Freddie Mills was quite capable of whipping it out and saying, "Wrap a big smile around that." He'd expose himself in front of anybody. He didn't bother to go to the gents.'

All this and events following 24 November 1964 took on a whole new dimension. So what *did* happen that 24 November? Well, at Freemason's Hall in Great Queen Street, London, Freddie was initiated into the Chelsea Lodge (No. 3098). This was then – and still is today – a Freemasons' Lodge for entertainers, meeting formally five times a year for ritual ceremonies.

Mills was proposed as an Initiate by Andy Ho and his nomination was seconded by the musician Judd Solo. Ho was entitled to be a member of this Lodge because, in addition to being a partner in Freddie's club, he had also appeared in numerous movies, if only in walk-on parts and cameo roles. Monkhouse was there that evening and was one of the first to congratulate Freddie on becoming a 'Brother', owing allegiance to one another, in all undertakings legal. Singer Issy Bonn was Master of the Lodge. The Master asked Mills, 'Do you seriously declare on your honour that, unbiased by the improper salutations of friends against your own inclination, and uninfluenced by mercenary and other unworthy motive, you freely and voluntarily offer yourself as a Candidate for the mysteries and privileges of Freemasonry?'

He replied, in front of all members in their regalia, 'I do.'

Bonn told Mills that Freemasonry was 'founded on the purest principles of piety and virtue,' adding, 'it possesses great and invaluable privileges, and in order to secure these privileges to worthy men, and we trust to worthy men alone, vows of fidelity are required...' After taking the 'solemn oath', this *celebrated* lecher kissed the Bible, known in Freemasonry as the Sacred Law.

Months earlier, Mills had been interviewed by the Lodge's management committee, a routine procedure when someone was seeking to join the fraternity. Before this meeting, rigorous inquiries would have been made to establish his character, taking every precaution to try to ensure that he wouldn't be a disgrace to that particular Lodge and Freemasonry in general. Ho, as the proposer, attended that meeting and spoke highly of Mills' 'good name', a man who was 'adored' by households all over the country. Ho expressed his opinion that it would be a 'coup' for the Chelsea Lodge to have Mills among its fold.

Mills was asked his reasons for seeking to become a Mason. Whatever he answered to that question, it wouldn't have been for self-advancement in business or to ingratiate himself with senior police officers, or indeed for self-aggrandisement, otherwise his application would have come up against the buffers promptly. Ho would have primed him what to say and what to meticulously eschew. Certainly he would have had to pledge that he believed in God; that was an imperative. Today it would be sufficient to merely declare a belief in a superior being.

It is difficult to accept that at least a couple of members of the Lodge, all being involved in some form of entertainment and showbiz, hadn't witnessed Mills' extraordinary outré behaviour or at least heard the outrageous stories doing the rounds on the ever-current and updated grapevine about this incorrigible roué. Mills was worse than a rake; he was a dissolute dog, to put it bluntly. A dog with the purr of a cat when required and the instinct of a wolf, always. Certainly Ho knew enough about Mills to make him an undesirable for such an august and morality-based institution, with royalty at its helm. Indeed, at his initiation, Mills was informed that 'to so high an eminence has its credit been advanced [Freemasonry] that in every age monarchs themselves have been promoters of the Craft, have not thought it derogatory to exchange the sceptre for the trowel...'

Writer Dea Langmead wrote a letter to author James Morton about a visit to Mills' club, in part describing it like this: 'I seem to remember some black ties and also suits – no hard and fast rules, apparently – I know I went with a "suit" – and there were tables and a small dance floor and a live band. There were girls sitting at the bar and cute waitresses and various brawny, muscular men, and a strange air of it not being quite a top-class venue. I think I felt a bit shivery and daring in being there at all, as if rubbing shoulders with the underworld, and if it had been a bit pricey I wouldn't have been invited.'

Refocusing on the 'Nudes' murders, there are some critical alleged confessions in the public domain by singer Michael Holliday and pianist Russ Conway that give immense circumstantial credence to what I heard years earlier from a pivotal and inviolate source, 'Jack'. Mills and Holliday would hire hostesses from one of the West End clubs for a 'sex party'. These orgies would convene in Holliday's luxury apartment or the flat of one of the prostitutes.

The girls, for a brokered fee, had to be prepared to participate in sado/masochistic games, allowing themselves to be spanked, belted and tied-up. When the two men tired of that sequence of the 'party', they would then have sex with each other, while the girls egged them on and indulged in lesbian tricks, sometimes using riding crops to spur on the proceedings. Now, consistent through every sexual anecdote about Mills' proclivities has been his requisite for oral sex and this was an obligation for the girls who were rented; it was a clause in the verbal contract before any arrangement was finalised.

If a few girls couldn't be rounded up from the nightclubs, Freddie would say to Michael, 'Leave it to me. I know where I can collect a carload from the street. You get the bed warm and I'll be back with a harem in half an hour.' And he would be, with what he chuckling called a 'chorus line-up'.

Now to the seminal issue: on one occasion, a prostitute, plucked from the streets, passed out while Mills was being over-vigorous while enlarged in her mouth; there is no means of sanitising this, unfortunately. The story goes that she gasped and her eyes shot up into her head, but Mills wouldn't stop. Apparently, in Holliday's version, 'he was too far gone.' Holliday claimed to have endeavoured to pull him off, but Mills was beyond the rubicon and the whore died. Panic time!

Holliday is reputed to have repeated this version of horrific events to two people: world-renowned pop pianist Russ Conway and singer Dorothy Squires, whose marriage to Roger Moore, later of *James Bond* fame, was in the process of being shipwrecked on the rocks of infidelity. Now this indecent anecdote is independent of Mandy Rice-Davies's alarming experience and *facts* known to Bob Monkhouse.

When the two men realised that the woman was dead, Holliday, in frenetic, demented mode, wanted to call an ambulance and the police. Mills is said to have replied, 'Don't be such a fucking twat! If this gets out, we're both finished for ever. Even though it was an accident, there'll be no way back, for you just as much as for me. We're in this together, up to our necks.' If all accounts are correct, Mills assured Holliday that he could dispose of the body without it being 'a problem'. Horrified, Holliday didn't want any more to do with it and left Mills to see through his plan. Fortunately for them, there was no one else present; there was only one girl at this 'death party'.

In part, this outrage is related in *The Soho Don* by Michael Connor (Mainstream Publishing, 2002) and *Gangland Soho* (2008), already mentioned, by James Morton. But neither of them had access to an officer who worked the 'Nudes' case, so were not familiar with the method of disposing of the body nor the connection with the 'Jack the Stripper' murders. The body of the prostitute who died in the company of Mills and

Holliday went into the Thames, as a precursor, one might reasonably surmise.

Holliday, not surprisingly, was unnerved by the whole experience and Mills' disregard, verging on contempt, for human life, and this was why he sought a camaraderie 'confessional' with his confidants Conway and Squires, who both resented being drawn into a conspiracy of silence over something of such magnitude. Placed in such an invidious quandary of betraying their long-standing friend, Holliday, or betraying him by doing their moral and public duty, they opted temporarily and reluctantly to remain staunchly true to their companion, but their moratorium was quickly overtaken by unforeseen events.

Conway strenuously advised Holliday to cut all ties with Mills, but this wasn't easy to accomplish: there was still a strong emotional bond between the two men and Freddie could be both possessive and aggressive, so the cooling process had to be achieved by almost imperceptible increments.

Mills sensed Holliday's affections for him were waning, so promised to tone down the 'rough stuff', but when he was in a 'sexual fever' – Jack's phrase – he couldn't restrain himself and yet a second woman died during a bedroom romp. She, too, was dropped up river into the Thames. Both deaths were written off as suicides without even a post-mortem: fingerprints identified them as prostitutes with a string of convictions for soliciting. Doubtlessly they were dismissed as just more of the capital's flotsam. Holliday was so distressed that he decided he had only two alternatives: to go to the police or take his life. He chose the latter and overdosed.

For centuries the Thames in London has been an attraction for suicides, and bodies regularly fished from the river, in the murky past, were perfunctorily logged as 'selfies', unless there were external physical injuries to suggest foul play. In Victorian times, London's Thames was known as 'A Helping Hand for Prostitutes'. A poem, 'Bridge of Sighs' by Thomas Hood (1844), begins:

> One more Unfortunate,
> Weary of breath,
> Rashly importunate,
> Gone to her death!
>
> Take her up tenderly,
> Lift her with care;
> Fashion'd so slenderly
> Young, and so fair!

One has to understand the 1960s and keep Mills' killings within context to appreciate how it was possible for him to continue so long undetected. Prostitutes drowning themselves was commonplace. To begin with, there would be no marks or wounds on the bodies to hint at violence. 'Deep Throat' murder – choked by a penis – was unheard of and almost impossible to detect; not something any pathologist of the time would have thought of looking for. The only marks on the first two prostitutes Mills killed were weals and bruises on their buttocks, consistent with the trade the women were running, in the eyes of the law. In this sense, one should not judge the police harshly. They were simply playing the percentages when bogged down with an insurmountable workload.

Although Mills was said to be devastated by Holliday's death, there must also have been a veiled sense of relief and a feeling that he was now in the clear. The only eyewitness had removed himself, so the ambivalence for Mills would have been of grief and gratitude, a volatile tug of war. As for being in the clear, he hadn't taken into account his own intrinsic propensity for dangerous sex by enforcement; that would never change because it was embedded in his dark side, to which Bob Monkhouse alluded. In that respect, Holliday's death didn't change a thing. The reality is that Mills was already on the treadmill to becoming a serial killer before the first body in the official tally came in with the morning tide.

Despite the demise of Holliday, there were still people around who guessed the harrowing truth about Mills, but to them he was of more value on the streets than behind bars. Blackmail could be very lucrative, especially if you were one of the 'elite' senior police officers with plenty of 'covering fire', or a much-feared gang master with London's West End your fiefdom.

## CHAPTER 18

# HER DEATH WAS GREATLY EXAGGERATED

O n Sunday, 21 March 1965, the national newspapers ran a story intimating that the west London serial killer had almost certainly struck again. Scotland Yard named the probable victim as prostitute Susan 'Goldie' Smith, a twenty-five-year-old brunette.

Smith, who had been a close friend of Frances Brown (Margaret McGowan), had been missing from the streets of west London, her regular stamping ground, for seventeen days. If alive, how was she living and where? She was last seen leaving the Warwick Castle pub in the Portobello Road, Notting Hill. This, of course, was the pub where most of the geese (medieval English slang for whores) socialised during a boozy truce before going into cut-throat war on the streets.

My assignment was to take the story a stage further. Before leaving the office I unsuccessfully tried contacting 'Jack'. The starting point, obviously, was the Warwick Castle. Sunday lunchtime trade was brisk. After buying a drink, I circulated. Of course it was far too early in the day for the geese to be up and about, preening themselves. As soon as I started flashing a photo of Goldie, the atmosphere darkened as the tipplers suspected me of being Old Bill.

'Do I look like a cop?' I asked plaintively.

''Course you do, you're wearing a suit,' said the joker in the pack. 'Being a short-arse don't fool anyone around here.'

Someone else chipped in, 'Sneaky Old Bill even uses dwarfs from circuses to trick people into rabbiting too much.'

But as soon as I started buying them all drinks the mood changed. All suspicion blown away. 'He can't be Old Bill; no copper ever puts his hands in his *own* pocket.' Laughter. I was in business, one of the muckers.

The drinkers at the bar began passing round the photo. 'Yeah, that's Goldie all right,' said one. 'Not been in lately, has she?' None of them read newspapers so they weren't aware of the public appeal from Scotland Yard.

'She used to come in every evening, then stopped, as sudden as *that*,' said the barman, snapping his fingers.

'I reckon she must have gone to a monastery to repent.'

'More likely to give them monks an evening service they'd never forget,' the joker quipped.

*Patience! Patience! Let them dictate the pace. There's no rush. Deadline is hours away.*

'I saw her only last Wednesday.' Silence. This sudden outburst of news came from a Jamaican who was at a table beside a frosted window. He was all smiles, dazzling white teeth and calypso carefree. I joined him, shook hands, then asked, 'Where?'

'In the Atlantic pub in Brixton High Street. She was sitting between two English men. One was about forty and the other forty-five.' His friend, Reoy Vincent, said, 'The police questioned me because they were told I knew Susan. My wife was sick with worry.'

Sheffield-born Susan was nicknamed 'Goldie' because of the gold-coloured dress she wore frequently.

The most useful information came from a man who, until that point, had remained silent. 'If you really want to find Goldie, go to the Atlantic pub at nine tonight. She's done a runner to Brixton with her fella, whatever you like to call him. None of my business. She carouses from nine till ten before wiggling her bum up and down the High Street. I've been with her a couple of times down there. She's value for money, despite being bloody ugly.' Raucous laughter. Naturally enough, he wouldn't give me his name.

I returned to the office chuffed and went into a corner of the busy newsroom with Ken James, who seemed more hyper and stressed than ever. I confided that I had good reason to believe that Goldie hadn't been murdered and I banked on finding her alive and well in Brixton, south London, that evening. I thought his frog eyes were going to jump out of their sockets. I believe his first words were framed as a question: 'How did you get this drunk so early on a Sunday?'

After giving him a clinical rundown of the verbal stepping-stone gravitation towards Brixton, I still don't think he harboured an abundance of confidence. How could I do it in a few hours if it was impossible for Scotland Yard with all their resources? The man's delusional (that's me). Despite his scepticism and reservations, he assigned me a car and photographer Len Blandford – I'd worked with him many times before and he was a gem of a professional, especially when it came to snatch-photography, snapping from the hip without the subject realising that the hanging camera was aimed at him/her and firing. Sneaky but an essential black art at times.

Before setting off to Brixton at around eight, I again tried to reach 'Jack', but without joy. No doubt he was on the Goldie hunt, too, I reasoned.

The evening was damp and cold. Very black. A starless canopy was over the capital like a chilly, wet flannel, slightly porous, allowing droplets of rain to slip through. Certainly there was no suggestion of spring in the air. I even believe Len thought this venture was an artifice of mine to escape the office, distancing ourselves from the typical crappy stories that tended to distinguish Sundays from the rest of the week.

'Do we have a plan?' he wondered, almost mockingly.

'Yes, we settle ourselves in a warm pub, just drinking and waiting.' This news cheered him no end. 'I've no complaints about that. *Any* old pub or one in particular?' Len was blessed with a wry sense of humour.

'The Atlantic,' I replied, leading the way. As soon as we were inside and had bought our drinks, which took some time because the place was heaving, I said, 'She should be here at nine,'

'Only time for one drink, then,' he observed sadly.

Another wrong assumption. Metaphorically, the clock struck nine. Nine-fifteen, still no gold rush. Was there another bar? I carried out a recce. No, there wasn't. 'Let's take a walk,' I suggested.

With Len shouldering his heavy camera gear, fitted with flash and all cocked, ready to fire, we were sucked out into the soulless High Street by the wind. Brixton bore no resemblance to paradise even on warm, sunny evenings. The immediate question was which way to wander. Without a word of communication, we mutually turned left. We couldn't have gone more than fifty yards when I saw a woman hurrying towards us, head down, windswept and with ridiculously high heels click-clacking along the pot-holed pavement. As her face became illuminated under an amber street lamp, I knew that this was *murder victim* Goldie.

'Susan?' I said, blocking her path.

Halting and surprised, she said, 'Yes,' looking from me to Len and then back to me. The *yes* carried the question, *And who the hell are you and what do you want?*

At that moment, as if scripted and synchronised, a car pulled up kerbside and out stepped none other than 'Jack'.

*Shit!* I thought, visualising Goldie being carted off without a chance to interview her, scoop evaporating into the ether.

After holding his Scotland Yard ID card to Goldie's pallid face, he ordered her not to move. Turning to me, he said, semi-seething, 'What the fuck are you doing here?'

'Same as you, it seems,' I answered equably.

'I don't want you buggering up this whole thing.'

'What's the beef?' I challenged. 'We've found her safe. Isn't that the issue, the good news for once and all that matters?'

'No!' he retorted, rattled. '*I'm* supposed to have rescued her.'

Ah! Now I began to see. 'So this was a put-up job, a Yard PR exercise. You pretend she's probably dead, then along comes the cavalry to the rescue and the press coverage is not only positive for a change but tinsel-wrapped with praise. The glory boys!'

'OK,' he said, cooling down, 'let's share the spoils. Jump in the back of my car, the pair of you', meaning Len and myself.

Turning to Goldie, he said tersely, 'I want you in the front' (I bet she'd heard that more than a few times).

'Where are you taking me?' she enquired nervously.

'Home,' he said. 'To *your* home.'

Without asking for her address, 'Jack' drove directly to a house in Kemerton Road, where she lived. *Strange.* If she was genuinely missing and Scotland Yard feared she'd been murdered and 'Jack' had only chanced upon her then, like us, how did he know her current address, without asking for directions? Another mystery within a mystery. *Careless, 'Jack'. Not like you to be so slipshod...* 'Slipshod', there's a Masonic term to ponder.

In the car, Goldie told me, 'I haven't read any of the newspapers today. I don't know what all the fuss is about. I left Notting Hill on 4 March to stay with a friend in Brixton. If I'd known all about the anxiety I was causing, I would have gone straight to the police' (of course you would have!). That's what prostitutes do; find me a nice policeman. Really! Equivalent to saying, 'If I'd known you were coming, I'd have baked a cake.'

'I don't think I have been in any danger,' she went on. 'But I'm glad you found me so this whole trouble can be cleared up.' She didn't look *glad,* more glum. She was probably counting the cost of losing a night's earnings, thanks to us.

As we pulled up in Kemerton Road, I asked 'Jack', 'What now?'

'I'll just take her inside, have a look around, see that everything's hunky-dory, then take her to Brixton police station and get her to make a short statement. Do everything by the book, just for the record. Admin, admin, worse than Chinese water-drip torture.'

So this was *doing everything by the book!*

Len and I were left to hack it back to our car, but no complaints from us; it had been a positive day's work. All wrapped up just in time to catch the first edition of Monday morning's *Sun.* Yet the whole affair wreaked of a stunt, a set-up. Of course the murder squad were aware that Goldie had come to no harm and had simply changed address.

To 'Big John' du Rose it was simply another cynical, publicity-grabbing exercise, regardless of the distress caused to others. What he hadn't planned for was 'Goldie' being found by a journalist and for the journalist's newspaper to steal the kudos right from under the nose of his elite boys. Although he didn't take kindly to being upstaged, he saw the advantages of having a journalist magpie to whom he could feed crumbs through a trusty conduit, 'Jack'.

*It takes a thief to catch a thief. But does it take a murderer to catch a murderer?* There are some people, with knowledge, who would argue that such a proposition is not so outlandish as it may at first seem, but that's a theme for another book, not this one.

*Tuesday, 23 March, 10 a.m.*

A reporter, holding up a phone in the newsroom, called to me, 'It's a Detective Sergeant Berry for you, Mike.'

The fact that 'Jack' had used his real name and rank warned me immediately that the call was either being electronically recorded or it was being listened to by others via some form of internal link.

'Hello,' I said neutrally.

'Is that Mr Litchfield? This is Detective Sergeant Berry.'

'So I understand,' I said. 'How are you today after your long night?'

'Sidestepping my small talk, he said, 'My boss [du Rose] wants to know what the blazes is going on?'

'About what exactly?' Returning serve on the volley.

'About what's on the front page of your newspaper.'

'It's self-explanatory,' I said.

A hiatus. He was obviously taking instructions.

'Look, there's no problem this end, Mike.' Now it was the chummy *Mike* approach, clearly decreed by Big John. 'It's just that we're in the dark as how you came to be in Brixton with such perfect timing.'

'I just did my job, Bob (if I was *Mike*, then it cut both ways). I spent time and money in the Warwick Castle at lunchtime.'

'And someone knew her movements and whereabouts?'

'Correct.'

'Did he show a particular interest in the "Nudes" case?'

'No.'

'He didn't fish around for more info on what you or we knew about the killer?'

'No, not at all.'

'Was he white?'

'No. A Jamaican.'

'Oh, well!' He'd lost interest. At least I'd just learned that the police had reason to *know* that the killer was a Caucasian. 'As I said, the boss isn't upset by your story,' – I contained my mirth – 'but he wishes you'd operate through us so that we don't go treading on each other's toes. But we do want to keep you on board.'

Well, well, from suspect to honorary member of the murder squad. Some promotion! The objective, of course, was to keep me corralled. No chance!

'Got it?' 'Jack' said, the inflexion unmistakable.

I had *got it*. 'Jack' was coding me the message to stay in close contact with him. In the circumstances I couldn't tell him I'd twice tried reaching him before setting off for Brixton the previous evening.

'I'll bear that in mind,' I said, quickly adding, 'Incidentally, what's happened to Goldie?'

'She was driven home in the early hours after being given an official warning about soliciting. We went through the motions. Waste of valuable breath, though. She'll be out on the High Street tonight, like clockwork, tanked up on scotch or vodka. But with luck she'll avoid the west London creeper.'

'Anything else?'

'Not yet. Soon, maybe.'

Call over.

'Another complaint?' James boomed from his squeaky leather throne, beaming with good cheer for a change.

'No, just the Yard trying to pick my brains.'

'No wonder the call was so short.'

Usual boring newsroom banter, reminiscent of my school playground – a cloistered quad – during morning milk break.

* * *

The Heron Trading Estate comprised thirty-five factories constructed around a sports ground for the workers. There was lots of waste ground and weedy undergrowth between the buildings, plus a network of private roads. Altogether more than seven thousand men and women were employed on this industrial estate in Acton. Also it was freely used day and night by the general public, sometimes as a shortcut but more often as a quiet place during darkness for sexual activity in cars or on the ground around the sports area.

Referring to the inch-by-inch search of this estate during many weeks, du Rose was to report, 'Finally, and strangely enough, at the remotest end of the search area, we came up with the paint-pattern we were seeking. This was found a short distance from where Bridie O'Hara's body had probably lain for two weeks before being moved. It appeared to have been hidden at the site of a transformer at the rear of a factory... It faced a paint-spray shop!'

He went on, 'All the globules of paint matched and the substances that made up the dust on Bridie's body were in the right proportions. When the area was tested, it was found that the spray-pattern became fainter as one moved further from this spot and eventually disappeared after a few hundred yards, so it was clear that the bodies on which the pattern was shown had been kept within close range of this particular paint shop.'

The police scientists were able to pinpoint the exact spot where O'Hara's body had been kept, yet all this scientific data proved useless, as admitted by du Rose: 'It transpired eventually that the paint shop was purely incidental to the killing. It did not lead us to the killer, although he must have had some association with the factory estate.'

Untrue. It was the other way round: the prostitutes had carnal *knowledge* of the estate: it was one of their regular haunts for enacting business and they directed clients there. This popular choice of venue among the demimonde was logical. Few people, if any, were around on the industrial site at night and the access road and sports ground were deserted.

However, the investigation did turn up one macabre and eerie coincidence. A former employee of the Heron Industrial Estate was the one-time Special Constable and serial killer John Christie, of that chilling address, 10 Rillington Place, the epicentre of numerous movies and books. His victims numbered at least eight, but he was not in the frame this time: he'd been hanged at Pentonville Prison on 15 July 1953, aged fifty-four.

## CHAPTER 19

# THE BEGINNING OF THE END

On Friday, 16 July 1965, Andy Ho was just in the laborious process of opening Freddie Mills' Nite Spot when he had an unexpected early 'customer'.

The hostesses were just gathering, gossiping with the barman, who was arranging champagne glasses and giving them a polish to ensure they glittered like crystal. His next task would be to count the number of champagne bottles. Generally, Friday nights were best for trade – for the girls-for-hire as well as the club, though business was always slack during the summer months and little was predictable.

Henry Grant, the head waiter, was fussily re-arranging tables. The tall, burly 'customer' approached the doorman, Bob Deacon, and said he wanted to speak with Ho. The response was a dismissive Mr Ho was busy. This was followed by a Raymond Chandler sequence. 'He's not too busy to see me,' said 'Jack', Scotland Yard ID card pointed like a loaded gun at Deacon's eyes.

Ho, blanching and agitated, was quickly produced from his den, most probably anticipating being hit by another summons. The club had been going through a rough patch with legal actions against the proprietors for breach of licensing laws and other niggly but time-consuming legalities. But 'Jack' was on a very different mission. Stooping to bring his large head close to the little Chinaman's face, he hissed, 'I have a message from my boss for Mr Mills. Tell him, "We know." Got it?'

'Jack', known humorously among his colleagues as 'Tombstone Face', could turn anyone to stone when treating them to his intimidating stare.

Ho was so frightened that 'Jack' had to repeat himself, ending with, 'Have you got that now?'

Ho answered querulously, reassuring that he'd heard correctly and the message was *we know*. 'Jack' emphasised that the message was from his boss, adding, 'Mr Mills will know who that is. Clear?'

'Yes, sir; yes, sir; very clear.'

'Jack' turned on his heels and departed. After going to his unmarked car, parked in Tottenham Court Road towards the Leicester Square end, he climbed behind the wheel and waited. Further up the road two more murder-squad pool cars were poised. A further two were waiting in the Bayswater Road, plus a couple of vans near Notting Hill Gate.

Just before eleven o'clock, Mills' silver-grey Citroen passed 'Jack' and turned into Goslett Yard, a mews behind the club. 'Jack' and the others waited and waited. 'Jack' knew that the message would have been passed to Mills the moment he walked into the club. He also knew that Freddie would realise that 'Jack' was merely the messenger and the menacing warning had come from fellow Freemason du Rose.

Now what will he do? 'Jack' was thinking. The expectation was that he would react exactly as he was known to respond under duress: he would down between three and six double whiskies in machine-gun rapidity, then go out on the prowl, a sexual predator. Maybe he would go to another nightclub to hire a hostess or, if in a hurry and desperate for carnal relief, drive west for a quick street-pickup.

Midnight arrived and the cabaret began. Mills always liked to watch the cabaret and lead the boisterous applause, boosting morale. Just after twelve-thirty, the Citroen nosed out into Tottenham Court Road, turning left. Driving erratically, obviously drunk, he headed at speed for Oxford Street, which in those days was an unimpeded thoroughfare all the way to Marble Arch. The other two murder squad cars in Tottenham Court Road were also on the move. A trick they employed was to keep passing the car being followed in order to allay any suspicion that the subject might have about being tailed.

Mills circled Marble Arch and cruised along Queensway and into the Bayswater Road, where he was almost immediately flagged down by a streetwalker. He slowed to almost a standstill, made an appraisal, then accelerated away. This whore was tall. The 'Nude' killer was known to favour his victims short and more vulnerable.

Just before Notting Hill Gate Tube station, Mills slammed on the brakes, halted and performed a tight classic movie U-turn in one manoeuvre. *He's sussed us,* 'Jack' lamented to himself. The now not-so-undercover cops had no option but to copy.

Mills headed back to his club. Around four-thirty he was on the move once more, this time crossing Waterloo Bridge and making for home at a leisurely, despondent pace. As for 'Jack' and his team, the night hadn't been a washout, although they were bushed from lack of sleep. The main achievement was that Freddie had got the *message*. He was a marked man and, most importantly, he knew he was.

On the following Monday morning, du Rose received a phone call from Bob Monkhouse, who said that Freddie Mills wanted a meeting with him, just the two of them, and not in a police station or anywhere near Scotland Yard.

'When?' du Rose replied curtly.

'Anywhere, anytime. At your convenience, but it's urgent,' said Monkhouse.

Du Rose mulled over the proposition at length. Of course there was no possibility of his declining, but the venue could be all-important; it needed to be genuinely neutral territory and somewhere they both felt comfortable, especially Mills. Finally du Rose settled on the intimate Champagne Bar at the Connaught Rooms, part of Freemasons' Hall, the HQ of the Grand Lodge of England, in Great Queen Street. 'Seven o'clock tonight.'

'Freddie will be there,' Monkhouse guaranteed.

To reach the snug Champagne Bar you mounted the steps at the imposing entrance, turned right on entering the stately edifice and it was a few yards along on the left. The bar's décor comprised a number of alcoves decorated in pastel-shaded elegance that provided privacy, despite their close proximity to the small bar, which was manned by a white-jacketed young employee who wasn't a Freemason but who was immensely popular with the fraternity he served.

Du Rose arrived early, suited and FBI smart and clean-cut, though on the portly side. Freddie breezed in at seven, shook hands vigorously with the barman and larked about, pretending to spar with him. Du Rose had already bought a glass of bubbly for Freddie and they greeted one another cordially, brother to brother.

Du Rose intimated that he was pleased that Freddie had made contact rather than the other way round: 'we're coming for you.' The *coming for you* would have resonated with Freddie, punching home the enormity of the consequences of this proposed heart-spilling encounter.

Freddie's mood changed almost immediately, as if a black cloud had suddenly eclipsed the sun on an otherwise bright summer evening. Agitated and emotional, he began rambling, gulping down painkillers with the champagne, which du Rose advised him was a bad idea, but Freddie wasn't listening, just talking. What followed was a sob story without the sobs.

Everything had gone wrong in his life, ever since TV work had dried up and he'd gone into property speculation and then the restaurant and nightclub business. 'What a bleeding fiasco that's been!' But the worst bleeding had come from du Rose's own bloodsuckers, he said. 'Leeches, the whole lot of them!' At this point, du Rose asked for clarification.

'As if you don't know!' Freddie had said scornfully, believing that du Rose was taking him for a fool.

Du Rose had pleaded innocence, leading to a muffled barrage of expletives. 'You must know all about those bastards Virgo [Wally, Commander of the Serious Crime Squad] and Drury [Kenneth, Head of the Flying Squad]. They're rotten to the core. Your crowd's contaminated, Johnny. How the fuck did they get into Masonry? I thought we were supposed to be brothers in arms.'

'Only in lawful pursuits,' du Rose had reminded him.

'Exactly! So how come those two crooks are tolerated?' Freddie retorted, seething. 'What's lawful about blackmail?' He claimed that 'for years' he'd been 'bled dry' by Scotland Yard's blackmailers and money collectors. This certainly has the ring of truth. A few years later, both Drury and Virgo were gaoled for corruption, accepting bribes. Every Wednesday, for example, a detective constable from West End Central police station would visit each retailer of porn material in Soho and collect a brown envelope stuffed with cash, a pre-arranged fee. Anyone who failed to pay had his premises raided by officers from West End Central and all magazines and films would be confiscated. The only way the porn pedlars could then stay in business was to buy back the material from the police at an extortionate price. If an official complaint was lodged, that person would be arrested, with guns or drugs planted in his shop and home; alternatively, he could be visited by the gangsters who worked for the Kray twins. By undertaking 'rough-up' jobs for crooked senior police officers, the Krays were able to remain at large, much to the chagrin of the honest few among the Scotland Yard hierarchy, such as 'Nipper' Read, who did finally, through dogged persistence, topple the Krays and their seemingly impervious wall of protection.

Du Rose probed around the wrinkly edges of what Virgo, and Drury allegedly 'had on' Freddie in order for such alleged blackmail to be possible.

July was 'out of season' for Freemasonry, so the building was quiet and they had the Champagne Bar to themselves, except for the discreet barman, who kept his distance.

Freddie seemed daunted by the subject he was there to ventilate, so du Rose ordered a whole bottle of champagne, which was delivered to their table. Not until he was under the influence was Freddie able to talk fluently and without inhibition about his sexuality. Freddie lusted after men and boys as well as women, especially 'women of the night', as he called them. Homosexuality was still illegal and for indulging in such acts the penalty was usually imprisonment and social disgrace, becoming a pariah; this would especially have been the case for Freddie among his rugged, tough, very macho boxing pals. 'It would kill Chrissie if it ever came out,' he wailed, tormented by his own chemistry that couldn't be changed. 'Eternal embarrassment to his whole family, including his children,' was something else he muttered haplessly.

## THE BEGINNING OF THE END

Du Rose was as good a listener as any venerable priest in a confessional. Freddie was carrying too much baggage and was mentally staggering through life, spirit and resistance broken. Twice he'd been caught in public lavatories embarking on acts of indecency with youths, but Virgo and Drury had performed a magician's vanishing trick with the paperwork so that the cases never reached court. But Freddie had paid the price financially, selling his investments, one by one, as the blackmail demands continued unabated. He said Virgo had told him that the money wasn't for him or Ken (Drury), but to pay off the 'bent bastards' who knew 'all about' Mills and his illicit lifestyle.

Du Rose asked Freddie if he believed what he'd been told. Freddie vacillated, then said, 'Shit, no! They're stitching me up, the pair of the cockroaches; they're the biggest villains in town. Bigger even than you!' He said he'd foolishly believed that once they were all Freemasons together, they'd be on his side, but it was nothing like that. Because of his inherent 'weakness', he was seen as a 'blackberry bush', ripe for picking until there was no juicy fruit left and that was his position now, verging on penury. His investment properties had gone, he'd been compelled to remortgage his home, unbeknown to Chrissie, and the nightclub was hurtling 'down the lift-shaft as if the cable [had] snapped. He was down to his last few grand, which would soon be siphoned off and Chrissie would be left with nothing. All very informative, but not the subject matter du Rose was hoping would be on the agenda. So it was time to press the nuclear button.

'We're here, Freddie, because of my message, right?' said du Rose. 'You see, I'm aware of the much bigger story. Now's the time to unload, if I were you. It'll be a great relief to you. I'll do all I can to ease the pressure and see that Chrissie is supported, believe me.'

Du Rose was bluffing; he didn't *know*. He had his suspicions, the rumours were rife, the Citroen registration number had been logged several times in the red-light zones of west London, but the police had no forensic evidence to clinch the case against Freddie, even though he'd discussed oral sex lasciviously with du Rose's cop decoys, including the one he was to marry and settle down with in Great Yarmouth, Norfolk on his retirement. What he did believe, however, was that Mills was *ready* to be caught.

It is well known that many serial killers reach a crucial point where they long to bring their run of kills to an end but are incapable of stemming the animal urges which overrule their wishes for retirement. There was considerable disagreement between the various team leaders. They were confused by the apparent different MOs: some bodies went into the Thames, others were tossed on to wasteland. Were there two killers out there, one a copycat? What *was* consistent was the killer's *signature*; that never changed and couldn't have been copied, except by someone as physically endowed as Mills. The 'Nudes' killer always murdered with his penis. Today, the signature element is fully understood by criminal profilers; no such experts back then, however.

After a long, lingering pause, Freddie said very self-consciously, 'I never meant it to happen.'

'*What*, Freddie?' du Rose asked as casually as possible, as if referring to a minor motoring offence.

'I didn't mean to kill any of them; not the first, not the last.'

For du Rose, here was the salivating moment, journey's end, one foot on the peak of Everest.

'I paid for it, John,' said Freddie. 'Those women knew what they were doing. I didn't force them into anything they weren't prepared to do. They wanted the money. They just couldn't take it.'

'But you were too big for them?' This wasn't said pruriently, but Mills became a bonfire of shame. 'You could always have stopped,' Du Rose pressed on.

'Not when I was aroused full throttle; I was too far gone, then.'

Mills was told that he could explain all that in his statement. Mills replied that he'd thought this through 'very carefully' and needed time 'to put his house in order'.

Naturally, du Rose wanted to know exactly what Freddie had in mind. The answer was that he had to 'make peace' with Chrissie. He'd only gone with whores because his penchant was something that he couldn't expect his wife to indulge in and that the very notion would have disgusted her. By pleading guilty and having the medical evidence of death presented merely as asphyxia, without further elaboration, Chrissie and the family (he had two daughters and a stepson) wouldn't hear the gross facts – nor would the media.

Du Rose wasn't convinced. He also believed that Freddie would have a chance of a successful plea of manslaughter, because for murder intent to kill had to be established beyond all reasonable doubt. But Freddie wouldn't countenance such a defence: there would be a feeding frenzy by the press the world over and his name would be forever mud. He couldn't possibly contemplate putting his family and staunch friends and fans through such a wringer. 'All I want is a week's respite,' he said, before quickly adding, 'perhaps a fortnight.'

Du Rose balked at this, saying emphatically, 'No, ten days is top whack.'

Freddie snapped up the offer; his bargaining power was zero. 'I don't want you arresting me at home or the club. I'll come to you at Shepherd's Bush.'

'When?'

'Say a week this Wednesday. In the morning. By noon.'

Du Rose proffered his hand across the table. Freddie grasped it like a lifeline. 'I won't let you down,' said Freddie. 'I'll have everything sorted by then.'

Du Rose was tempted to ask why Freddie stripped the prostitutes and what he did with the clothing, but decided those questions could wait. He didn't want to push his luck.

Mills wasn't to know, though he might have guessed, that the briefcase du Rose had casually placed on the floor between them was a specially adapted tape recorder, hi-tech for 1965, certainly an early model James Bond gadget. By 1970 they were in common use by investigative reporters on some Sunday newspapers. When the handle was upright, the device was switched off. As soon as the handle was flicked down, recording began. They were powerful enough to record every word spoken in an average-sized room. Down the sides of the briefcase were camouflaged vents, resembling the head of a shower in miniature, where the pinhead mics were housed. I was using one regularly from 1970.

Du Rose, of course, was fully aware that a confession wouldn't be sufficient for a conviction as evidenced by the Archibald debacle. Something of forensic value would have to be discovered, possibly in the boot of the Citroen or on any of the seats; just a fingerprint of one of the victims on any part of the interior could be sufficient, alongside his confession. Mills was also in the habit of borrowing vehicles from among his extensive network of friends and hangers-on. He could have killed on the nights when driving someone else's car or a van, but this would suggest some degree of premeditation and finessing, and du Rose believed Mills when he claimed never setting out with murder on his mind.

Giving Mills some slack cut both ways. Du Rose now had a few days to fine-tune a strategy. Of course Mills would be watched and followed. If he took his car to a valet service for it to be vacuumed inside, washed and polished on the outside, the police would intervene, but Freddie would be aware that he was under strict surveillance from now on.

On the Sunday morning, around ten, Mills drove to the home

of the Kray twins in the East End. He knew they wouldn't be at church! He was followed by 'Jack'. This wasn't seen as a significant development: like Freddie, the Krays were boxing fanatics. They had attended the opening of Freddie's nightclub as 'celebrity' guests. . Perhaps he was asking them to advise him on a solicitor? 'Jack' assessed the visit as a social call: du Rose agreed. Nothing to worry about. Nothing...

On the morning of Friday, 23 July, Mills drove to the home of Mrs Mary Gladys Ronaldson at 316 Queenstown Road, Battersea, south-west London. Mrs Ronaldson was an old friend of Freddie's and ran an amusement arcade in the Battersea funfair. They had a cup of tea together in the kitchen and when he left he was carrying something long and slim, wrapped in brown paper. Only after his death would it transpire that he was concealing a .22-calibre FN automatic rifle, one of those that made up the armoury of Mrs Donaldson's shooting range at the funfair. He had promised to return it on Sunday afternoon.

On Saturday, 24 July, Mills was still recovering from a bout of pneumonia and he went to bed for a siesta at four p.m., while Chrissie was shopping. He was downstairs again by seven-thirty for dinner, but returned to bed after eating. Therefore, Chrissie was shocked to see him dressed for the club some fifteen minutes before ten. Later, Chrissie was to say that she didn't think him 'well enough to go' and tried to dissuade him, but to no avail. A little ritual of theirs was to have supper together at the club every fortnight on a Saturday. So Chrissie promised to join him later at *their* table.

By eleven forty-five, Mills was dead in his car, which was parked in Goslett Yard. Mills, aged forty-six, was slumped forward on the back seat. The offside window was wound down. He'd been shot through the right eye with a single slug from a .22 rifle. A .22 rifle was leaning against the offside rear seat, well away from Mills, the butt resting on the floor. Just before two a.m., Mills was certified dead at Middlesex Hospital in Mortimer Street, just off the Tottenham Court Road. Detective Inspector Harold Walton took charge, announcing that it was now a murder investigation and Goslett Yard, the nightclub and the Citroen were crime scenes.

Professor Keith Simpson conducted the PM. The lethal shot had shattered and scattered skull and brain. There was no exit hole. His conclusion, stunning many pathologists, experienced murder squad officers and Mills' family, was that there was 'nothing from the medical examination of this wound or of the body generally to give cause for suspicion of foul play... The wound shows nothing out of keeping with deliberate self-infliction.'

So despite what Detective Inspector Walton said from his immediate assessment of the crime scene, there was no murder investigation.

Dr Gavin Thurston presided over the inquest, dispensing with a jury (odd) and recorded unilaterally a verdict of suicide, even though the police evidence substantiated that two shots had been fired at the scene, one of them penetrating the Citroen's chassis. Mills had simply been practising, he speculated! Curious, indeed.

Chrissie Mills would not accept the verdict. Police officers and pathologists throughout the country were quick to point out that they'd never heard of anyone committing suicide by shooting themselves through an eye. In the mouth, temple or under the chin, yes. But in the eye? – unthinkable! Simpson decided the entry of the bullet was a 'contact wound'. But as at least one other pathologist, of equal standing if indeed not more qualified than Simpson, stressed: a contact wound always leaves scorch marks and there was none on Mills' face. He added, 'I've never seen a deliberate self-inflicted gunshot wound to the eye. This should raise the suspicion that a third party was involved [...] There is nothing in the description of the entrance wound to confirm that this was a close-range wound which had been self-inflicted.' They were the findings of Professor Jack Crane, State Pathologist for Northern Ireland and Professor of Forensic Medicine at Queen's University, Belfast.

No suicide, then?

Wrong.

Freddie Mills did commit suicide. And he was murdered. Confused? Read on.

Freddie's death was suicide by proxy, murder by appointment and self-financed. Yes, Mills paid a hit man to kill him because he couldn't bring himself to do it himself.

When Freddie went to the Krays, he told them he'd decided he could take no more of 'this crappy life', which had become 'a living hell' for him. He wanted out but he didn't have the 'bollocks' for it; he needed someone else to take the responsibility. Someone who wouldn't tell him when, where or how the end would come.

At first, the twins thought Mills was 'gagging around, taking the piss'. When they realised he was serious, one of them said that there was too much heat on them to do it, but they knew a man who would, if the price was right. The price quoted was a grand. 'All upfront; none of your half in advance and the rest on delivery, none of that malarkey!' They thought it the best giggle they'd had in years.

Their man for the job was Jimmy Moody, a twenty-four-year-old wannabe Mafia-styled hit man, who went on to live his warped dream. When in Brixton prison, awaiting trial for robbery, he escaped with Gerard Tuite, an IRA bomb-maker, and another inmate. He remained on the run for thirteen years, a Provisional IRA hit man and latterly more attached to the Richardson brothers than the Krays. On 1 June 1993, he was gunned down and killed by another hit man in the Royal Hotel in Hackney. He died as he had lived.

One of the Krays' 'collectors' was sent to Freddie's nightclub for the grand. After handing over the money, Mills was told he should leave his rifle in the boot of the Citroen. The boot should remain unlocked. At least Freddie knew he wasn't going to be knifed, poisoned, cremated alive or even asphyxiated... Only the time, date and place remained unmapped for him; perhaps that was a sufficient mystery to make his final hours bearable. It was rumoured that the Krays told Moody that Freddie had paid them five hundred pounds. They kept the rest for themselves, as an introduction fee. They'd never done anything honourably in their entire lives. So why should anyone have expected them to behave differently for a legend who they believed had lost his bottle? Freddie really was out for the count this time.

This was a story the Krays didn't keep to themselves, but it was regaled only to their criminal clansmen with the strict rule of *omertá* imposed. Naturally, 'Mad' Frankie Fraser was the only one to break the circle of censorship. In 1991, he was shot outside the Turnmills nightclub in Clerkenwell, east London – the bullet, fired from a .22 rifle, hit him in the right eye and it was a miracle he survived. No one before, as far as I know, has ever made the connection with the Freddie Mills assassination. An eye for an eye, the penalty of breaching the code of silence.

As a footnote, it's worth looking at the research by Detective Superintendent William Baldock, who wrote in a report that '...a lack of teeth, allied to the difficulties experienced in manipulating the jaw during fellatio, when the mouth or throat is fully occupied, would have prevented the victim from biting the murder weapon. From the commencement of choking, death could be as quick as six seconds.'

Probably the most shameful episode of this whole rollercoaster was du Rose's attempt to implicate an innocent man, Mungo Ireland, who committed suicide on 3 March 1965. The forty-five-year-old night security guard lived with his wife at 132 Tildesley Road, Putney. He had worked on the Heron estate, but was in Dundee, the city of his birth, when Bridie O'Hara was murdered. In a suicide note to his wife, he wrote:

> I can't stick it any longer. It may be my fault but not all of it. I'm sorry Harry [his brother] is a burden to you. Give my love to the kid.
> Farewell,
> Jock.
> P.S. To save you and the police looking for me, I'll be in the garage.

There was never any evidence to link Ireland with the murders; he was simply a convenient patsy for the unscrupulous du Rose. The message in the suicide note was transparently a reference to the breakdown of his marriage to wife Elizabeth. Du Rose tried to convey it as Ireland being under unbearable pressure because he knew the great, unbeatable detective was about to come knocking on his door. What risible prattle!

Mills didn't leave a suicide note. Always a showman, when the curtain came down on his turbulent life he ensured that it immediately rose again with a whodunit drama to compete with Agatha Christie's *The Mousetrap* as a West End long-runner. Even in death, he packed a punch. But one shouldn't forget his real legacy. He was 'Deep Throat'.

Let us not forget his victims, either. They were prostitutes, but aren't we all in one way or another? For me, the biggest question of all still remaining is what would a jury have made of it all? Surely it would have been the most bizarre case ever tried at the Old Bailey. A sell-out. And do you know, I have a sneaking feeling that cheeky chappie Freddie would have walked...

Over a period of time 'Jack' leaked me the story of Freddie's final hours. He showed me a transcript of the tape-recording. I briefed Ken James. He scoffed, 'Would du Rose come clean?' – Not a chance. 'Would "Jack" or anyone be prepared to talk "on the record"?' – Doubt it. 'A bloody good story, but we'd get buried. Even the Krays would sue us!'

James resigned to go into public relations with Gillette. Rupert Murdoch bought *The Sun* and turned it into a red-top tabloid, with topless Page Three girls its trademark. I went off Mafia-hunting overseas for *Time/Life*. Du Rose wrote an autobiography and lied, then died. But Freddie wasn't left to rest in peace. Countless people had countless theories. One generation faded away, until there were those who would say vacuously, 'Freddie *who*?'

Well, now you know. He was a man who could soak up a lot of pain, but he couldn't live with disgrace and ridicule. He was a big man. Too big for his own good... and certainly for a few unfortunate women of the night in west London.